*Lewis Theobald
and the
Editing of Shakespeare*

Lewis Theobald
and the
Editing of Shakespeare

Peter Seary

Clarendon Press · Oxford
1990

Oxford University Press, Walton Street, Oxford OX2 6DP
Oxford New York Toronto
Delhi Bombay Calcutta Madras Karachi
Petaling Jaya Singapore Hong Kong Tokyo
Nairobi Dar es Salaam Cape Town
Melbourne Auckland
and associated companies in
Berlin Ibadan

Oxford is a trade mark of Oxford University Press

Published in the United States
by Oxford University Press, New York

British Library Cataloguing in Publication Data
Seary, Peter
Lewis Theobald and the editing of Shakespeare.
1. Drama in English. Criticism. Theobald, Lewis, 1688–1744
I. Title   822'.009
ISBN 0-19-812965-3

Library of Congress Cataloging in Publication Data
Seary, Peter
Lewis Theobald and the editing of Shakespeare/Peter Seary.
p. cm.
1. Shakespeare, William, 1564–1616—Editors. 2. Theobald, Mr.
(Lewis), 1688–1744.   I. Title.
PR3071.S44 1990   822.3'3—dc20   89-23103
ISBN 0-19-812965-3

Set by Downdell Limited, Oxford
Printed and bound in
Great Britain by Biddles Ltd,
Guildford and King's Lynn

To the Memory of
F. E. L. Priestley

Preface

THIS study of Lewis Theobald is in part devoted to footnotes and their making. The emphasis may seem beyond apology, given Theobald's prominence in Pope's *Dunciad*. But Theobald was the first to edit Shakespeare systematically, and from his work flowed all successive editions of Shakespeare, such studies of the language as Johnson's *Dictionary*, as well as studies of Elizabethan thought, manners, and society. The hero of *The Dunciad* is, in short, also the founder of modern scholarship devoted to Renaissance English literature.

Scholarship devoted to English literature supposes that English literature is worth reading and worth understanding. In the opening decades of the eighteenth century opinion was divided on this fundamental issue: why study English literature rather than the classics of Greece and Rome? What were perceived as classical ideals could, and did, clash with popular taste and with movements ultimately associated with the rise of nationalism. Thus the close study of English language and literature is connected with the politics of increasing national self-consciousness and self-confidence and with aspects of English romanticism. These generalizations are, however, far removed from the personalities of the critics and scholars themselves, who were caught up in a web of assumptions and disputes determined by their social class, education, ambitions, and their stature among their peers.

This book has a number of major concerns: early eighteenth-century assessments of Shakespeare as a dramatist, with particular reference to how Theobald's views either differed from or matched those of his contemporaries; attitudes to scholarship in the opening decades of the eighteenth century; the conflicting personalities of critics and scholars; and, finally, Theobald's scholarly techniques as seen from both eighteenth-century and twentieth-century perspectives. I have attempted to relate all these matters to Theobald's chief work, his edition of Shakespeare, and to his reputation.

In these tasks I have abandoned a strict chronological structure. Although all modern editions of Shakespeare are indebted
to him, Theobald is inextricably associated with Pope's *Dunciad*
and with Johnson's censures in his Preface to *Shakespeare*. It was
therefore necessary to acknowledge the prevalent view of him
as a supreme Dunce before writing about him as a scholar. To
reconcile these two views is impossible, although it is possible
to trace their evolution. This process has, however, required
more flexibility than a chronological framework would have
allowed. Hence the Introduction considers the vagaries of
Theobald's reputation, with particular reference to the damage
caused by Johnson. Chapter 2 is mainly biographical and
establishes the social context of Theobald's career, and
Chapter 3 establishes the critical concerns relevant to the
Shakespearian scholarship of the period. The next four
chapters delineate conflicts among critics and critical attitudes
and their consequences for scholarship. Chapters 4–6 focus on
Pope and Theobald; Chapter 7 deals with Theobald's discussions of textual problems in Shakespeare in his correspondence
with William Warburton, and with his manœuvres to maintain
control over the editorial content of his edition. Theobald's
achievements in his edition are described and assessed in
Chapters 8 and 9. The final chapter reverts to biography, and
to Theobald's reputation in the light of his accomplishments.
The concerns of the appendices are self-evident, although it
may be helpful to note here that Appendix D addresses the
validity of Warburton's claims to parts of Theobald's Preface
to *Shakespeare*, particularly those passages having to do with
definition of editorial functions. Correct attribution of these
passages is important to the history of English literary scholarship and necessary in an assessment of Theobald's contribution.

My initial stimulus to examine Theobald's career came from
a chance purchase of David Garrick's copy of Theobald's
Shakespeare Restored and a reading of David Nichol Smith's
Introduction to *Eighteenth Century Essays on Shakespeare*. I have
learned much from studies of Theobald by John Churton
Collins, T. R. Lounsbury, and R. F. Jones. Although I have
been anticipated in some details and in the tenor of some discussions, this study adds to theirs a further consideration of the
causes of Johnson's denigration of Theobald and its influence

on modern views of him, a more detailed account of Theobald's uneasy relations with William Warburton as revealed in their correspondence, and an examination of Theobald's use of palaeographic arguments and of his attempts to determine compositors' copy as guides to emendation. I also indicate some of Johnson's similarities to Theobald in his critical and scholarly approaches to Shakespeare. In this last, I am partly indebted to Arthur Sherbo's *Samuel Johnson, Editor of Shakespeare* (Urbana: University of Illinois Press, 1956). In a number of instances Maynard Mack (in his *Alexander Pope: A Life* (New York: Norton, 1985)) and I have independently considered identical materials, and have formed differing opinions of their significance.

I aim to demonstrate that Theobald independently evolved a canon of editorial principles, and that in the establishment of the text he sought to replace taste with fact or probability. To these great merits he adds a responsiveness to Shakespeare's figurative style that distinguishes him from his contemporaries and that anticipates modern criticism. Theobald's excitement as he engaged in the then novel application of scholarly techniques to the editing of Shakespeare has—I trust—been captured. Unfortunately, Theobald writes indifferent prose, probably because, as J. R. Sutherland has suggested, he was steeped in the prose of the Elizabethans. None the less, I quote him extensively to illustrate the originality of his methods and to demonstrate the range of considerations that lie behind his editorial decisions. His ability to relate individual observations to a comprehensive view of Shakespeare's stylistic habits is best demonstrated by full quotations. Also, Theobald has not often been read carefully, and it seems useful to relate what he himself had to say: extensive quotation provides the best evidence of the quality of his mind. I have indicated some of the mundane detail of his life because, like Johnson, he did not work 'under the shelter of academick bowers' and his devotion to scholarship was 'amidst inconvenience and distraction'.

I have received financial assistance in aid of research from the Canada Council and the Office of Research Administration of the University of Toronto. To these bodies I am very grateful. I am indebted to the editors of the *University of Toronto Quarterly* and to the University of Pennsylvania Press for permission to use previously published material, and to the Viscountess Eccles, Four Oaks Farm; Ralph W. Franklin, Director, Beinecke Rare Book and Manuscript Library; Werner Gundersheimer, Librarian, Folger Shakespeare Library; Donald W. Koepp, Librarian, Princeton University Library; and D. G. Vaisey, Bodley's Librarian, for permission to reproduce MS material in their collections. I also wish to thank for their friendly help the staffs of the Bodleian Library, the British Library, the Folger Shakespeare Library, and the University of Toronto Library. I particularly wish to thank the following for providing pertinent information: J. H. Baker, St Catharine's College, Cambridge; W. W. S. Breem, Librarian and Keeper of Manuscripts, The Library, The Honourable Society of the Inner Temple; J. D. Fleeman, Pembroke College, Oxford; T. O. Haunch, Librarian, United Grand Lodge of England, Freemasons' Hall; Alan Jutzi, Assistant Curator, Literary Manuscripts, The Huntington Library; Gary Taylor, Brandeis University; The Revd G. C. Taylor, St Giles-in-the-Fields; Laetitia Yeandle, The Folger Shakespeare Library.

I have benefited from the criticism and encouragement of many friends and colleagues. Rachel Trickett, with great hospitality, spent afternoons discussing aspects of Theobald with me. The late Professor Clifford Leech favoured me with meticulous comments on my first draft. James Woodruff made an extended loan of the first edition of Johnson's *Shakespeare* and of a house to read it in, when I had need of both. William Blissett, Martine Watson Brownley, Patricia Brückmann, Frederick Flahiff, William Halewood, Robin Jackson, Randall McLeod, and Sheldon Zitner at different times read drafts and gave advice and encouragement. I am also indebted to the anonymous readers for the Press for general and specific suggestions for improving my script. My brother, Richard Seary, generously made available a computer for word processing. F. E. L. Priestley, to whose memory the book is dedicated, gave support and assistance in more ways than can be adequately indicated here.

P.S.
New College, University of Toronto

Contents

Abbreviations

Shakespearian act, scene, and line references follow *The Riverside Shakespeare*, ed. G. Blakemore Evans *et al.* (Boston: Houghton Mifflin, 1974), which is the basis of the *Harvard Concordance to Shakespeare* (Cambridge, Mass.: Belknap Press, 1973). Unless otherwise stated, the place of publication for works printed before 1900 is London. References to eighteenth-century editions of Shakespeare are to volume and page. Dates prior to 2 September 1752 are given Old Style, but with the year beginning 1 January.

Arden	*The Arden Edition of the Works of William Shakespeare*, gen. eds. W. J. Craig, R. H. Case, Una Ellis-Fermor, Harold Brooks, and Harold Jenkins, London: Methuen/ Cambridge, Mass.: Harvard University Press. Cited by editor, title, and date.
Boswell, *Life*	James Boswell, *Life of Johnson*, ed. G. B. Hill, rev. L. F. Powell, 6 vols., Oxford: Clarendon Press, 1934–64.
Censor	Lewis Theobald, *The Censor*, 2nd edn., 3 vols., 1717.
Complete Works	*William Shakespeare: The Complete Works*, gen. eds. Stanley Wells and Gary Taylor, eds. Stanley Wells, Gary Taylor, John Jowett, and William Montgomery, Oxford: Clarendon Press, 1986.
Correspondence	*Correspondence of Alexander Pope*, ed. George Sherburn, 5 vols., Oxford: Clarendon Press, 1956.
Dawson	Giles E. Dawson, 'The Copyright of Shakespeare's Dramatic Works', in *Studies in Honor of A. H. R. Fairchild* (University of Missouri Studies, xxi/1), ed. C. T. Prouty, Columbia: University of Missouri Press, 1946.
Dunciad	Alexander Pope, *The Dunciad Variorum with the Prolegomena of Scriblerus* (1729), in The Twickenham Edition of the Poems of Alexander Pope, V, ed. James Sutherland, 3rd edn., rev., London: Methuen, 1963.

Greg, *Bibliography*	W. W. Greg, *A Bibliography of the English Printed Drama to the Restoration* (printed for the Bibliographical Society), 4 vols., Oxford: Oxford University Press, 1939–59.
Greg, *Editorial Problem*	W. W. Greg, *The Editorial Problem in Shakespeare*, 3rd edn., Oxford: Clarendon Press, 1954.
Greg, *First Folio*	W. W. Greg, *The Shakespeare First Folio*, Oxford: Clarendon Press, 1955.
Jones	R. F. Jones, *Lewis Theobald: His Contribution to English Scholarship, with some Unpublished Letters*, New York: Columbia University Press, 1919.
LS	*The London Stage, 1660–1800: A Calendar of Plays, Entertainments & Afterpieces, Together with Casts, Box-Receipts and Contemporary Comment*, pts. 1–5, ed. William Van Lennep, Emmett L. Avery, Arthur H. Scouten, George Winchester Stone, Jr., and Charles Beecher Hogan, 11 vols., Carbondale: Southern Illinois University Press, 1960–8.
McKerrow	R. B. McKerrow, 'The Treatment of Shakespeare's Text by his Earlier Editors, 1709–1768', *Proceedings of the British Academy*, London: Oxford University Press, 1933.
New Shakespeare	The New Shakespeare, ed. John Dover Wilson, *et al.*, Cambridge: Cambridge University Press. Cited by editor, title, and date.
Nichols, ii	*Illustrations of the Literary History of the Eighteenth Century*, ii, 1817.
OED	*The Oxford English Dictionary, being a corrected re-issue . . . of A New English Dictionary on Historical Principles*, 13 vols., Oxford: Clarendon Press, 1933.
Oxford Shakespeare	*The Oxford Shakespeare* (Oxford English Texts), gen. ed. Stanley Wells, with Gary Taylor, John Jowett, and Christine Avern-Carr. Cited by editor, title, and date.
Riverside	*The Riverside Shakespeare*, ed. G. Blakemore Evans, *et al.*, Boston: Houghton Mifflin, 1974.

Sherburn	George Sherburn, *The Early Career of Alexander Pope*, Oxford: Clarendon Press, 1934.
Sisson	C. J. Sisson, *New Readings in Shakespeare*, 2 vols., 1956, repr. London: Dawsons of Pall Mall, 1961.
Smith	D. Nichol Smith (ed.), *Eighteenth Century Essays on Shakespeare*, 2nd edn., rev., Oxford: Clarendon Press, 1963 (1st edn., Glasgow: J. MacLehose, 1903).
Spence	Joseph Spence, *Observations, Anecdotes, and Characters of Books and Men*, ed. James M. Osborn, 2 vols., Oxford: Clarendon Press, 1966. Cited by anecdote number.
SR	Lewis Theobald, *Shakespeare Restored: or, A Specimen of the Many Errors, as well Committed, as Unamended, by Mr. Pope in his Late Edition of this Poet*, 1726.
Textual Companion	Stanley Wells, Gary Taylor, with John Jowett and William Montgomery, *William Shakespeare: A Textual Companion*, Oxford: Clarendon Press, 1987.
Watson	John Dryden, *Of Dramatic Poesy and Other Critical Essays*, 2 vols., (Everyman's Library), ed. George Watson, London: Dent, 1962.
Wilson, *MS of 'Hamlet'*	John Dover Wilson, *The Manuscript of 'Hamlet'*, 2 vols., 1934, repr. Cambridge: Cambridge University Press, 1963.
Wilson, *New Bibliography*	F. P. Wilson, *Shakespeare and the New Bibliography*, rev. and ed. Helen Gardner, Oxford: Clarendon Press, 1970.
Yale	*Johnson on Shakespeare* (The Yale Edition of the Works of Samuel Johnson, vii, viii), ed. Arthur Sherbo, with an introduction by Bertrand H. Bronson, New Haven: Yale University Press, 1968.
Zimansky	*The Critical Works of Thomas Rymer*, ed. C. A. Zimansky, New Haven: Yale University Press, 1956.
1709	*The Works of Shakespear*, ed. Nicholas Rowe, 6 vols., 1709.
1725	*The Works of Shakespear*, ed. Alexander Pope, 6 vols., 1725.

1. Introduction: Theobald and the Johnsonian Shadow

THE modern tradition of editing Renaissance English classics begins with Nicholas Rowe's *Shakespear* (1709), but it was Alexander Pope's *Shakespear* (1725) and Lewis Theobald's *Shakespeare Restored: or, A Specimen of the Many Errors, as well Committed, as Unamended, by Mr. Pope in his Late Edition of this Poet* (1726) that raised editorial practice as a subject for detailed consideration, thus beginning a series of misunderstandings and disputes among poets, critics, and scholars over their respective roles in the literary process. The ideal of the scholar-critic had yet to be recognized, and Pope, as an upholder of the ideal of the gentleman-reader in the tradition of Sir William Temple, Francis Atterbury, the Hon. Charles Boyle, and the third Earl of Shaftesbury, tried in *The Dunciad Variorum* (1729) to discredit Theobald and his methods. Theobald responded by publishing his own *Shakespeare*,[1] an enterprise that might have established his reputation had not his assistant, William Warburton, subsequently become a friend of Pope. Eventually Warburton published his *Shakespear* (1747), whose Preface defamed Theobald by repeating Pope's charges of dullness and stupidity. Scholarly vituperation was commonplace, and it is likely that Theobald's reputation would have withstood these onslaughts if Samuel Johnson in his Preface to *Shakespeare* (1765) had not accepted Warburton's account of Theobald and represented him as 'a man of narrow comprehension and small acquisitions, with no native and intrinsick splendour of genius, with little of the artificial light of learning, but zealous for minute accuracy, and not negligent in pursuing it'. Johnson acknowledges that Theobald 'collated the ancient copies, and rectified many errors', but adds: 'A man so anxiously scrupulous might have been expected to do more, but what little he

---

[1] Theobald's *Shakespeare* was published in Jan. 1734, but the title-page is dated 1733.

did was commonly right.'[2] Elsewhere in his Preface Johnson characterizes Theobald as weak, ignorant, mean, faithless, petulant, and ostentatious.[3]

Theobald must appear at best an enigmatic figure: most modern editors acknowledge the brillance of his emendations while accepting the unflattering accounts of his intellect given by Pope and Johnson. Peter Alexander exemplifies the difficulties that result from an attempt to reconcile the two views:

> To assess the relative merits of the editors would be an invidious and perhaps odious task; but whatever the judgement given after such a scrutiny, the claims of Theobald would have to be weighed with care. Yet Theobald is the first hero of the *Dunciad*, a poem by . . . the outstanding man of genius who has given his time to editing Shakespeare. But in editing Shakespeare the race has not always been to the swift or the battle to the strong. Those who have done most to elucidate Shakespeare are not of the type of which Bentleys, Porsons, and Housmans have been made; and Dr. Johnson could describe Theobald as a man of narrow comprehension and small acquisitions, though there is no modern edition of Shakespeare that does not include many of the happy suggestions first proposed by Theobald.[4]

Other scholars have taken sides. John Churton Collins considered Theobald's fate 'without parallel in literary history':

> no poet in our own or in any language has ever owed so great a debt to an editor as Shakespeare owes to this man. He found the text of the tragedies and comedies . . . in a condition scarcely less deplorable than that in which Aldus found the choruses of Æschylus . . . and he contributed more to its certain and permanent settlement than all the other editors from Rowe to Alexander Dyce.[5]

In addition to lavishing praise on Theobald's emendations and exclaiming against the injustice of his treatment, Collins indicated that in his edition Warburton had presented a number of Theobald's emendations as his own. Nevertheless, in his influential Introduction to *Eighteenth Century Essays on Shakespeare* (1st edn., Glasgow: J. MacLehose, 1903), Nichol Smith dismissed the views of Collins and presented Theobald as an intermit-

---

[2] *1765*, vol. i, sig. D^r [Yale, vii. 95–6].

[3] Ibid., sigs. D^v–D2^r [Yale, vii. 96].

[4] 'Restoring Shakespeare', *Shakespeare Survey*, 5 (1952), repr. in *Shakespeare Criticism 1935–1960*, ed. Anne Ridler (Oxford: Oxford University Press, 1970), 118.

[5] 'The Porson of Shakespearian Criticism', *Essays and Studies* (1895), [263].

tently inspired dunce almost totally dependent on Warburton for his success.

In direct conflict with Nichol Smith's account are those of T. R. Lounsbury and R. F. Jones. Lounsbury shared Collins's views and in *The Text of Shakespeare* (New York: Scribner, 1906) undertook a thorough examination of Pope's misrepresentations. Jones's major contribution was a demonstration of the influence of Richard Bentley's techniques in classical scholarship on Theobald's editorial practice.[6] The findings of Jones and Lounsbury have left their mark on the Twickenham Edition of *The Dunciad*. However, neither Lounsbury nor Jones challenged Nichol Smith who, although familiar with their work, did not feel the need to alter his conclusions when the second, revised edition of *Eighteenth Century Essays on Shakespeare* was published (Oxford: Clarendon Press, 1963). When assessing Theobald's qualifications as an editor, he maintained that 'we must subscribe to the deliberate verdict of Johnson'.[7] The point is argued at length in Smith's Introduction to the *Essays*, which again concludes that Theobald owed the merits of his edition (which are allowed) to Warburton. But Smith fails to explain the generally accepted inferiority of Warburton's own edition of 1747, a work in which, it has been said, 'Warburton reveals himself . . . as without doubt the stupidest man ever to edit Shakespeare'.[8]

Johnson's statements about Theobald have been the decisive factor in shaping Theobald's later reputation, and Nichol Smith is certainly right to insist that strong evidence is required before Johnson's judgement of Theobald may be rejected. Parts of this study consequently examine that judgement and the considerations that seemed to Nichol Smith to confirm it. But it is necessary to indicate immediately that Johnson's account should not be taken simply at face value.

Johnson's gratitude to Warburton apparently entailed acceptance of Warburton's portrayal of his predecessor.[9] In

---

[6] R. F. Jones, *Lewis Theobald: His Contribution to English Scholarship, with some Unpublished Letters* (New York: Columbia University Press, 1919), ch. 2.

[7] Preface to the 1st edn., repr. in 2nd edn., sig. π^r.

[8] Leading article, 'Shakespeare and the Judgments of Johnson', *The Times Literary Supplement* (22 May 1969), [545].

[9] T. R. Lounsbury noted that Johnson's gratitude to Warburton was a major factor in his depiction of Theobald. See *The Text of Shakespeare* (New York: Scribner, 1906), 546 ff.

1745 Johnson's *Miscellaneous Observations on the Tragedy of Macbeth* appeared, and Warburton, now famous as the friend of Pope and as a polemicist, went out of his way in his Preface to *Shakespear* (1747) to praise Johnson's work: 'as to all those Things, which have been published under the titles of *Essays, Remarks, Observations,* &c. on *Shakespear,* (if you except some critical Notes on *Macbeth,* given as a Specimen of a projected Edition, and written, as appears, by a Man of Parts and Genius) the rest are absolutely below a serious Notice.'[10] Johnson felt that Warburton had praised him 'when praise was of value to me'.[11] Moreover, the fact that this praise was forthcoming despite Johnson's initial admiration for Theobald in the *Miscellaneous Observations*[12] worked to Theobald's disadvantage because it magnified Warburton's seeming magnanimity. For in the same Preface Warburton had written:

Mr. *Theobald* was naturally turned to Industry and Labour. What he read he could transcribe: but, as what he thought, if ever he did think, he could but ill express, so he read on; and, by that means got a Character of Learning, without risquing, to every Observer, the Imputation of wanting a better Talent. By a punctilious Collation of the old Books, he corrected what was manifestly wrong in the *latter* Editions, by what was manifestly right in the *earlier*. And this is his real Merit; and the whole of it. For where the Phrase was very obsolete or licentious in the *common* Books, or only slightly corrupted in the *other*, he wanted sufficient Knowledge of the Progress and various Stages of the *English* Tongue, as well as Acquaintance with the Peculiarity of *Shakespear's* Language to understand what was right; nor had he either common Judgment to see, or critical Sagacity to amend, what was manifestly faulty. Hence he generally exerts his conjectural Talent in the wrong Place: He tampers with what is sound in the *common* Books; and, in the *old* ones, omits all Notice of *Variations* the Sense of which he did not understand.[13]

---

[10] Vol. i, p. xiii. The Folger Library possesses a set of Warburton's *Shakespear* (PR 2752 1747a c. 5) annotated by the editor for a second edition (which was never printed). The compliment to Johnson has been crossed out.

[11] Boswell, *Life*, i. 175–6; cf. Sir John Hawkins, *Apophthegms* in *Johnsonian Miscellanies*, ed. G. B. Hill (2 vols., Oxford: Clarendon Press, 1897), ii. 7: 'Of Warburton he always spoke well. He gave me, says he, his good word when it was of use to me.' For Johnson's difficulties in the 1740s, see chs. 13–16 of James L. Clifford's *Young Samuel Johnson* (London: Heinemann, 1955).

[12] Note III, Yale, vii. 8: 'some of his amendments are so excellent, that, even when he has failed, he ought to be treated with indulgence and respect.'

[13] *1747*, vol. i, p. xi.

The extent of Warburton's misrepresentations of Theobald, who had died in 1744, will become apparent in the examination of their Shakespearian correspondence. But if Theobald's industry in collation is disregarded, Warburton has provided a convenient summary of his own editorial shortcomings, as was demonstrated at length in the eighteenth century by Thomas Edwards in *The Canons of Criticism* (first published in 1747 as *A Supplement to Mr. Warburton's Edition of Shakespear*).

Johnson's gratitude to Warburton and his prolonged experience of both Warburton and Theobald as editors produced a conflict that continued to influence him from the publication in 1756 of his *Proposals for Printing the Dramatick Works of William Shakespeare* to the eventual appearance of his edition in 1765. Johnson once said that Warburton, cut into slices, would make 'two-and-fifty Theobalds'. This extravagance occurred in conversation in 1758, and followed an observation by Dr Burney that Johnson (in 'some volumes of his Shakespeare already printed, to prove that he was in earnest') 'seemed to be more severe on Warburton than Theobald'.[14] In fact, Burney was accurate. Johnson's notes on *The Merchant of Venice*, the play in question, generally quote Theobald without comment, but reprint Warburton to correct him. Buttressing this testimony of Johnson's opinion of Warburton as an editor is that of William Seward: 'Dr. Johnson, in some of the early sheets of his Edition of Shakespeare, was inclined to treat Warburton's Notes upon that Author very roughly. At the solicitation of Mr. Tonson and Mr. Millar, the sheets that contained any abuse upon the Bishop's Notes were cancelled.'[15] Contemporary support for this anecdote is found in William Kenrick's Preface to his *Review of Doctor Johnson's New Edition of Shakespeare* (1765).[16] Although even in his cancelled notes[17] Johnson was no more severe upon Warburton than Warburton habitually was in his

[14] Boswell, *Life*, i. 329.

[15] *European Magazine*, 24 (1793), 296. Warburton was consecrated Bishop of Gloucester in 1760.

[16] Kenrick asserts that Johnson was 'prevailed on by his printer prudentially to cancel several annotations, in which he had strongly expressed his dissent from that learned scholiast' (p. vii). Edmond Malone has a manuscript note by this passage in his copy of Kenrick's work: 'This is true' (Bodleian Library, Malone 142).

[17] In 1938 A. T. Hazen published a study of Johnson's cancelled notes, which had survived in Bishop Percy's set of Johnson's edition. See 'Johnson's Shakespeare, a Study in Cancellation', *Times Literary Supplement* (24 Dec. 1938), 820.

treatment of rivals, there can be no doubt of Johnson's low opinion of Warburton's editorial practice. None the less, in 'The Life of Pope' Johnson maintained that Warburton supplied 'the best notes' to Theobald's *Shakespeare*.[18]

There can be no question that as an editor of Shakespeare Theobald is infinitely superior to Warburton, and this fact was generally recognized in the eighteenth century. In *The Companion to the Play-house* (1764) David Erskine Baker says that Theobald's *Shakespeare* 'is . . . in general prefered to those Editions published by *Pope, Warburton,* and *Hanmer*'.[19] Even after the publication of Johnson's edition, Theobald's *Shakespeare* was pronounced by Joseph Warton 'to be *the best* till those of Steevens and Malone appeared'.[20] The reading public evidently agreed, since 'of the various Editions of Theobald . . . no less than 12,860 copies were sold'.[21] Malone's summary of Warburton's reputation as an editor of Shakespeare stands in marked contrast to that of Theobald: 'His unbounded licence in substituting his own chimerical conceits in the place of the authour's genuine text, has been so fully shewn by his revisers, that I suppose no critical reader will ever again open his volumes.'[22] In the nineteenth century the editors of the Cambridge Shakespeare comment that 'Theobald, as an Editor, is incomparably superior to his predecessors, and to his immediate successor, Warburton, although the latter had the advantage of working on his materials. . . . Many most brillant emendations . . . are due to him.' On Johnson's assertion that Warburton would make 'two-and-fifty Theobalds' they state: 'From this judgment, whether they be compared as critics or editors, we

[18] *Lives of the English Poets*, ed. G. B. Hill (3 vols., Oxford: Clarendon Press, 1905), iii. 167.

[19] Vol. ii, Art. 'Theobald'. (Sir Thomas Hanmer, sometime Speaker of the House of Commons, edited Shakespeare for the Clarendon Press in 1744 without taking any fee and with cuts and decorations provided at his own expense. His sumptuous edition was based on Pope's first edition and has occasionally brilliant, unsupported emendations. His annotated set of Pope's first edition, which served as printer's copy, is in the Bodleian Library.)

[20] Nichols, ii. 714 n. Cf. Warton's *Essay on the Genius and Writings of Pope*, 4th edn., corr. (2 vols., 1782), ii. 235–6.

[21] Nichols, ii. 714 n. Nichols's estimate is perhaps conservative: Edmond Malone, in a manuscript note (Bodleian Library, Malone 14, 'Shakespeariana', i. 238), believed Theobald's first edition numbered 1,360 copies and that there were 10,000 more copies from 1740 to 1774.

[22] Preface, 1790, vol. 1, pt. i, p. lxvii.

emphatically dissent.'[23] More recently, John Dover Wilson has paid witty tribute: 'no editor should pass Lewis Theobald without a salute—"*splendid-emendax*".'[24] Brian Vickers goes so far as to call Theobald 'the best all-round editor of Shakespeare in this period or any other',[25] while Gary Taylor acknowledges that he 'remains one of the finest editors of the last three centuries'.[26]

As an editor of Shakespeare Johnson is closer to Theobald than to any other of his predecessors, and he certainly found Theobald more useful than Warburton. It is not surprising that after his death Theobald's copy of the second folio, with his marginalia, passed eventually into Johnson's hands.[27] Of much greater importance is that Johnson, having begun by using Warburton as his copy-text (thereby following the usual eighteenth-century practice of emending the text of one's immediate predecessor), 'abandoned Warburton's edition beginning with *The Taming of the Shrew*, the eleventh play in his edition and the first play in volume three'.[28] At this point he adopted the 1757 edition of Theobald's *Shakespeare*, which may have been set up from a copy of Theobald's second edition (1740) containing manuscript corrections by Theobald.[29] Johnson used Theobald's 1757 edition for twenty-three of the plays, and vacillated between Theobald's and Warburton's texts in eleven others.[30] Many restorations of Shakespeare's text previously attributed to Johnson now have to be attributed to the editor of the 1757 edition.[31]

[23] *The Works of William Shakespeare*, ed. William George Clark, John Glover, and William Aldis Wright (1st edn., 9 vols., 1863–6; 3rd edn., 9 vols., 1891, repr. 1894), vol. i. pp. xxxii, xxxv n.

[24] General Introduction, *The Tempest*, New Shakespeare (1921; repr. 1969), p. xv.

[25] Introduction, *Shakespeare: The Critical Heritage Volume 2, 1693–1733* (London: Routledge & Kegan Paul, 1974), 1.

[26] General Introduction, *Textual Companion*, p. 54.

[27] This volume is now Folger No. 20. See Appendix E.

[28] G. Blakemore Evans, 'The Text of Johnson's *Shakespeare* (1765)', *Philological Quarterly*, 28 (1949), 426.

[29] This was suggested by R. F. Jones; see Evans, op. cit., 428 n. 10.

[30] See Arthur M. Eastman, 'The Texts from which Johnson Printed his *Shakespeare*', *Journal of English and Germanic Philology*, 49 (1950).

[31] For example, concerning *1 Henry VI*, Blackmore Evans writes (op. cit., 426): 'In *1 Henry VI* alone thirty-two readings which would otherwise be credited (or discredited) to Johnson must now be assigned to the anonymous reviser of the 1757 text. Of these thirty-two readings, seven may be considered worthwhile either as restorations or emendations, five of the seven finding a place in all modern editions.

Johnson's respect for Theobald as an editor, as revealed by his abandoning Warburton's edition in favour of Theobald's, is more substantially complimentary than his praise for Warburton. When his own editorial work was concluded, Johnson remarked in his Preface on the importance and difficulty of emending corrupt passages.[32] And of his own attempts at conjectural emendation, he added: 'As I practised conjecture more, I learned to trust it less; and after I had printed a few plays, resolved to insert none of my own readings in the text.'[33] Yet in his accounts of Theobald, the most successful of all the practitioners of conjectural emendation, Johnson seems either guilty of misrepresentation, or callous: '"O poor Tib.! (said Johnson) he was ready knocked down to my hands; Warburton stands between me and him."'[34]

In his *Proposals for Printing the Dramatick Works of William Shakespeare* (1756) Johnson remarks that among the previous editors of Shakespeare, Rowe and Pope 'were very ignorant of the ancient English literature', and Warburton 'was detained by more important studies'. But in his portrayal of Theobald he deferred to Warburton: 'Mr. Theobald, *if fame be just to his memory* [*my italics*], considered learning only as an instrument of gain, and made no further inquiry after his authour's meaning, when once he had notes sufficient to embellish his page with the expected decorations.'[35] Johnson may have thought Theobald mercenary, but it is unfortunate that such a statement should occur in a paragraph concerned with the elucidation of obscure words and phrases in Shakespeare by means of parallel readings. Theobald was the first to use this very important technique in the study of an English author, both in *Shakespeare Restored* and in his edition.[36] This Johnson must have known, since these illustrations were of use to him in his *Dictionary*

Johnson's total of two restorations and six emendations (only one later accepted) does not compare favorably.'

[32] *1765*, vol. i, sig. D7^r [Yale, vii. 104–5].

[33] Ibid., sig. E^v [Yale, vii. 108].

[34] Boswell, *Life*, i. 329 (1758).

[35] Yale, vii. 56.

[36] See *SR*, pp. viii, 128; Preface, *1733*, vol. i, p. xliii. The potential of this technique, which was borrowed from classical scholarship, was recognized, but scarcely realized, by John Urry and Timothy Thomas in the compilation of a glossary to Chaucer; see *The Works of Geoffrey Chaucer* (1721), sig. m^v and the glossary.

(1755). It is not surprising, however, that his representation of Theobald is biased, since his source was again Warburton's Preface: 'As to Mr. *Theobald*, who wanted Money, I allowed him to print what I gave him for his own Advantage: and he allowed himself in the Liberty of taking one Part for his own, and sequestering another for the Benefit, as I supposed, of some future Edition.'[37]

Nichol Smith is indubitably right when he says that Warburton's 'statement of the assistance he rendered Theobald is rude and cruel, but it is easier to impugn his taste than his truthfulness'.[38] An examination of Theobald's correspondence with Warburton on the subject of notes to Shakespeare will, however, clearly reveal that Warburton's truthfulness was no better than his taste. What is of more immediate interest is Johnson's loyalty to Warburton, despite his obvious mistrust of Warburton as an editor. As might be expected, Johnson's views were formed by an entirely non-Shakespearian matter, for, in addition to praising Johnson's *Miscellaneous Observations on Macbeth* in 1747, Warburton complimented Johnson on another performance that was much nearer his heart. In a letter to Boswell, Dr William Adams, the Master of Pembroke, Johnson's old college, related that shortly after Johnson had sent his famous letter (7 February 1755) to Lord Chesterfield on patronage, 'While this was the talk of the town . . . I happened to visit Dr. Warburton, who finding that I was acquainted with Johnson, desired me earnestly to carry his compliments to him, and to tell him, that he honoured him for his manly behaviour in rejecting these condescensions of Lord Chesterfield, and for resenting the treatment he had received from him, with a proper spirit'. Adams added that 'Johnson was visibly pleased with this compliment'.[39]

Warburton had reasons of his own for resenting Chesterfield: he had dedicated the third edition of *The Alliance between Church and State* (1748) to Chesterfield prior to enquiring about livings at Chesterfield's disposal. Chesterfield had replied (14

---

[37] *1747*, vol. i, p. x.

[38] Introduction, Smith, p. xlvi.

[39] Boswell, *Life*, i. 263. For a discussion of the importance of Johnson's letter to Chesterfield in his career, see Frank Brady, 'Johnson as Public Figure', in *Johnson After Two Hundred Years*, ed. Paul J. Korshin (Philadelphia: University of Pennsylvania Press, 1986).

September 1749) regretting that he could not be of any assistance.[40] Warburton's praise of Johnson's letter to Chesterfield
accounts, however, for Johnson's loyalty to Warburton and for
Johnson's acceptance of Warburton's denigration of Theobald.
None the less, when Johnson attempted a formal evaluation of
Warburton's *Shakespear* he was still hard pressed to be complimentary:

> Of the last editor it is more difficult to speak. Respect is due to high
> place [*Warburton was now Bishop of Gloucester*], tenderness to living
> reputation, and veneration to genius and learning; but he cannot be
> justly offended at that liberty of which he has himself so frequently
> given an example, nor very solicitous what is thought of notes, which
> he ought never to have considered as part of his serious employments,
> and which, I suppose, since the ardour of composition is remitted, he
> no longer numbers among his happy effusions.[41]

On another occasion Johnson remarked to Dr Adams:

> 'If . . . I had written with hostility of Warburton in my Shakespeare,
> I should have quoted this couplet:
>> ''Here Learning, blinded first, and then beguil'd,
>> Looks dark as Ignorance, as Fancy wild.''[42]
> You see they'd have fitted him to a *T*,' (smiling.) DR. ADAMS. 'But
> you did not write against Warburton.' JOHNSON. 'No, Sir, I treated
> him with great respect both in my Preface and in my Notes.'[43]

Johnson's loyalty to Warburton is both characteristic and
attractive. Indeed, because he had no knowledge of Theobald,
Dr Samuel Parr believed Johnson had accomplished the impossible and had spoken well of Warburton without insulting
those whom Warburton despised.[44] But, taken altogether,
sufficient contradictions and complications remain behind

[40] *The Letters of Philip Dormer Stanhope 4th Earl of Chesterfield*, ed. Bonamy Dobrée (6
vols., London: Eyre & Spottiswoode, 1932), 1398. Warburton added a note to this
letter, suggesting that he had enquired on behalf of his nephew. Previously (4 June
1745) Chesterfield had offered Warburton a domestic chaplaincy in Ireland, which,
however, Warburton declined. See ibid. 628, 632, 1078.

[41] Preface, *1765*, vol. i, sigs. D2ᵛ–D3ʳ [Yale, vii. 98].

[42] Richard Savage's *Wanderer*, ii. 170. L. F. Powell notes that the original reads: 'as
Frenzy wild.'

[43] Boswell, *Life*, iv. 288 (1784). Warburton thought Johnson's comments in his
edition 'full of insolence and malignant reflections'. See John Nichols, *Literary Anecdotes
of the Eighteenth Century*, v (1812), 595 n.

[44] See Boswell, *Life*. iv. 47 n. 2.

Johnson's 'deliberate verdict' on Theobald to prevent any easy acceptance of Johnson's assessment. Instead of relying on Johnson, it is necessary to examine afresh the evidence of Theobald's life as a man of letters.

2. *Theobald before* The Dunciad *(1729)*

LEWIS Theobald (1688–1744), the son of Peter Theobald, an attorney, and his second wife, Mary, was baptized on 2 April 1688 at Sittingbourne, Kent.[1] The family was financially insecure but socially well connected, and Lewis Watson, Baron Rockingham, was the child's godfather.[2] After the death of Peter Theobald in September 1690,[3] young Lewis was received into the household of his godfather and raised with Ned and George, the sons of the family. Rockingham was a conscientious godparent, and there are regular entries in his household accounts for payments 'Given My Co: [Mrs] Theobalds towards Lewiss & schooling', as well as for Christmas gifts of three pounds 'Given my Godson Lewis Theobalds', ten shillings 'for a p^r of black Woosted rowling Stockings', and bills for shoemakers.[4] The children's elementary schooling was first undertaken by the local clergyman, Mr Barriss, and a Mr Stevens.[5] After the death in May 1696 of Rockingham's wife, who left a legacy of £20 to her god-daughter, Lewis's sister Katherine,[6] Mrs Theobald seems to have become Rockingham's housekeeper and to have had responsibility for Rockingham's daughters, Moll, Kate, and Nan.[7] Rockingham maintained his

---

[1] Maidstone, Kent Archives and Record Office, 'Sedingbourn The Register of mariages, Baptisinges, & Burialls from the year of our Lord 1561' (hereafter cited as 'Sittingbourne Register'), p. 338/1/1.

[2] Rockingham noted in his account books under disbursements for Lady Day 1688 that he had 'Given' £2 10s. 'when I Christned Mr Theobald's child' (Lincoln, Lincolnshire Archives Office, MS Monson 10/1/A, 19, 'Family Household Book. The Earl of Rockingham, 1678–1701', fo. 91^r.)

[3] Sittingbourne Register, p. 338/1/1.

[4] Lincoln, Lincolnshire Archives Office, MS Monson 10/1/A, 19, fo. 183^r (June 1695), fo. 192^r (Dec. 1695), fo. 207^r (Dec. 1696).

[5] Ibid., fo. 199^r (July 1696): 'P^d Mr Stevens half a y^{rs} Allowance, & half a y^{rs} teaching . . . £5/10s.'

[6] Ibid., fo. 206^r (Nov. 1696).

[7] Ibid., fo. 224^r: 'P^d my Coz: Theobalds her bill p^t whereof for my d^r: Wife ye rest for ye 3 eldest Girles £12/0/0' (Nov. 1697); fo. 229^r: 'P^d Mrs Theobalds her bill for ye Girles before I gave e'm their Allowance £5/15/' (May 1698).

interest in the children's schooling, and we find him paying four shillings for 'Mr Locks book of Education'.[8] There follow payments for a writing master, and in June 1697 the boys went to a boarding school in Ewell run by a Mr Evans.[9] There are several bills paid for books and schooling for Theobald, and although he appears not to have shared in the dancing lessons given Ned and George (in this instance there is no bill for him specifically), it is evident that Rockingham expended a considerable sum on his godson. Mr Evans seems not to have been satisfactory as a schoolmaster, and at the end of Michaelmas Term 1699, after paying £45 for half a year's schooling for 'Ned & George &c.', Rockingham gave Evans an additional £10 'at the same time to oblige him to be ye more carefull of 'em'.[10] The following April the boys were moved to a school in Isleworth run by the Reverend James Ellis.

In later years Theobald gratefully acknowledged the kindness of his godparent (who in 1714 had been created Earl of Rockingham) in a Dedication: 'your Lordship vouchsaf'd to patronize the Author . . . almost from the Hour of his Birth . . . [P]ermit me, my Lord, to boast of that chearing Influence from your Goodness, which secured me against those Calamities, that might have crush'd me, thro' the Loss of a Father, and a decaying Fortune.'[11] Rockingham's generosity continued until the end of his life, and there are records in his last account book of gifts of four and five guineas to Theobald.[12] The experience of growing up in an aristocratic household, without being one of the family, may account for the fluctuations between boastful confidence and extreme diffidence that are found in Theobald's career. Unlike his exact contemporary, Alexander Pope, he had no expectations of being treated as an equal by the aristocracy, although he sustained an intimacy with at least three noble families.

The chief benefit of Theobald's upbringing was his education. In his Dedication to Rockingham he observes: 'You bestow'd an Education on me, I may justly style Liberal, since

8 Ibid., fo. 200^r (Aug. 1696).   9 Ibid., fo. 216^r.   10 Ibid., fo. 252^r.

11 Dedication, *Oedipus King of Thebes. A Tragedy. Translated from Sophocles with Notes* (1715), sigs. A3^v–A4^r.

12 Lincolnshire Archives Office, MS 10/1/A, 1 (Monson MS cxx), 'The Earl of Rockingham 1715–23', fos. 8, 23, 39, 78, 107, 144, 149.

for above seven Years you were pleas'd to make me a Companion for your Noble Sons.'[13] According to Thomas Hearne, Theobald had 'a very able schoolmaster'. The Reverend James Ellis was a graduate of Oriel College, Oxford, and kept his private school 'purely for grounding young Gentlemen, noblemen's sons or Gentlemen of some Rank, in Classick Learning, & fitting them for the University, in which Faculty he is of considerable Repute'.[14] Theobald did not proceed to university, however; like his father, he was destined to be an attorney, and throughout his life he maintained a desultory practice. Although his training in the law was a significant factor when he became a Shakespearian editor (as an attorney he would have been familiar with Elizabethan secretary script),[15] with Ellis he developed a love of literature and, equally significantly, a love of the scholarship that made classical literature accessible.

Before the Act of 1729 regulating the training and practice of attorneys,[16] when attorneys' bills were in court hand and Law Latin, the profession of attorney 'was held in such estimation that it was no disgrace to a gentleman, or to a younger son of one higher born, to be bred to it'.[17] But many rebelled against the drudgery of the profession, and clearly Theobald was one of these. In 1707, when he may have been apprenticing,[18] he published *A Pindaric Ode on the Union of Scotland and England* and *Naufragium Britannicum a panegyrical poem dedicated to the memory of*

---

[13] Sigs. A4^r–A4^v.

[14] *Remarks and Collections of Thomas Hearne*, ed. C. E. Doble *et al.* (11 vols., Oxford: Clarendon Press, 1885–1921), xi, ed. H. E. Salter (1921), 341; ii, ed. C. E. Doble (1886), 9. See also i, ed. C. E. Doble (1885), 19 n. 1.

[15] Dr J. H. Baker of St Catharine's College, Cambridge, in a letter to me (4 Sept. 1974) on behalf of the Selden Society, observes that 'attorneys often had to examine archives of some antiquity and one would expect them to be able to read the secretary-hand, which is easier to read than court-hand'. See also Appendix A.

[16] 2 Geo. II, c. 23.

[17] *Reflections or Hints . . . touching the Law, Lawyers, officers, attorneys, etc.* (1759), quoted in Robert Robson, *The Attorney in Eighteenth Century England, Cambridge Studies in English Legal History*, ed. H. A. Holland (Cambridge: Cambridge University Press, 1959), 13. See also ibid. 55.

[18] Details of Theobald's legal career appear to be non-existent. Although judges in 1704 ordered attorneys to belong to some Inn of Court or Chancery, the orders were impossible to enforce, and barristers campaigned successfully to exclude attorneys from the Inns of Court (Robson, op. cit., 2–7). W. W. S. Breem, Librarian and Keeper of Manuscripts, The Honourable Society of the Inner Temple, tells me in a letter (29 Feb. 1984) that it is possible that Theobald was a member of one of the Inns

Sir Cloudsly Shovel, Kt. (commemorating the murder by a woman of Admiral Sir Clowdisley Shovell after his shipwreck on the Scilly Islands in October 1707). The following year marks his first theatrical venture, an attempt at tragedy. He tells us, with slight inaccuracy, that *The Persian Princess; or, The Royal Villain* 'was writ, and acted, before I was full Nineteen Years Old; and I expect that Age shall stand as a Plea for many Errors with the candid Reader'.[19] The play was performed twice at Drury Lane, on 31 May and 1 June. The managers of the theatre were kind enough to grant him a benefit on the second night, instead of waiting for the customary third.[20] Perhaps the experience was chastening, for nothing more is heard from Theobald until 1713, when he seems to have determined to escape the law for the uncertain livelihood of a man of letters.

When he embarked on his career as a writer, the chief objects of Theobald's admiration were Joseph Addison and Alexander Pope. He began an association with Bernard Lintot early in 1713, about the same time that Pope and Lintot were negotiating the contract to publish *The Iliad.*[21] Lintot planned an extensive list of classics in English, and, like Pope, Theobald hoped to establish himself with translation. As far as a knowledge of Greek and Latin was concerned in this undertaking, he was exceptionally well prepared by his schooling under Ellis. His first production for Lintot drew upon the great success of Addison's *Cato* and was entitled *The Life and Character of Marcus Cato of Utica . . . From whose History the late Famous Tragedy of Cato was drawn, and is Acted with such wonderful Applause at the Theatre in*

of Chancery, each of which was affiliated with one of the four Inns of Court, but that the Inns of Chancery were dissolved and no early membership list of any one of them is now extant. Other surviving records of attorneys are incomplete, and Theobald's name does not appear in the Book of Attorneys dating from 1656 in the Public Record Office, nor in the *Lists of Attornies and Solicitors Admitted in Pursuance of the late Act for the Better Regulation of Attorneys and Solicitors Presented to the House of Commons, Pursuant to their Order of the 26th Day of January 1729* (1729).

[19] Dedication, *The Persian Princess or, The Royal Villain* (1715), sig. A5ᵛ.

[20] *LS*, pt. 2, i. 172.

[21] Sherburn, p. 129 and n., dates Pope's agreement with Lintot 23 Mar. 1714. But when Pope's proposals for his translation of *The Iliad* were issued in Oct. 1713 (see Introduction, *The Iliad of Homer*, trans. Pope, Twickenham Edition, vii, ed. Maynard Mack *et al.* (London: Methuen, 1967), p. xxxvi and n. 5), Lintot was already involved in taking subscriptions, and it therefore seems that the agreement was signed in March 1713. See also Septimus Rivington, *The Publishing Family of Rivington* (London: Rivingtons, 1919), pp. 57, 61.

Drury Lane (1713). A second, enlarged edition, with a title-page emphasizing Theobald's knowledge of the Greek and Latin sources, appeared almost immediately. This was followed in turn by *Plato's Dialogue of the Immortality of the Soul. Translated from the Greek* (1713), the work Cato is said to have read on the last night of his life, and for which, in May 1713, Theobald was paid five guineas. These two works probably initiated his friendship with Addison. They were followed in 1715 by a translation from the French of *Monsieur Le Clerc's Observations upon Mr. Addison's Travels through Italy*, which, however, was printed for Edmund Curll. The interest in Homer generated by Pope's impending translation probably accounts for *A Critical Discourse upon the Iliad of Homer; written in French by Monsieur de la Motte . . . and translated into English by Mr. Theobald* (1714).

More directly related to his own ambitions was his contract with Lintot to translate Aeschylus for the sum of ten guineas. The translation, although completed, was never published.[22] On 21 April 1714, Theobald entered into a further agreement with Lintot. At fifty shillings for every 450 Greek verses, he undertook to translate into blank verse, with explanatory notes, Homer's *Odyssey*, Sophocles' *Oedipus Tyrannus, Oedipus Coloneus, Trachiniae*, and *Philoctetes*. In addition, he was to translate the Satires and Epistles of Horace into couplets at a rate of one guinea for every 120 lines. Although the contract called for a penalty of £50 upon the default of either party, in practice there must have been considerable flexibility. Theobald's association with Lintot actually resulted in five published works: in addition to those noted above, he translated Sophocles' *Electra* (1714),[23] dedicated to Addison, and *Oedipus King of Thebes* (1715). The first book of *The Odyssey* was printed by William

---

[22] Giles Jacobs, *The Poetical Register* (2 vols, 1723), i. 259, states that Theobald 'finish'd a Translation of the Seven Tragedies of ÆSCHYLUS'. In *The Dunciad* (1729), iii. 311 n., Pope says that Theobald 'printed a specimen of [Aeschylus] many years ago, of which I only remember that the first Note contains some comparison between *Prometheus* and *Christ crucify'd*'. Theobald has several references to his translation: *Electra* (1714), 71 n. 6; *SR* (1726), 194; *1733*, vii. 44 n.; and in his correspondence (12 Feb. 1734, 5 Mar. 1734, 18 Oct. 1735). Selections were printed: in *The Censor*, 60 (9 Mar. 1717), ii. 207–9, and in *The Grove* (1721), 315–21.

[23] This version was apparently acted: see vol. xvi of Bell's *British Theatre*: *Electra. A Tragedy, as Translated from Sophocles; with Notes, by Mr. Theobald. . . . as performed at the Theatre-Royal in Drury-Lane. Regulated from the Prompt-Book. . . . by Mr. Hopkins, Prompter* (1777), [4]. *LS*, however, has no notice of a performance.

Bowyer for Lintot in January, 1716.[24] In 1715, Theobald broke
with Lintot; however, he continued his ambitious programme
of translation with Aristophanes' *The Clouds* (1715) and *Plutus:*
or the World's Idol (1715), which were printed for Jonas Brown.
His efforts to establish himself with the public by these translations were totally unsuccessful, but it is worth noting that
those from Greek drama were 'highly esteemed' by Richard
Porson.[25]

In addition to his translations of this period, Theobald
published three poems. The first, *The Mausoleum. A Poem.*
Sacred to the Memory of her Late Majesty Queen Anne (1714), was dedicated
to Charles Boyle, Fourth Earl of Orrery, who was earlier the
antagonist of Richard Bentley in the Phalaris controversy and
later one of Theobald's most consistently generous patrons.
The poem itself has no interest, except for its passing tributes to
Addison and Pope. *A Poem written on the Recovery of the Duke of*
Ormond from a Dangerous Illness, mentioned by Theobald in the
Dedication of the *Persian Princess* (1715) to the Duchess of
Ormond, also seems to have been written in the hope of
patronage. More significant is *The Cave of Poverty. A Poem.*
Written in Imitation of Shakespeare (1715). Here, Theobald reveals
an interest in Shakespeare unusual in the early eighteenth
century: the poem displays a familiarity with *Venus and Adonis*
and adopts Shakespeare's stanza. As would be expected, there
are also obvious reminiscences of passages in Shakespeare. The
poem's 121 stanzas are divided into two parts: the first describes
the Queen of Poverty's cave, where she torments mankind.
The second depicts two brass horns that convey poverty's
complaints to the ears of the queen. In this part, Theobald's
financial struggles are reflected within the conventions of heroic
rejection of fate.

In 1715 Theobald launched *The Censor*, a tri-weekly periodical

---

24 Theobald's contracts with Lintot, now in the British Library (Add. MS 38729,
fos. 234–5), are described in Nichols, ii. 707–8; see also John Nichols, *Literary Anecdotes*
of the Eighteenth Century, i (1812), 80 n.; viii (1814), 174 n.; and J. C. Eade, 'Lewis
Theobald's Translation Rates: A Hard Bargain', *Library*, 1, 6th series (June 1979),
168–70. On-line ESTC records 1 copy of *The Odyssey of Homer. Book I. Translated from the*
Greek; with notes. By Mr. Theobald. [P]rinted for J. Roberts, 1717.

25 See *Reliquiae Hearnianae: The Remains of Thomas Hearne*, ed. Philip Bliss, 2nd ed.
(3 vols., 1869), iii. 137 n. 1. John Churton Collins thought the translations from the
Greek 'very meritorious' ('The Porson of Shakespearian Criticism', *Essays and Studies*
(1895), 276 n. 1).

that ran from 11 April to 17 June (No. 30), discontinued publication, and then was resumed from 1 January to 30 May 1717
(No. 96). A second edition was collected in three volumes in
1717. Although patrons of the collected edition included
Orrery and the Earl of Burlington, the papers were not a great
success, partly because they '*followed too close upon the Heels of the
inimitable* Spectator' and Theobald found it '*a hard Task to come
after such a Writer*'.[26] The persona of the *British Censor*, although
'lineally descended from *Benjamin Johnson* of surly Memory',[27]
has, however, an ingenuous charm—presumably unintended
—and allows Theobald to explore his interests in criticism,
scholarship, translation, and Shakespeare. *The Censor* may be
regarded as an extended tribute to Addison; but in No. 33 (5
January 1717), after ridiculing the critic John Dennis as *Furius*,
Theobald extols Pope's *Iliad*, saying that 'The spirit of *Homer*
breaths all through this Translation'.[28] The whole of this
panegyric eventually found its way, with minor changes, into
the 'Testimonies of Authors' in *The Dunciad* (1729).

1715 also marks Theobald's renewed connection with the
theatre. He contributed a Prologue to *A Woman's Revenge; or, A
Match in Newgate*, an afterpiece adapted from Aphra Behn by
Christopher Bullock and performed on 24 October at John
Rich's recently opened theatre in Lincoln's Inn Fields.[29] A
production of Theobald's *The Perfidious Brother* followed on 21
February 1716. The play 'was got up with indefatigable Application, in Twelve Days time from the first Reading, which is
less than ever any Tragedy was known to be got ready in'.
Although it ran for four nights and the author's benefit grossed
£25 17s. in money at the door and £81 7s. in tickets, the play
was not a financial success for Rich's company.[30] It was also
the subject of controversy. A watchmaker called Mestayer
had brought Theobald an outline of the tragedy and then
claimed Theobald had stolen his work; in his Preface to the
printed version (1715) Theobald maintained he had 'labour'd
at it Four Months almost without Intermission' and had

---

[26] Preface to 2nd edn. (3 vols., 1717), vol. i, sig. A6ʳ.
[27] *Censor*, 1 (11 Apr. 1715), i. [1].
[28] Ibid. ii. 18–19.
[29] *LS*, pt. 2, i. 372.
[30] Ibid. i. 390.

'created it anew: For even where the Original Matter is continued, I have brought it to Light, and drawn it as from a *Chaos*'.[31] Mestayer subsequently published his version, ironically dedicated to Theobald. Although Theobald's account seems accurate, the affair reflects badly on him.

The real benefit of these ventures was that Theobald began a lifelong friendship with John Stede, Rich's promoter for more than twenty years. He also became associated with John Rich himself, and the results were, for better or worse, to affect London theatres for the next fifty years. But it is his intimacy with Stede that has importance for his future work as an editor of Shakespeare. In the Bodleian Library there are three manuscript prompt-books for Theobald's *The Perfidious Brother*, Elkanah Settle's *The Lady's Triumph*, and Thomas Southerne's *Money the Mistress*, dating from early in 1716, 1718, and 1726. The great majority of the prompt-notes for all three plays and the texts of *The Perfidious Brother* and *The Lady's Triumph* are in Theobald's handwriting.[32] As an assistant to Stede, he acquired a familiarity with the ways of the theatre and with the treatment and appearance of dramatic manuscripts. Both were of incalculable importance in Theobald's conjectural emendations of Shakespeare. Because of this experience he was able, with a preciseness available to few other editors, to strip away the veil of print and imagine the nature of the manuscript before a compositor, as well as the kind of misreadings such a manuscript might induce.

He also tried his hand at an oriental tale, *The History of the Loves of Antiochus and Stratonice* (1717). The Preface, which discusses his scholarly sources and critical principles, has been admired: 'It is an unusually dignified, modest, and aesthetically informative essay'; but the novel itself, although recognized as an early contribution to exotic Eastern fiction and presaging *Rasselas*, is a failure.[33]

Theobald's involvement with Rich's theatre provided John Dennis with a handle in his retaliation for Theobald's satire on

---

[31] Sig. A3[r].

[32] Bodleian Library, MS Rawl. poet. 136. The prompt-books are described in detail by Edward A. Langhans, 'Three Early Eighteenth-Century Manuscript Promptbooks', *Modern Philology*, 65 (1967). See below, p. 145.

[33] Malcolm J. Bosse, Introduction, *The History of the Loves of Antiochus and Stratonice*, *Foundations of the Novel* (New York: Garland, 1973), 5, 8.

him as *Furius* in *Censor* No. 33. Countering Theobald's praise of
Pope's Homer, Dennis asserts: 'There is a notorious Ideot, one
Hight *Whachum*, who from an under-spur Leather to the Law,
is become an under-strapper to the Play-House.'[34] By 1717
Theobald's connection with Lincoln's Inn Fields was well
known. The rivalry between Lincoln's Inn Fields and Drury
Lane provided Theobald with further opportunities to serve
Rich. In order to woo audiences away from Drury Lane, in
1715 Rich's relatively young, inexperienced company began to
offer musical interludes and afterpieces consisting of farces or
pantomimic 'Entertainments of Dancing in Grotesque Characters'. The importance of the supplementary bill was increased
on 22 April 1717, when Rich himself, under the stage name of
Lun, made his debut as Harlequin in 'an Italian Night Scene'
entitled *The Cheats; or, The Tavern Bilkers*.[35] Theobald's first
definitely known contribution to these additional entertainments is *Pan and Syrinx*, a one-act opera with music by John
Ernest Galliard performed on 14 January 1718. It was revived
in 1726 and had a total run of nineteen performances. This was
soon followed by *Decius and Paulina* on 22 March 1718, an
operatic masque included in the performance of Elkanah
Settle's *The Lady's Triumph* and expanded for a revival of
Charles D'Avenant's *Circe* in 1719. Again the experiment was
worthwhile, with fifteen performances in all.[36] Although John
Rich was the recipient of occasional benefit nights for these
productions, Theobald was also sporadically well paid for his
assistance as librettist.[37]

---

[34] *Remarks upon Pope's Homer* (1717) in *The Critical Works of John Dennis*, ed. E. N.
Hooker (2 vols., Baltimore: Johns Hopkins Press, 1939–43), ii. 122. *Whachum* alludes
to the persona of *The Censor*.

[35] See Emmett L. Avery, 'The Repertory: The Afterpiece', *LS*, pt. 2, i. cxvii–cxx,
and Leo Hughes, 'Afterpieces: or, That's Entertainment', in *The Stage and the Page:
London's 'Whole Show' in the Eighteenth-Century Theatre*, ed. Geo. Winchester Stone, Jr.
(Berkeley: University of California Press, 1981), 60–2.

[36] Numbers of performances derive from the *Index to the London Stage, 1660–1800*,
compiled by Ben Ross Schneider, Jr. (Carbondale: Southern Illinois University Press,
1979).

[37] British Library, Egerton MS 2265, Lincoln's Inn Fields Accounts (1724/25),
fo. 52 (10 Dec. 1724): 'Mr J. Rich on acct. of M^r. Theobalds—[£]10/10/0'; fo. 117
(16 Mar. 1725): 'Repaid M^r. J. Rich a bill he paid M^r. Theobalds [£]25/1/7'; British
Library, Egerton MS 2266 (1726/27), fo. 111^v (27 Feb. 1727): 'The Savage &
Proserpine the 9th Night for M^r. J. Rich as Author [£198 7*s.* 6*d.*] [*LS*] Reced of
M^r. J. Rich for the Charges [£]40/0/0'; fo. 133 (8 Apr. 1727): 'M^r. Theobalds on act
[£]30/0/0'.

The golden age of English pantomime began in 1723. Rich had been sufficiently encouraged by the success of his performance in *The Tavern Bilkers* to stage other pantomimes. Probably with Theobald's collaboration, he began to explore in *Amadis; or, The Loves of Harlequin and Colombine* (24 January 1718) what was to become the most popular form of pantomime, a *mélange* of classical themes, lavish spectacle, song, dance, and mimed *commedia dell'arte* sub-plots. The success of the rival Drury Lane *Harlequin Doctor Faustus* on 26 November 1723, with 'All the Scenes, Machines, Habits, and other Decorations being entirely New',[38] prompted Rich (perhaps with Theobald) to stage *The Necromancer; or, Harlequin Doctor Faustus* (20 December), which grossed £162 1*s.* the first evening and remained in the repertory for 341 performances. This extraordinary success was followed by a series of pantomimes devised by Theobald that became the mainstay of Rich's fortunes until his death in 1761: *Harlequin a Sorcerer, with the Loves of Pluto and Proserpine* in which was 'shewn the boldest Piece of Machinery that ever yet was seen upon the Stage' (21 January 1725; 443 performances), *Apollo and Daphne; or, the Burgomaster Trick'd* (14 January 1726; 362 performances), *The Rape of Proserpine; or, The Birth and Adventures of Harlequin*, which, according to *Mist's Journal* (18 February 1727), 'is of the Nature of Pantomimes, partly grotesque, and partly vocal, but far exceeds all ever yet shewn, in the Magnificence and Beauty of the Scenes, the Number and Richness of the Habits, as well as the Fable, which is purely poetical, as the Italian Operas ought to be' (13 February 1727; receipts £216 12*s.*; 462 performances), and *Perseus and Andromeda; or, The Spaniard Outwitted* (2 January 1730; 448 performances).[39]

The vitality of pantomime fascinated Theobald, but not to the exclusion of his other interests. In the midst of the bustle

[38] *LS*, pt. 2, ii. 746.

[39] *LS* and *Index to the London Stage* (a distinction has been made between the *Perseus and Andromeda* performed at Drury Lane and that staged at Lincoln's Inn Fields). For general accounts of pantomime in this period, see Emmett L. Avery, 'Dancing and Pantomime on the English Stage, 1700–1737', *Studies in Philology*, 21 (1934); Avery, 'The Defence and Criticism of Pantomimic Entertainments in the Early Eighteenth Century', *English Literary History*, 5 (1938); Roger Fiske, *English Theatre Music in the Eighteenth Century* (London: Oxford University Press, 1973); Viola Papetti, *Arlecchino a Londra: La Pantomima Inglese 1700–1728* (Naples: Instituto Universitario Orientale, 1977).

associated with earning his living, he continued to aspire to the dignity of a poet while sustaining the temperamental inclinations of a literary critic, a scholar, and an antiquary. At the forefront of these interests was Shakespeare. On 10 December 1719 his adaptation of *Richard II*, a relatively unpopular play, was performed at Lincoln's Inn Fields in a run of seven performances, followed by three more in 1721. The adaptation was dedicated to the Fourth Earl of Orrery.[40] Theobald's Preface makes it apparent that he rewrote the play as a neo-Aristotelian experiment: '*The many scatter'd Beauties, which I have long admir'd . . . induced me to think they would have stronger Charms, if they were inter[w]oven in a regular Fable . . . maintaining the* Unity *of* Action, *or supporting the* Dignity *of the* Characters.'[41] The result is no better or worse than most Restoration and eighteenth-century adaptations of Shakespeare. Theobald was able to retain about one-quarter of the original's language. The value of this enterprise as good theatre was learned at the box-office. *The London Stage* records the sums taken during the revival of 1721: on 7 January the receipts were £86 9s., but there was an afterpiece, *Amadis; or, The Loves of Harlequin and Colombine*. On 4 February the play was performed without an afterpiece, and the receipts were £23 9s. At its final performance, again without afterpiece, the receipts were £11 14s. 6d. At this time, the theatre needed about £40 to break even.[42] Theobald might have consoled himself with the thought that this dismal showing of the play at the box-office was not due solely to his alterations. For example, on 14 November the receipts for *Othello*, which was not adapted, were £11 19s. But his belief in the power of a regular fable to enforce 'stronger Charms' was not supported by experience. On the other hand,

[40] [John Mottley], in 'A List of all the Dramatic Authors, with some Account of their Lives; and of all the Dramatic Pieces ever published in the English Language, to the Year 1747' appended to Thomas Whincop's *Scanderbeg: or Love and Liberty* (1747), 294, records Orrery's generosity on this occasion: 'My Lord asked Mr. *Theobald* if he took Snuff; which he answering in the Affirmative, his Patron made him a Present of a very handsome Box, made of *Egyptian* Peeble, the Top and Bottom, the Rims and Hinges being of Gold, all together, perhaps, of about twenty Pounds Value, which Mr. *Theobald* could not but think a very genteel Acknowledgment of the Compliment he had made his Lordship; but how agreeable was his Surprize when he came home, and found a Bank Bill of one hundred Pounds inclosed in it?'

[41] Sig. Aa^r.

[42] See *LS*, pt. 2, i. xcvii.

the power of pantomime, whatever its source, was again proved.

Theobald's chief concern in his Preface to *Richard II* is to put Shakespeare '*at least, upon the Foot of a tolerable Scholar*'.[43] He believed throughout his life that Shakespeare's learning was underestimated. In the Preface he calls on a wide range of reading to prove Shakespeare's knowledge of Greek and Latin by parallel passages. His discussion is lengthy and sensible, but at this early stage in his thought about Shakespeare he was unaware of North's translation of Plutarch. As a result, he is less cautious in his pronouncements on Shakespeare's knowledge of the classics than he was to be in his edition.

Theobald also continued to admire Pope and to seek his friendship. Indeed, in a translation of Ovid's *Metamorphoses*, said by John Dennis to be 'vile', there is a suggestion of cooperation, if not actual friendship, between them. Pope's *Vertumnus and Pomona* (first printed in *Miscellaneous Poems and Translations*, 1712) was included in book xiv, otherwise translated by Theobald, the result being labelled 'by Mr. Pope and Mr. Theobald'.[44] Although technically a collaboration, since Pope's permission was presumably sought and granted, this joint translation need not imply friendship, although Theobald's earlier expressions of admiration for Pope would not have been displeasing to the latter, especially when coupled with an attack on Dennis.[45] In 1721 Theobald published *The Grove; or, a Collection of Original Poems, Translations, &c*, a compilation from different authors, including himself, in which his praise of Pope is continued. The volume was published by subscription, so Pope probably knew Theobald was the editor, although this fact was not publicly announced until 1732, when the remaining sheets were reissued with a different title-page.[46] In any event, Pope took the unusual step, for him, of subscrib-

---

[43] Sig. Aa2ᵛ.

[44] *Ovid's Metamorphoses. In Fifteen Books. A New Translation. By Several Hands* (2 vols., 1717), ii. [312]. The compiler was G[eorge] Sewell, and Edmund Curll was one of the publishers. Dennis's characterization appears in *Remarks upon Pope's Homer* (1717), in *Works*, ed. Hooker, ii. 122.

[45] See Sherburn, p. 183, and Norman Ault, *New Light on Pope* (London: Methuen, 1949), 164.

[46] *A Miscellany of Original Poems, Translations, &c. Collected and Published by Mr. Theobald* (1732).

ing for four copies on Royal Paper of the miscellany, which also contained lavish tributes to him:

> So much, dear *Pope*, thy *English Illiad* Charms,
> Where Pity melts us, or where Passion warms,
> That after-Ages shall with Wonder seek,
> Who 'twas translated *Homer* into *Greek*.[47]

Theobald's life in the 1720s (and, indeed, generally) seems to have been one of fleeting affluence followed by endemic financial emergencies. His devotion to literature and the stage was constant, however, and he showed no enthusiasm for the practice of law. He appears to have been perpetually hopeful and a regular client of usurers. When pressed for repayment, he would either borrow from John Rich or be allowed a benefit either at Lincoln's Inn Fields Theatre or Drury Lane, since he was on good terms with the managers of both theatres, despite their intense rivalry. In this fashion he went from crisis to crisis until the end of his life, but with a grace that his friends found charming and that had them rallying to his support. Undoubtedly typical is a letter of 13 May 1727:

S[r]:

M[r]. Concanen[48] was so kind to inform you I was under some Difficulties: but, I thank God, I have hopes of getting over them. A considerable sume I have already paid; & another Means, by w[ch]: I expect to disengage myself, is a Benefit Play.[49] This, as you'll see, S[r]., by the inclosed packet, I have contracted for wth the Drury Lane Theatre. I flatter myself, upon so pressing an Emergency, you will be so good to exert your Interest for my Service: & to that End I have enclosed 12 of my Box Tickets. I have chose a play, w[ch]: as I think I have heard you intimate, is a Favourite of Madam Towne's: tis greatly my Desire to have the Ladies my Friends in this Cause. Excuse haste, & the Trouble of this Address in

S[r].

Y[r]: most humble Serv[t].[50]

---

[47] 'To Mr. Pope on his Translation of Homer', p. 265; see also pp. 284–6.

[48] Matthew Concanen (1701–49), Irish poet and journalist, founder of the Concanen Club, eventually Attorney-General of Jamaica, and a steady friend of Theobald.

[49] Beaumont and Fletcher's *Rule a Wife and Have a Wife* followed by *The Strollers* and performed 24 May 1727. *LS*, pt. 2, ii. 928, records that the performance was 'At the particular Desire of several Persons of Quality'.

[50] Yale University, Beinecke Rare Book and Manuscript Library, James M. and Marie-Louise Osborn Collection).

The great tragedy of Theobald's life was that he never received a pension or sinecure that would have allowed him a life of scholarship. In 1730, after the death of the poet laureate, Laurence Eusden, the women in his household[51] spurred him up 'to put in for the withered laurel'. With Lord Gage he 'attended Sir Robert Walpole; was commanded by him to attend at Windsor; had his warmest recommendations to the Lord Chamberlain; nay, procured those recommendations to be seconded even by his Royal Highness: and yet, after standing fair for the post at least three weeks, had the mortification to be supplanted by *Keyber*'. By this time he was hard at work on Shakespeare and, as he writes, 'would fain sit down to my little studies with an easy competency'.[52] Because of the failure of this and other solicitations, he was forced to continue to take advantage of his theatrical connections to earn a living. He was fortunate, however, in the assistance of his friends.

It was some time in early 1727 that a 'Noble Person', probably Charles Boyle, Fourth Earl of Orrery, presented him with a manuscript of what was believed to be a lost play by Shakespeare. Altogether Theobald acquired three manuscripts of the play, which he revised for the stage with the title *Double Falshood; or, The Distrest Lovers*.[53] The play proved a financial success, after opening on 13 December 1727 at Drury Lane and yielding Theobald three benefit nights and a run of thirteen performances. It was revived in 1729 for the 'Benefit of the Author of *Shakespeare Restor'd*', and again in 1740–1 there were three more performances, the last of which, on 15 May 1741 at Covent Garden, was 'By Command of their Royal Highnesses the Prince and Princess of Wales, Prince George, and the Lady Augusta. Benefit the last Editor of Shakespear' with receipts of £100.[54] In addition to the profits from his benefit nights,

[51] I have not been able to discover the identity of his wife or the date of their marriage. They had a son who, in Aug. 1739, was old enough to be employed in the Office of the Pells. See below, ch. 10 n. 26.

[52] Letter to William Warburton, Nichols, ii. 617 (Dec. 1730).

[53] For a comprehensive account of this play and the evidence for associating it with Shakespeare, see John Freehafer, '*Cardenio*, by Shakespeare and Fletcher', *PMLA*, 84 (1969). See also below, p. 135 and Appendix C.

[54] *LS*, pt. 2, ii. 949–50, 951, 954; pt. 3, ii. 873, 917. On this last occasion the Prince did not attend the performance. See also B. S. Hammond, 'The Performance History of a Pseudo-Shakespearean Play: Theobald's *Double Falshood*', *British Journal for Eighteenth Century Studies*, 7 (1984).

Theobald received the extraordinary sum of one hundred guineas for the copyright of the play from John Watts, a London stationer probably acting for Jacob Tonson.[55]

Theobald's part in the repertory of Lincoln's Inn Fields suggests that he had both a catholic taste and, when his other activities are remembered, great energy. His contribution to Rich's pantomimes was undoubtedly important, although the chief attractions of these performances were Rich's skill as a mime and the spectacular effects of the stage-managers. He would, of course, have had ample opportunity to influence Rich—and it seems that what distinguished Rich from the other mimes of his day was a concern to exhibit a progressive revelation of character.[56] However, not until Pope published his edition of *Shakespear* in 1725, followed by Theobald's long, unfavourable review, *Shakespeare Restored* (1726), did Theobald become of consequence to literary history, first as the hero of *The Dunciad*, and then as an editor of Shakespeare. Before these events, Theobald's greatest success was as a deviser of Rich's mimes.

For Pope, it was an affront to have the inadequacies of his *Shakespear* exposed by one who blatantly catered to the vulgar tastes of the town. Indeed, Theobald seemed determined to emphasize this fact by dedicating *Shakespeare Restored* to Rich. It was, no doubt, a gesture designed 'to carry the Sentiments of *Friendship* and *Gratitude*' in the 'Acknowledgment of some Obligations receiv'd,' but Theobald's choice of Rich as a dedicatee and his candour manage to surprise even twentieth-century scholars. In fact, both Rich and Theobald tended to be apologetic about pantomime and their roles in it. Theobald was inclined to blame the debauched taste of the town for the popularity of mime but, as a good critic should, kept an open mind and was able to recognize the real pleasure it afforded: 'perhaps, the very Frame of our Nature is concern'd; and the Dissecters of an *Eye* and *Ear* can tell us to what Membranes, or

---

[55] See Appendix C and Freehafer, op. cit., 513. Freehafer points out that Theobald received only 6 guineas for his adaptation of Webster's *The Duchess of Malfi* as *The Fatal Secret* (1735).

[56] See Elvena M. Green, 'John Rich's Art of Pantomime as Seen in his *The Necromancer, or Harlequin Doctor Faustus*: A Comparison of the Two Faustus Pantomimes at Lincoln's-Inn-Fields and Drury Lane', *Restoration and 18th Century Theatre Research*, 4 (1965), 51.

Organs, we owe the Communication of *Pleasures*, in which the *rational Soul* has no Share.'[57] Rich acknowledged that his 'Theatre has of late ow'd its Support in great Measure' to pantomime, but maintained 'whenever the Publick Taste shall be disposed to return to the Works of the *Drama*, no one shall rejoice more sincerely than my self'.[58] But the theatre-going public, from the monarchy down, demanded these afterpieces: 'George I and George II enjoyed what was tantamount to an animated comic book in their predilection for 2,027 performances of pantomimes, farces, drolls, musicals, and nondescript "entertainments"—a number nearly equalling the 2,361 performances of tragedies, and about half the number (5,823) of performances of comedies.'[59]

This enthusiasm for afterpieces and other entertainments was known in a general way at the time, as was Theobald's part in the proceedings. In the opening lines of *The Dunciad* (1729) Pope writes: 'BOOKS and the Man I sing, the first who brings | The Smithfield Muses to the Ear of Kings' (i. 1–2). Pope's note on the second line is explicit: '*Smithfield* is the place where Bartholomew Fair was kept, whose Shews, Machines, and Dramatical Entertainments, formerly agreeable only to the Taste of the Rabble, were, by the Hero of this Poem and others of equal Genius, brought to the Theatres of Covent-Garden, Lincolns-inn-Fields, and the Hay-Market, to be the reigning Pleasures of the Court and Town.' Of course, Pope himself was in some ways fascinated by the vitality of pantomime, and *The Dunciad*, Book III revels in the descriptions of *The Necromancer; or, Harlequin Doctor Faustus* and Theobald's *The Rape of Proserpine*:

> He look'd, and saw a sable Sorc'rer rise
> Swift to whose hand a winged volume flies:
> All sudden, Gorgons hiss, and Dragons glare,
> And ten-horn'd fiends and Giants rush to war.
> Hell rises, Heav'n descends, and dance on Earth,
> Gods, imps, and monsters, music, rage, and mirth,

---

[57] *SR*, sigs. A3ᵛ, A2ᵛ.

[58] Dedication, *The Rape of Proserpine*, 3rd edn. (1727), pp. v–vi. The receipts for the second night this afterpiece was staged (14 Feb. 1727) were £203 19*s*. (*LS*).

[59] George Winchester Stone, Jr., 'The Making of the Repertory', in *The London Theatre World, 1660–1800*, ed. Robert D. Hume (Carbondale: Southern Illinois University Press, 1980), 188. See also Louis D. Mitchell, 'Command Performances during the Reign of George I', *Eighteenth-Century Studies*, 7 (1974).

> A fire, a jig, a battle, and a ball,
> Till one wide Conflagration swallows all.
>
> (iii. 229–36)

Much of the good humour of *The Dunciad* of 1729 comes from a tacit understanding that Theobald's doings in the theatre are not equiponderant with Pope's larger theme, even as the traditional image of the world as theatre is invoked; and part of the witty confusion of Book III is that theatrical scenes are described in apocalyptical terms, while the apocalypse itself concludes with a theatrical image:

> Thy hand great Dulness! lets the curtain fall,
> And universal Darkness covers all.
>
> (iii. 355–6)

The value of Theobald's experiments with pantomime was that they confirmed his respect for the audience's imaginative response to a play. Whether this response was produced by diction, song, spectacle, or special effects was less important than that it should be produced at all. This first rule of dramaturgy was driven home by the necessity of earning a living. It also created a sympathetic respect for the achievement of Shakespeare and tempered Theobald's view of the importance of neo-Aristotelian rules—although this last consequence of his experience has not been generally recognized.

3. The Critical Approach to Shakespeare

A MAJOR charge against Theobald as a critic has been that he is one of the 'pedant theorists' with a 'complacent belief in the rules'.[1] In so far as Theobald is a theorist, he is so in the manner of Dryden in the 1670s, when Dryden was rebelling against the neo-Aristotelian constraints of Thomas Rymer. Dryden emphasized the necessity of pleasing an audience, and maintained that English audiences delighted in character as revealed through language. In the essay *Of Dramatic Poesy* (1668) he had supposed that the rules of French neo-Aristotelianism lead to 'the beauties of a statue, but not of a man, because not animated with the soul of poesy, which is imitation of humour and passions'.[2] For Dryden, the vitality of dramatic language was far more important than the rules pertaining to plot, and he thought that 'in most of the irregular plays of Shakespeare . . . there is a more masculine fancy and greater spirit in the writing than there is in any of the French'.[3] In *The Tragedies of the Last Age* (1678) Rymer also seemed to reject French formalism: 'I would not examin the *proportions*, the *unities* and *outward* regularities, the *mechanical part* of Tragedies.' The style in which he gave his reasons is, however, the best guide to his belief: ' 'tis not necessary for a man to have a nose on his face, nor to have two legs: he may be a *true* man, though aukward and unsightly, as the *Monster* in the *Tempest*.' This was simply a hit at Dryden's trope on the beauties of a statue. In fact, Rymer did subscribe to the rules of formalism: 'in the contrivance and *oeconomy* of a Play, *reason* is always principally to be consulted.'[4] Rymer also differs from Dryden in more fundamental matters.

Instead of delight in character and language, Rymer insists

---

[1] Smith, p. xix.
[2] Watson, i. 56.
[3] Ibid. 66.
[4] Zimansky, pp. 18, 20.

on the moral purpose of tragedy as found in 'the *Fable* or *Plot*, which all conclude to be the *Soul* of a *Tragedy*; which, with the *Ancients*, is always found to be a *reasonable Soul*; but *with us*, for the most part, a *brutish*, and often worse than *brutish*'. Rymer's moral stance ensured that his criticism would be treated with respectful caution: opponents had to admit the validity of an explicit moral purpose, such as he claimed to find in the fables of Greek tragedy, 'unless they will, in effect say, that we have not that *delicate tast* of things; we are not so *refin'd*, nor so *vertuous*; that *Athens* was more *civiliz'd* by their *Philosophers*, than we with both our *Philosophers* and *twelve Apostles*'. His requirements are probability of action (with private experience or history as a standard of comparison) and the illustration of a moral order through observance of what he was the first to call '*Poetical Justice*'.[5] Indeed, a moral purpose in the design of the fable is Rymer's chief critical concern.[6]

Dryden and Rymer never engaged in an outright critical war, but they delineated the two main conflicting critical approaches to drama in the eighteenth century. Rymer's continued hostility to Dryden's emphasis on character and language is obvious in *A Short View of Tragedy* (1693), especially in his attack on *Othello* where at best it is asserted, 'The verse rumbling in our Ears are of good use to help off the action.'[7] Dryden's 'Heads of An Answer to Rymer'—a set of notes jotted down in the fly-leaves of *The Tragedies of the Last Age*—were not published until 1711, when they appeared in a Preface to the works of Beaumont and Fletcher published by Jacob Tonson. Although not well known in the early eighteenth century, they were read by Theobald,[8] who seems to have been particularly impressed by Dryden's belief that

Amongst us, who have a stronger genius for writing, the operations from the writing are much stronger: for the raising of Shakespeare's passions are more from the excellency of the words and thoughts than the justness of the occasion; and if he has been able to pick single

[5] Zimansky, pp. 18, 19, 26; see also 75.
[6] Ibid. 23.
[7] Ibid. 136.
[8] Theobald refers to the edition of Beaumont and Fletcher in his correspondence and identifies the editor as Nicholas Rowe (Nichols, ii. 620). Johnson printed the 'Heads' in his 'Life of Dryden', unaware of their previous publication.

occasions, he has never founded the whole reasonably; yet by the genius of poetry, in writing he has succeeded.

Dryden was able to find support for his views on the supreme importance of dramatic language over plot in the work of the French critic, René Rapin: 'Rapin's words are remarkable: " 'Tis not the admirable intrigue, the surprising events, the extraordinary incidents that make the beauty of a tragedy; 'tis the discourses when they are natural and passionate." So are Shakespeare's.'[9]

The rival claims of plot design and affective language as the chief concern of critics were at their height in the first three decades of the eighteenth century. Even such a dedicated follower of Rymer and the French neo-Aristotelians as Charles Gildon felt genuine inner conflict when he confronted the issue:

It must be own'd, that Mr. *Rymer* carried the Matter too far, since no Man, that has the least Relish of Poetry, can question [Shakespeare's] *Genius*: For, in spite of his known and visible Errors, when I read *Shakespear*, even in some of his most irregular Plays, I am surpriz'd into a Pleasure so great, that my Judgment is no longer free to see the Faults, tho' they are never so Gross and Evident.[10]

Gildon, however, was not alone when he proceeded to attack the 'very formidable Party among us, who are such Libertines in all manner of Poetry, especially in the *Drama*, that they think all regular Principles of Art an Imposition not to be born' and reasserted, on behalf of Rymer, that '*Aristotle* . . . and his best Commentator [André Dacier] are very large on this Head, to prove, that all the *fine Diction*, the *Manners* well express'd, and the Sentiments Natural and Just are of no manner of Value if the Fable be faulty, or the Action maim'd.'[11]

Like Dryden, Theobald was aware that conformity with neo-Aristotelian dictates conferred respectability. Yet, like Dryden,

---

[9] Watson, i. 216–17, 220; Dryden's reference to Rapin (who had been translated by Rymer in 1674) comes from *Réflexions sur la poëtique d'Aristote* (Paris, 1674), ii. xxi.

[10] 'Essay on the Art, Rise, and Progress of the Stage', in *The Works of Mr. William Shakespear. Volume the Seventh* (1710), p. v. (This volume was published by Curll as a supplement to Tonson's *Shakespear*, 1709, ed. Nicholas Rowe.)

[11] Ibid., pp. xi–xii, xxxii; the Dacier reference is to 'Remarques sur le chapitre VI', *La Poétique d'Aristote . . . Avec des remarques* (Paris, 1692), 99: 'Aristote n'assigne que le quatriéme rang à la diction, à l'Elocution. En effet on peut dire que de toutes les parties essencielles à la Tragedie, la diction est la moins importante.'

he was also prepared to qualify critical theory in the light of theatrical experience. A playwright must please his audience, and he was keenly aware of his own delight in literature, especially Shakespeare, for whose writings he had a 'Veneration, almost rising to Idolatry'.[12] When neo-Aristotelian rules conflicted with the sources of his pleasure, he was prepared to consider the possibility that other principles of dramaturgy, having their own validity, might be involved. He believed that Shakespeare is a poet 'whose Honour must never dye till Taste and Judgment are withered in our Country'.[13]

Theobald's Shakespearian criticism emphasizes language and character and minimizes neo-Aristotelian preoccupations with plot or fable. *Censor* No. 7 (25 April 1715) is remarkable as the first examination of *King Lear* in relation to the play's source in Holinshed's *Chronicles* (1577).[14] Theobald cannot ignore Shakespeare's failure to observe the unities, but he stresses Shakespeare's affective power: 'with all its Defects and Irregularities [*Lear*] has still touch'd me with the strongest Compassion, as well in my Study, as on the Stage.' Shakespeare is a master of character and language, and Theobald intends

not to charge [*King Lear*] with those Errors, which all this Author's Plays lie under, thro' his being unacquainted with the *Rules* of *Aristotle*, and the *Tragedies* of the *Ancients*; but to view it on the beautiful Side, to remark the Propriety of *Lear*'s Character, how well it is supported throughout all the Scenes, and what Spirit and Elegance reigns in the Language and Sentiments.

The rest of the paper is taken up with Holinshed's history of Lear, but before concluding Theobald indicates that in his next paper on *Lear* he will

Examine how *Shakespear*, by Incidents naturally arising out of his Fable, has encreas'd the Distress of the History; wherein he has kept up to the Tenor of it; and how artfully he has preserv'd the Character

---

[12] *SR*, p. iii.

[13] *Censor*, 26 (8 June 1715), i. 184.

[14] By the time he printed his edition of *Shakespeare* Theobald had discovered *The True Chronicle History of King Leir* (1605); he was at pains to prove that Shakespeare 'may stand acquitted from the least Suspicion of Plagiarism, in the Opinion of his Readers' (*1733*, v. 217 n.). He also knew of Shakespeare's use of Samuel Harsnett's *Declaration of Egregious Popish Impostures* (1603) (ibid. 163–4 n.).

of *Lear*, and given him Language and Manners conformable to his recorded Conduct and Infirmities.[15]

Censor No. 10 (2 May 1715) resumes Theobald's examination. His purpose is to forestall any objections in the manner of Rymer to the improbability of Lear's conduct by a demonstration of its historical basis. He observes that Shakespeare 'has been just, to great Exactness' in following Holinshed: 'He has copied the *Annals*, in the Partition of his Kingdom, and discarding *Cordelia*; in his alternate Monthly Residence with his two Eldest Daughters, and their ungrateful Returns of his Kindness; in *Cordelia*'s marrying into *France*, and her prevailing with her Lord for a sufficient Aid to restore her abus'd Father to his Dominions.'[16] In the catastrophe, Theobald observes, 'the Poet has given himself a Liberty to be Master of the Story: For *Lear* and *Cordelia* are taken Prisoners, and both lying under Sentence of Death, the latter is hang'd in the Prison, and the former breaks his Heart with the Affliction of it.'[17] This information was necessary for those readers familiar only with the happy ending provided by Nahum Tate in the interests of poetic justice in his alteration of *Lear* (1681). Like Johnson, Theobald is inclined to point various morals in *Lear*; in so doing, he was intent on disproving Rymer's assertions that Shakespeare has no moral value because of his failure to observe poetic justice.

Although Joseph Warton in 1754 deprecated Shakespeare's double plot, Theobald, in 1715, is not concerned by this violation of a neo-Aristotelian rule and anticipates Johnson in Shakespeare's defence:

The two Episodes of *Edgar* and *Edmund* are little dependant on the Fable, (could we pretend to pin down *Shakespear* to a Regularity of Plot,) but that the Latter is made an Instrument of encreasing the Vicious Characters of the Daughters, and the Former is to punish him for the adulterous Passion, as well as his Treachery and Misusage to *Gloucester*.

---

[15] *Censor*, 7, i. 47, 47–8, 52.

[16] Ibid. 10, i. 67. Cf. Johnson's general note on the play, *1765*, vi. 158 [Yale, viii. 703]: 'On the seeming improbability of *Lear*'s conduct it may be observed, that he is represented according to histories at that time vulgarly received as true.'

[17] *Censor*, 10, i. 67.

He adds that 'in the last Instance, the Moral has some Connection to the main Scope of the Play'. Indeed, Theobald is prepared to dismiss all objections by neo-Aristotelian critics to Shakespeare's irregularity of plot:

> As to the General Absurdities of *Shakespear* in this and all his other Tragedies, I have nothing to say; they were owing to his Ignorance of *Mechanical* Rules and the Constitution of his Story, so cannot come under the Lash of Criticism; yet if they did, I could without Regret pardon a Number of them, for being so admirably lost in Excellencies.[18]

The major fault of *Lear* for Theobald, as for Johnson, was Shakespeare's violation of poetic justice, and like Johnson he was sentimental enough to regret the deaths of Cordelia and Lear and to give his support to Tate's ending. Theobald was probably influenced, again like Johnson, by his belief that 'the Vulgar . . . where their Passions are concern'd, are certainly no ill Judges':[19]

> Yet there is one [fault] which without the Knowledge of Rules he might have corrected, and that is in the *Catastrophe* of this Piece: *Cordelia* and *Lear* ought to have surviv'd, as Mr. *Tate* has made them in his Alteration of this Tragedy; Virtue ought to be rewarded, as well as Vice punish'd; but in their Deaths this Moral is broke through.[20]

The most pleasing part of Theobald's criticism is his appreciation of Shakespeare's artistry in the presentation of Lear's character: 'had *Shakespear* read all that *Aristotle*, *Horace*, and the Criticks have wrote on this Score, he could not have wrought more happily. . . . There is a Grace that cannot be conceiv'd in the sudden Starts of [Lear's] Passion, on being controul'd; and which best shews itself in forcing Us to admire it.' This assertion is illustrated by lengthy quotations from the play, after which Theobald concludes: 'I cannot sufficiently admire

---

[18] *Censor*, 71, 72.

[19] Ibid. 70 (2 Apr. 1717), iii. 43.

[20] Ibid. 10, i. 72. Cf. Johnson, *1765*, vi. 159 [Yale, viii. 704]: 'since all reasonable beings naturally love justice, I cannot easily be persuaded, that the obervation of justice makes a play worse. . . . In the present case the publick has decided. *Cordelia*, from the time of *Tate*, has always retired with victory and felicity. And, if my sensations could add anything to the general suffrage, I might relate, that I was many years ago so shocked by *Cordelia*'s death, that I know not whether I ever endured to read again the last scenes of the play till I undertook to revise them as an editor.'

[Lear's] Struggles with his Testy Humour, his seeming Desire of restraining it, and the Force with which it resists his Endeavours, and flies out into Rage and Imprecations; To quote Instances of half these Beauties, were to copy Speeches out of every Scene.'[21]

Theobald's criticism is weakest when he is intent on countering Rymer's assertion that Shakespeare has no moral value.[22] The same is true of Dryden's criticism, when, for example, he recommends *All for Love* (1678) for 'the excellency of the moral': 'For the chief persons represented were famous patterns of unlawful love; and their end accordingly was unfortunate.'[23] Johnson's justification of the Edmund sub-plot in *Lear*, on the grounds that it enables Shakespeare 'to impress this important moral, that villany is never at a stop, that crimes lead to crimes, and at last terminate in ruin',[24] reaches no higher than Theobald's representation of *Othello* in *Censor* No. 16 as 'a compleat Common-place Book of Cautions against entertaining rash Suspicions'. It is likely that Theobald felt the inadequacy of this comment, for in his following paragraph he counterbalanced its effect by drawing attention, once again, to Shakespeare's artful presentation of character:

As I never see the Rage of the *Moor*, when he is once work'd up by the Villany of *Iago*, without the greatest Pity; so I am as strongly pleas'd to observe the Art of the Poet, with what a curious Happiness he has trac'd this Passion, what little Baits he has laid to feed *Othello*'s Suspicion, and what Sentiments of Resentment he has fir'd him with, at every new Suggestion of being injur'd. His very Resolution against Jealousy speaks him prepar'd for Doubts, and bent to sift the Truth.[25]

In *Censor* No. 36 (12 January 1717) Theobald evolves a more subtle context for discussing moral significance. He is chiefly concerned with the relation of character to action, and with the influence of poetic justice on the tragic emotions of pity and fear. The most original feature of the essay is his willingness to admit the complexity of any attempt to see character in relation to action or dramatic situation. Although Rymer had appealed

[21] *Censor*, 10, i. 72–3, 73–4, 74.
[22] See *A Short View of Tragedy* (1693), Zimansky, pp. 131–6.
[23] Preface, Watson, i. 222.
[24] *1765*, vi. 159 [Yale, viii. 704].
[25] *Censor*, 16 (16 May 1715), i. 116–17. Theobald quotes III. iii. 48–65.

to history or private experience when ridiculing dramatic characters and their actions, he impeded analysis of psychology and
motive in criticism by emphasizing the paramount importance
of a moral fable (that is, a fable that observes poetic justice)
while, at the same time, insisting on simplicity in its assessment: 'there is not requir'd much Learning, or that a man
must be some *Aristotle*, and *Doctor* of *Subtilties*, to form a right
judgment in this particular; common sense suffices.'[26] Rymer
implied that, when confronted with moral considerations, any
departure from his standards of simplicity should be regarded
as a sign of indifference or evasion on the part of the critic; the
eagerness of later critics to point morals that might be discovered
in Shakespeare (despite his neglect of poetic justice) represents
an attempt both to vindicate Shakespeare and to avoid com-
promising complexity. However, the resulting simplification
severely limited critical appreciation of Shakespearian tragedy,
and in *Censor* No. 36 Theobald insists on the complexity inherent
in any moral assessment of character, motive, and action: 'We
meet with, in Conversation, Men of so *mix'd* a Character, that
we know not whether to determine them *Good* or *Bad*; their
Virtues and Imperfections are so confus'd and blended.' For
Theobald moral judgement is unavoidably complex, because

The most Sublime and Common Actions of our Lives are influenc'd
by the Operation of *inferior* and *subservient* Qualifications; There are
Incidents in which often our Frailties are active, without involving us
in any flagrant Guilt; and there are Others, where our meanest
Accomplishments carry us up to Exploits, in which our Virtue is very
little concern'd.[27]

He places moral judgement in a psychological context and
departs from Rymer's insistence that poetic justice in the fable
determines the moral value of tragedy. This new emphasis
leads, as in much Romantic criticism of Shakespeare, to
analysis of character and motive, and poetic justice itself
becomes more complex than it is in Rymer:

The Praise and Censure . . . of Things must be establish'd not from
the Consequences, but the Springs and Motives from which such
Consequences were deriv'd. An Historian cannot comment judi-

ciously upon *Facts*, without viewing them in this Light; and a *Dramatic* Writer will be very defective in his *Poetical* Justice, if he has not the strictest Regard to these intermediate Qualities.[28]

The results of Theobald's approach are first found in a discussion of Sophocles' *Oedipus* and its reworkings by Corneille, Dryden, and Lee. The modern dramatists 'have entirely mistaken the *Character* of *Oedipus*, and the *Conduct* of the *Grecian* Poet' owing to their failure to observe 'this Mixture of Character'. Instead of seizing on poetic justice as the crowning glory of *Oedipus*, in the manner of Rymer, Theobald maintains that Sophocles, at any rate, 'meant not to propose his Hero an Object of Horror for the Commission of Parricide and Incest; neither does he involve him in Calamities merely as Judgments for those Crimes, which in him were involuntary, and rather the Guilt of his Fate than Nature'. Whereas Rymer virtually ignored catharsis in his criticism and Dryden tended to restrict pity to the sufferings of the virtuous and fear to the punishment of villains,[29] Theobald associates both pity and fear with the fate of the hero by stressing the importance of 'some involuntary Fault' or '*uncontroulable Impulses*' implicitly related to the 'intermediate Qualities' in his character. Otherwise we 'view the Offender with Detestation, and may have some Pleasure to see him punish'd for his Crimes, but his Misery will never stir us up to Compassion, because he has only what he deserv'd'. For morality through observance of poetic justice, Theobald substitutes catharsis and, as an important corollary, a continuing, sympathetic concern for the hero, whose 'Praise and Censure' derive 'not from the Consequences [of his actions], but [from] the Springs and Motives from which such Consequences were deriv'd'. It is this carefully constructed argument that allows him to conclude his paper with reference to *Othello*, 'a Play most faulty and irregular in many Points, but Excellent in one Particular'. In his reading of the play,

the Crimes and Misfortunes of the *Moor* are owing to an impetuous Desire of having his Doubts clear'd, and a Jealousie and Rage, native to him, which he cannot controul, and which push him on to Revenge. He is otherwise in his Character brave and open; generous

---

[28] Ibid. 36.
[29] See 'Heads of An Answer to Rymer', Watson, i. 213.

and full of Love for *Desdemona*; but stung with the subtle Suggestions of *Iago*, and impatient of a Wrong done to his Love and Honour, Passion at once o'erbears his Reason, and gives him up to Thoughts of bloody Reparation: Yet after he has determin'd to murther his Wife, his Sentiments of her suppos'd Injury, and his Misfortune are so pathetick, that we cannot but forget his barbarous Resolution, and pity the Agonies which he so strongly seems to feel.[30]

Theobald's emphasis on representation of character and his neglect of rules pertaining solely to plot make him one of the earliest proto-Romantics. His criticism adumbrates such later works as William Richardson's *Philosophical Analysis and Illustration of Shakespeare's Remarkable Characters* (1774) and Thomas Whately's *Remarks on Some of the Characters of Shakespeare* (1785). These in turn anticipate the Romantic criticism of Hazlitt.[31]

Theobald's most important qualification as a future editor of Shakespeare is yet to be mentioned. He is almost alone among his contemporaries in his ability to respond appreciatively to highly figurative language. In the 'Author's Apology for Heroic Poetry and Poetic Licence' (1677) Dryden had provided a basis for the defence of figurative writing, but his most memorable statement concerning Shakespeare's style occurs in the Preface to *Troilus and Cressida* (1679):

the tongue in general is so much refined since Shakespeare's time that many of his words, and more of his phrases, are scarce intelligible. And of those which we understand, some are ungrammatical, others coarse; and his whole style is so pestered with figurative expressions, that it is as affected as it is obscure.[32]

Similar views are expressed by Addison:

The Judgment of a Poet very much discovers itself in shunning the common Roads of Expression, without falling into such ways of Speech as may seem stiff and unnatural. . . . [A] false Sublime . . . among our own Countrymen, *Shakespear* and *Lee* . . . often hurts the Perspicuity of the Stile, as in many others the Endeavour after Perspicuity prejudices its Greatness.[33]

[30] *Censor*, 36 (12 Jan. 1717), ii. 36–41, *passim*. Theobald quotes IV. ii. 48–64. Cf. Rymer, *A Short View of Tragedy* (1693), Zimansky, pp. 136 ff.

[31] See also Brian Vickers, 'The Emergence of Character Criticism, 1774–1800', *Shakespeare Survey*, ed. Stanley Wells, xxxiv (Cambridge: Cambridge University Press, 1981), 11–21.

[32] Watson, i. 239.

[33] *Spectator*, 285 (26 Jan. 1712).

In addition to the influence of Longinus' *On the Sublime*, Theobald's translation of Aeschylus probably fostered his receptiveness to just those aspects of Shakespeare's style his contemporaries found reprehensible. In *Censor* No. 60 (9 March 1717) Theobald indicates explicitly his attitude to the language of Aeschylus and Shakespeare, and also gives further evidence of his critical independence:

the *Tragick* Poets, so esteem'd by Antiquity, were *Three* in Number; The Criticks of every Age have more particularly determin'd in favour of *Two* of these. . . . The Reason that *ÆSCHYLUS* is not so often nam'd as the *Divine SOPHOCLES*, the *Sententious EURIPIDES*, is, that your *Adepts* in Learning have been startled with this Traditional Notion of his *Bombast*, and *Harshness* of *Diction*. But as I have read him, without a *blind* Admiration, I view him as I do my Countryman *SHAKESPEAR*: I can find some Things in him I could wish had been temper'd by a softer Hand; but must own at the same Time, that where he is most *harsh* and *obsolete* he is still *Majestick*.[34]

Theobald is careful to support his views with quotations from Longinus and Dionysius of Halicarnassus, when disregarding 'whatever may be the Sentiments of more *Polite* Readers', but it is his responsiveness to metaphorical language and to verbal texture generally that allows him to state:

As to particular Irregularities, it is not to be expected that a Genius like *Shakespear*'s should be judg'd by the Laws of *Aristotle*, and the other Prescribers to the Stage; it will be sufficient to fix a Character of Excellence to his Performances, if there are in them a Number of beautiful Incidents, true and exquisite Turns of Nature and Passion, fine and delicate Sentiments, uncommon Images, and great Boldnesses of Expression.[35]

Clearly Nichol Smith is mistaken when he calls Theobald 'a critic of the same type as Gildon', one who 'had a profound respect for what he took to be the accredited doctrines' and who 'believed in the rules. He complied with the taste of the town when he wrote pantomimes, but he was a sterner man when he posed as a critic. He would then speak of the "general absurdities of Shakespeare", and the "errors" in the structure of his plays.'[36] That Theobald, like Dryden, was prepared to believe

---

[34] *Censor*, 60, ii. 203–4.
[35] Ibid. 70 (2 Apr. 1717), iii. 43.
[36] Smith, pp. xix, xviii.

that observance of the rules might intensify dramatic impact is evident in his alteration of *Richard II*.[37] The failure of his version to keep the stage may have contributed to his ultimate indifference to the rules; in his Preface to *Shakespeare* (1733) Theobald again discusses Shakespeare's powers of character-ization,[38] but makes no reference to the unities. In his corres-pondence he remarks of *The Tempest*: 'I have already thrown in a note on the nice preservation of the three unities'[39]—but the note does *not* appear in the edition. In the interval between *The Censor* and publication of his edition Theobald came to the conclusion that Shakespeare's neglect of the unities was deliber-ate and not owing to ignorance. He probably came to accept entirely Shakespeare's indifference to the rules; in a note to Berowne's expostulation in *Love's Labour's Lost*, 'That's too long for a play' (V. ii. 878), Theobald comments:

Besides the exact Regularity to the Rules of Art, which the Author has happen'd to preserve in some few of his Pieces; This is Demon-stration, I think, that tho' he has more frequently transgress'd the *Unity* of *Time*, by cramming Years into the Compass of a Play, yet he knew the Absurdity of so doing, and was not unacquainted with the Rule to the contrary.[40]

'Absurdity' does not imply strong criticism on Theobald's part; along with 'irregularities' and 'errors', it refers to those aspects of Shakespeare's dramaturgy generally recognized by his contemporaries as being liable to neo-Aristotelian censure or ridicule, rather than implying an absolute judgement by Theobald. For example, after quoting at length a passage from Rymer's *Short View of Tragedy* inveighing against improbabilities in *Othello*, Theobald comments: 'such Reflexions require no serious Answer. This Tragedy will continue to have lasting Charms enough to make us blind to such Absurdities, as the Poet thought were not worth his Care.'[41] Shakespeare, Theo-bald realized, was working under different principles—the imaginative appeal of dramatic characters revealed through language—and what seemed 'absurd' to Rymer and his school

---

[37] See above, p. 22.   [38] *1733*, vol. i, pp. xx-xxv.
[39] Nichols, ii. 309 (6 Dec. 1729) to Warburton.   [40] *1733*, ii, 181 n.
[41] *1733*, vii. 372 n. Cf. Theobald's argument, anticipating Johnson, that 'the Audience are always willing to help their own Deception . . . to allow as much Time . . . as . . . necessary . . . in the Conduct of [the] Fable' (*1733*, iv. 18 n.).

was, Theobald supposed, ultimately irrelevant. Such attitudes, of course, appeared to many of his contemporaries to constitute critical irresponsibility—such as might be expected of a deviser of pantomimes pandering to popular taste.

Pope's *Shakespear* (1725) was inevitably disappointing to Theobald, both critically and textually. The differences between Pope and Theobald in their critical approaches to Shakespeare are partly suggested by their differing views of Rymer. Theobald eventually made explicit what is implicit in his early criticism in *The Censor*: Rymer 'taught me to distinguish betwixt the *Railer* and the *Critick*. The Outrage of his Quotations is so remarkably violent, so push'd beyond all Bounds of Decency and sober Reasoning, that it quite carries over the Mark at which it was levell'd.'[42] Pope, on the other hand, is recorded as saying of Rymer: 'He is generally right, though rather too severe in his opinions of the particular plays he speaks of, and is on the whole one of the best critics we ever had.'[43] Pope's Preface to *Shakespear* is consistent with this statement.

Pope begins his Preface in a manner that suggests uncertainty about the status of Shakespeare's achievement:

> It is not my design to enter into a Criticism upon this Author; tho' to do it effectually and not superficially, would be the best occasion that any just Writer could take, to form the judgment and taste of our nation. For all *English* Poets *Shakespear* must be confessed to be the fairest and fullest subject for Criticism, and to afford the most numerous, as well as most conspicuous instances, both of Beauties and Faults of all sorts.[44]

The deliberate balance established in the first paragraph persists in the body of the Preface, allowing Pope to organize his materials while still withholding his final judgement of Shakespeare. Pope is obviously eager to praise Shakespeare, but he also appreciates the force of objections by neo-Aristotelian critics. 'I cannot', he writes, 'but mention some of his principal and characteristic Excellencies, for which (notwithstanding his defects) he is justly and universally elevated above all other Dramatic Writers.'[45] This sentence has an ambiguity charac-

---

[42] Preface, *1733*, vol. i, p. xlviii.
[43] Spence, No. 480.
[44] *1725*, vol. i, p. i.
[45] Ibid., p. ii.

teristic of the Preface: is Shakespeare the greatest of dramatists? Or is he 'elevated above all other Dramatic Writers' solely in the areas of his 'principal and characteristic Excellencies'— without considering the effect of his 'defects' on his art as a whole?[46] Gildon had argued that 'if *Shakespear* had had those Advantages of Learning, which the perfect Knowledge of the Ancients wou'd have given him, so great a *Genius* as his, wou'd have made him a very dangerous Rival in Fame, to the greatest poets of Antiquity', but 'tho' I must always think our Author a Miracle, for the Age he liv'd in . . . I am oblig'd, in Justice to *Reason* and *Art*, to confess, that he does not come up to the Ancients, in all the Beauties of the *Drama*.' Moreover, 'to put his Errors and his Excellencies on the same Bottom, is to injure the Latter.'[47] If Pope does not say all this, neither does he reject it; as Nichol Smith has observed: 'Pope was a discreet man, who knew when to be silent.'[48]

Pope's praise of Shakespeare focuses on the man as a natural genius; the plays are referred to primarily as a means of illuminating the mind of their author, not as independent works of art. Pope finds Shakespeare more original than Homer: 'The Poetry of *Shakespear* was Inspiration indeed: he is not so much an Imitator, as an Instrument, of Nature; and 'tis not so just to say that he speaks from her, as that she speaks thro' him.' Shakespeare also possesses unrivalled '*Power* over our *Passions*', and 'he is not more a master of the *Great*, than of the *Ridiculous* in human nature; of our noblest tendernesses, than of our vainest foibles; of our strongest emotions, than of our idlest sensations!' Finally, Shakespeare excels 'In the coolness of Reflection and Reasoning', which leads Pope to the declaration that 'he seems to have known the world by Intuition, to have look'd thro' humane nature at one glance, and to be the only Author that gives ground for a very new opinion, That the

---

[46] Austin Warren, *Alexander Pope as Critic and Humanist* (1929; repr. Gloucester, Mass.: Peter Smith, 1963), 148–9, who sees in the Preface 'an almost ecstatic appreciation of great excellence', misrepresents this passage: 'Pope exalts the English playwright not only above his fellows but above the great Greek tragedians: "he is justly and universally elevated above all other dramatic writers." '

[47] 'Essay on the Art, Rise and Progress of the Stage', *Works of Shakespear. Volume the Seventh* (1710), pp. iii–iv.

[48] Smith, p. xix.

Philosopher and even the Man of the world, may be *Born*, as well as the Poet.'[49]

·Pope may seem intent on obviating all censure of Shakespeare. Such, however, was not his purpose: 'It must be own'd that with all these great excellencies, he has almost as great defects; and that as he has certainly written better, so he has perhaps written worse, than any other.' There is no question that the 'great excellencies' outweigh the 'almost as great defects'; what remains deliberately undetermined is his view of the consequences of this combination for the work of art. Pope traces many of the plays' faults to their audiences: 'It must be allowed that Stage-Poetry of all other, is more particularly levell'd to please the *Populace*, and its success more immediately depending upon the *Common Suffrage*.' The tastes of his audiences are responsible for Shakespeare's 'low' characters: 'The Audience was generally composed of the meaner sort of people; and therefore the Images of Life were to be drawn from those of their own rank: accordingly we find, that not our Author's only but almost all the old Comedies have their Scene among *Tradesmen* and *Mechanicks*.'

Similar considerations determined the choice of plots and the language of the plays:

In Tragedy, nothing was so sure to *Surprize* and cause *Admiration*, as the most strange, unexpected, and consequently most unnatural, Events and Incidents; the most exaggerated Thoughts; the most verbose and bombast Expression; the most pompous Rhymes, and thundering versification. In Comedy, nothing was so sure to *please*, as mean buffoonry, vile ribaldry, and unmannerly jests of fools and clowns.

Here, Pope's style is reminiscent of Rymer; and it was with Rymer in mind that he continues:

the common Audience had no notion of the rules of writing, but few even of the better sort piqu'd themselves upon any great degree of knowledge or nicety that way. . . . [O]ur Authors had no thoughts of writing on the model of the Ancients: their Tragedies were only Histories in Dialogue; and their Comedies follow'd the thread of any Novel as they found it, no less implicitly than if it had been true History.[50]

<hr>

[49] *1725*, vol. i, pp. ii–iv.   [50] Ibid., pp. iv–vi.

Shakespeare, of course, is one of 'our Authors'. This point is of crucial importance and hinges on Rymer's assertion, when promoting poetic justice, that the Greek dramatists 'found that *History*, grosly taken, was neither proper to *instruct*, nor apt to *please*; and therefore . . . refin'd upon the History; and thence contriv'd something more *philosophical*, and more *accurate* than *History*.'[51] Pope's judgement of the plays remains implicit; unlike Rymer, he avoids censure of Shakespeare: 'To judge therefore of *Shakespear* by *Aristotle*'s rules, is like trying a man by the Laws of one Country, who acted under those of another.' The excuse that Shakespeare 'writ to the *People*' is not intended, however, to balance his supposed total ignorance of 'the best models, the Ancients.'[52]

Pope's respect for 'the rules of art remains unaffected by Shakespeare's example. He does not see Shakespeare as one who would '*snatch* a Grace beyond the Reach of Art' because to do so, in this instance, would be to make popular taste the criterion of excellence. Pope's position is apparent when he accounts for the plays' defects as arising 'from our Author's being a *Player*, and forming himself first upon the judgments of that body of men whereof he was a member'. The players 'have ever had a Standard to themselves, upon other principles than those of *Aristotle*. As they live by the Majority, they know no rule but that of pleasing the present humour.' Pope does continue to defend Shakespeare, but, in so doing, gives the plays up to censure: 'As to a wrong choice of the subject, a wrong conduct of the incidents, false thoughts, forc'd expressions, &c. if these are not to be ascrib'd to the foresaid accidental reasons, they must be charg'd upon the Poet himself, and there is no help for it.' His recapitulation of excuses is finally most damning:

But I think the two Disadvantages which I have mentioned (to be obliged to please the lowest of people, and to keep the worst of company) if the consideration be extended as far as it reasonably may, will appear sufficient to mis-lead and depress the greatest Genius upon earth.[53]

Pope's failure to consider the possibility of valid principles in

---

[51] *Tragedies of the Last Age* (1678), Zimansky, p. 23.
[52] *1725*, vol. i, pp. vi–vii.
[53] Ibid., pp. vii–viii, ix.

Shakespeare's approach to the drama marks his separation from the new criticism of the eighteenth century. It also marks his diametrical opposition to Theobald. He is glad, once again, to separate the plays from their author, and, after a discussion of interpolations, cuts, and alterations by the players, to blame 'whole heaps of trash' and 'additions of trifling and bombast passages' on Shakespeare's fellows.[54]

Pope generally disliked Shakespeare's style. In a comment to Joseph Spence on Nicholas Rowe's *Jane Shore* (1714) he remarked: 'It was mighty simple in Rowe to write a play now, professedly in Shakespeare's style, that is, professedly in the style of a bad age.' Shakespeare was affected and bombastic: he 'generally used to stiffen his style with high words and metaphors for the speeches of his kings and great men. He mistook it for a mark of greatness. This is strongest in his early plays, but in his very last play, his *Othello*, what a forced language has he put into the mouth of the Duke of Venice!'[55] On another occasion Pope observed that the style of *Gorboduc* was much purer than that in some of Shakespeare's first plays: 'Sackville imitates the manner of Seneca's tragedies very closely, and writes without affectation or bombast—the two great sins of our first tragic writers.'[56] A consequence of these views is that in Pope's edition Macbeth's 'innocent sleep, | Sleep that knits up the ravell'd sleave of care' (II. ii. 33–4) is placed in a footnote as an interpolation unworthy of Shakespeare, as is

> Will all great Neptune's ocean wash this blood
> Clean from my hand? No; this my hand *will rather*
> *The multitudinous seas incarnadine,*
> *Making the green one red.*   (ii. ii. 57–60)

Pope's text reads: 'this my hand will rather | Make the green ocean red.'[57] He also felt that Shakespeare was guilty of excessively low language in tragedy. Consequently, the Porter's lines (II. iii. 1–21) are relegated to a footnote, while in *Romeo and Juliet* over 200 lines are either 'bottomed' or omitted. In the canon as a whole, over 1,550 lines suffer this editorial disgrace.

There is no question of Pope's admiration for Shakespeare as

---

[54] Ibid., p. xvi.

[55] Spence, No. 421. As yet there had been no scholarly attempt to ascertain the order of Shakespeare's plays.

[56] Ibid., No. 415.   [57] *1725*, v. 541.

an untutored genius, but it is his unwillingness to affront the predilections of his more enthusiastic readers by stating his views on Shakespeare's rank as a dramatic artist that produces the calculated ambiguity of the final paragraph of the Preface. There the explicit meaning as well as the further implications of his balanced sentences leave the scales of judgement wavering:

> I will conclude by saying of *Shakespear*, that with all his faults, and with all the irregularity of his *Drama*, one may look upon his works, in comparison of those that are more finish'd and regular, as upon an ancient majestick piece of *Gothick* Architecture, compar'd with a neat Modern building: The latter is more elegant and glaring, but the former is more strong and more solemn. It must be allow'd, that in one of these there are materials enough to make many of the other. It has much the greater variety, and much the nobler apartments; tho' we are often conducted to them by dark, odd, and uncouth passages. Nor does the Whole fail to strike us with greater reverence, tho' many of the Parts are childish, ill-plac'd, and unequal to its grandeur.[58]

The paragraph reflects Pope's careful reading of the critics before writing the Preface, especially the antepenultimate page of Rymer's *The Tragedies of the Last Age*: 'I have thought our Poetry of the last Age as rude as our Architecture.'[59] In *An Essay on Criticism* (1711), when advocating overall design, rather than language, as the valid object of critical attention, Pope had also used an architectural analogy:

> Thus when we view some well-proportion'd Dome,
> (The *World*'s just Wonder, and ev'n *thine* O *Rome*!)
> No single Parts unequally surprize;
> All comes *united* to th'admiring Eyes;
> No monstrous Height, or Breadth, or Length appear;
> The *Whole* at once is *Bold*, and *Regular*.   (247–52)

---

[58] *1725*, vol. i, pp. xxiii–xxiv. An attempt was made by John Butt to discover positive evidence of Pope's taste in Shakespeare in the system of stars and commas which distinguish in his edition those scenes and passages he approved (*Pope's Taste in Shakespeare*, Shakespeare Association Pamphlets (Oxford: Oxford University Press, 1936)). Butt's assumption that Pope was not indebted to his predecessors (pp. 5, 13) has been shown to be false. See Peter Dixon, 'Pope's Shakespeare', *Journal of English and Germanic Philology*, 63 (1964), and 'Edward Bysshe and Pope's 'Shakespeare' ', *Notes and Queries*, 209 (1964). The elaborate index to Pope's *Shakespear* is also to be discounted, since it was compiled by Elijah Fenton and some other, unknown 'Index-maker'. See *Correspondence*, ii. 130, 213–14, 244.

[59] Zimansky, p. 76 (p. 142 of the 1st edn., 1678).

Theobald concentrated on language in his criticism and, unavoidably, in his textual scholarship. Moreover, the rules he was prepared to neglect were those of Aristotle, Dacier, and Rymer pertaining to design. It was on this basis that he was prepared to assert, when engaging in a discussion of textual emendation in *Shakespeare Restored* (1726), that '*SHAKESPEARE* stands, or at least ought to stand, in the Nature of a Classic Writer.'[60] It was *Shakespeare Restored* that assured Theobald's position in *The Dunciad*, and it is no surprise to discover there evidence of a mind essentially unreceptive to Shakespeare:

> Here one poor Word a hundred clenches makes,
> And ductile dulness new meanders takes;
> There motley Images her fancy strike,
> Figures ill-pair'd, and Similes unlike.
> She sees a Mob of Metaphors advance,
> Pleas'd with the Madness of the mazy dance:
> How Tragedy and Comedy embrace;
> How Farce and Epic get a jumbled race;
> How Time himself stands still at her command,
> Realms shift their place, and Ocean turns to land.
>
> (i. 61–70)

It was probably in deliberate contrast to the final paragraph of Pope's Preface that Theobald again asserted Shakespeare's classic status by beginning his Preface to *Shakespeare* (1733) with the declaration: 'THE Attempt to write upon SHAKESPEARE is like going into a large, a spacious, and a splendid Dome.' He made a concession to neo-Aristotelianism and to Pope when he added, 'thro' the Conveyance of a narrow and obscure Entry'.[61]

The major significance of the differing critical approaches of Pope and Theobald to Shakespeare is to be found in their editions of his plays. Where Pope found matter requiring apology, Theobald found dramatic poetry of the highest order. Contempt for the artistry of an author is likely to produce in the editor a profound sense of the dullness of his duties. On the other hand, admiration for the achievements of the author tends to produce in the editor a delighted excitement as he frees the text from corruption or obscurity. In either case, critical postulates affect scholarly procedures and scholarly accomplishments.

[60] p. v. [61] Vol. i, p. i.

4. Pope and Scholarship: The Edition of Shakespear (1725)

WHEN he was young, it was Pope's light-hearted affectation to despise commentators; his old friend, Henry Cromwell, might take him for a critic, but Pope would 'by no means be thought a Commentator'.[1] Before his death he had supplied a commentary to Homer, edited Shakespeare, annotated *The Dunciad*, and assured copious annotation for the rest of his works by appointing William Warburton their editor. The trappings of scholarship came to have a horrid fascination for him, while his contempt for scholars apparently grew; he could be 'So humble, he has knock'd at *Tibbald's* door'[2] *and* lampoon Theobald in *The Dunciad*. He was enthralled by Richard Bentley's notorious edition of *Paradise Lost* (1732) and alternated between extremes of ridicule and admiration:

> Avaunt—is Aristarchus yet unknown?
> Thy mighty Scholiast, whose unweary'd pains
> Made Horace dull, and humbled Milton's strains.
> Turn what they will to Verse, their toil is vain,
> Critics like me shall make it Prose again.

> (*The Dunciad*, iv (1743). 210–14)

After Pope's infectious enjoyment of his ridicule of Bentley, it is surprising to come across the following in Thomas Newton's Preface to his edition of *Paradise Lost* (1749):

[Mr Warburton] very kindly lent me Mr. Pope's Milton of Bentley's edition, wherein Mr. Pope had all along with his own hand set some mark of approbation, rectè, benè, pulchrè &c, in the margin over-

---

[1] *Correspondence*, i. 101.

[2] *Epistle to Dr. Arbuthnot* (1735), l. 372 (that Pope did visit Theobald is confirmed by a letter (12 Jan. 1757) from Warburton to Richard Hurd (Nichols, ii. 741 n.), quoted below, Appendix D n. 7).

against such emendations of the Doctor's, as seemed to him just and reasonable. It was a satisfaction to see what so great a genius thought particularly of that edition, and he appears throughout the whole to have been a very candid reader, and to have approved of more than really merits approbation.[3]

In an age that takes close reading for granted, it is easy to underestimate the distrust or contempt in the early eighteenth century for the minute scrutiny of texts. Pope's distrust of this activity reflects at its best a commitment to humanistic ideals about the value of literature as a means of perceiving moral order and harmony in life, but appears at its worst as a confusion of the aims of criticism and scholarship. It is, however, usually difficult to charge Pope with deliberately confusing the purposes of criticism and scholarship, since any particular instance of seeming wilfulness, if not the immediate product of his convictions, may at least be defended in their light. Moreover, Pope's unwillingness (or inability) to separate the functions of criticism and scholarship is especially understandable in a poet who made translation one of his major undertakings, and who, as a consequence, was open to critical or scholarly attacks.[4] His own frequently personal attacks on those he considered bad writers are often the result of his preoccupation with the ultimate moral purposes of literature.

In both aesthetic and moral contexts, Pope is hostile to those who neglect overall design and concentrate instead on language. Critics who seemed to judge on the basis of consideration of the parts of a composition, rather than on consideration of the whole, were seen as descendants of the carping critics of language in chapter 25 of *The Poetics*. J. C. Scaliger's hypercriticism of

---

[3] Vol. i, sig. a4[r].

[4] Contemporary marginalia in a subscription set of *The Iliad* that apparently belonged to the Earl of Aberdeen and is now in my possession give some indication of this. Such comments are found as 'bad', '4 lines for one', 'not nice', 'futile', 'unequal', 'weak', 'superfluous', 'a bad word', or simply 'no'. In addition, Pope is accused of being 'affected', 'quaint', and of having 'nothing of the original'. The lines (i. 161–2),

> But to resume whate'er thy Av'rice craves,
> (That Trick of Tyrants) may be born by Slaves,

are graced with 'oh stuff' and 'party'—the second referring to 'That Trick of Tyrants', which is underlined. Other lines are labelled 'poor fit for a lover' and 'abominable'. In his final comment, on 'High on the Deck was fair *Chruseïs* plac'd' (i. 406), the annotator concludes with a note of triumph: 'there was no deck'.

Homer had irritated Dryden, while the application to drama of
the verbal criticism of François Malherbe in the *Sentiments de
l'Académie française sur le Cid* (Paris, 1658) by Richelieu, Chapelain,
and Scudéry was remembered by Rymer as 'the *doubts*, the
remarks, and eternal triflings of the *French Grammaticasters*'.[5]
Such criticism grew in England with the renewed demand for
printed plays after the Restoration. As the Hon. Edward
Howard remarked: 'the Press being in some manner the Stages
Tyring-House, where all Ornaments are thrown off, save native
design and Language', plays 'suffer a more severe Correction
from the Reader'.[6] Carping criticism was evidently a Restoration pastime, for Dryden refers in the Epilogue to the second
part of *The Conquest of Granada* (1672) to critics who 'weigh |
Each Line, and ev'ry word, throughout a Play' (13–14) and in
'The Author's Apology for Heroic Poetry' (1677) admonishes
his readers: 'we are fallen into an age of illiterate, censorious,
and detracting people who, thus qualified, set up for critics.'[7]

The close affinity of Pope's views with those of Dryden is
apparent in *An Essay on Criticism* (1711), where the magnanimity
of the truly literate and moral 'Men of Breeding' is contrasted
with the narrow concerns of the verbal critic:

> Whoever thinks a faultless Piece to see,
> Thinks what ne'er was, nor is, nor e'er shall be.
> In ev'ry Work regard the *Writer's End*,
> Since none can compass more than they *Intend*;
> And if the *Means* be just, the *Conduct* true,
> Applause, in spite of trivial Faults, is due.
> As Men of Breeding, sometimes Men of Wit,
> T'avoid *great Errors*, must the *less* commit,
> Neglect the Rules each *Verbal Critick* lays,
> For *not* to know some Trifles, is a Praise.
>
> (253–62)

Despite his championing the importance of language in drama,
Dryden almost invariably associated verbal criticism with

---

[5] See Scaliger, *Poetices* (Lyons, 1561), bks. v–vi; Dryden, Preface to *Examen Poeticum*
(1693), Watson, ii. 158; *The Tragedies of the Last Age* (1678), Zimansky, p. 18.

[6] The Epistle to *The Usurper* (1668), sigs. A2^r–A2^v.

[7] Watson, i. 196. For examples of the carping criticism Dryden had in mind, see
the Introduction by Maximillian E. Novak to *The Empress of Morocco and its Critics*,
Augustan Reprint Society (Los Angeles: William Andrews Clark Memorial Library,
1968).

hostility and malice. After he had published his translation of
Virgil (1697) and Luke Milbourne's *Notes on Dryden's Virgil*
(1698) had appeared, Dryden had reason to connect verbal
criticism with malevolent, quasi-scholarly pedantry; the same
associations were made for Pope early in his career by his
sympathy for Dryden (see *An Essay on Criticism*, ll. 458–63) and
were reinforced by John Dennis's *Reflections Critical and Satyrical,
Upon a Late Rhapsody, Call'd, An Essay on Criticism* (1711) and
Remarks Upon Mr. Pope's Translation of Homer (1717).[8] But
whereas the '*Verbal Critick*' (however narrow, misguided, or
malevolent) of *An Essay on Criticism* (1711) was concerned with
criticism of language as literary criticism, in the annotations of
The Dunciad Variorum (1729) Pope uses 'verbal criticism' to
mean textual criticism. The phrase's shift in meaning is probably owing at least in part to his experience of those critics of
his translation who mingled matters of scholarship and critical
taste in their attacks on his text.

Dryden's dislike of verbal critics as literary critics does not
greatly influence his view of commentators. There are occasional slighting references to 'Dutch commentators', and as a
translator he feels the need to defend himself in particular
passages for having 'discovered some beauty yet undiscovered
by those pedants, which none but a poet could have found',[9]
but normally he does not go beyond condescension to scholars.
Indeed, although he had no high regard for Thomas Creech's
translation of Lucretius, Dryden does refer to his 'excellent
annotations' and to those of Barten Holyday, 'whose interpretation and illustrations of Juvenal are as excellent as the
verse of his translation and his English are lame and pitiful'.[10]
For Pope, who was privately educated (and for many others of
his generation), assumptions about the taste and worth of
scholars were more uncompromisingly formed by the Phalaris

---

[8] Although Dennis indulged in unforgivably personal abuse in both pamphlets,
Pope made a number of changes to his texts in the light of Dennis's criticisms. See
J. V. Guerinot, *Pamphlet Attacks on Alexander Pope 1711–1744* (London: Methuen,
1969), 7–11, 54–5. (Of course, it is possible that Pope's dislike of verbal criticism as
literary criticism began as a boy, when his father, who 'was pretty difficult in being
pleased', would 'send him back to new turn' his verses! See Spence, No. 11.)

[9] Preface to *Sylvae* (1685), Watson, ii. 19.

[10] Ibid. ii. 29; 'Original and Progress of Satire' (1693), ibid. ii. 136; cf. ibid. ii.
152–3.

dispute in the 1690s between Richard Bentley and Sir William Temple, the Hon. Charles Boyle (later Fourth Earl of Orrery), and Francis Atterbury.[11]

At its most superficial (and most popularly influential) level, the dispute over the epistles of Phalaris amounted to a contest between scholarship and polite taste as to which was the better arbiter of the worth of a work of literature. Despite previous scholarly doubt about the authenticity of the epistles, Sir William Temple, the quintessence of good taste, declared them genuine, representative of the general superiority of the Ancients, and, indeed, 'to have more race, more spirit, more force of wit and genius, than any others I have ever seen, either ancient or modern'.[12] As a result of this praise, the epistles were chosen to be edited by the Hon. Charles Boyle, then an undergraduate at Christ Church, and the edition appeared in 1695. In the meantime, Bentley had confided to his friend, William Wotton, that the epistles could be proved to be spurious, and Wotton, in anticipation that his *Reflections upon Ancient and Modern Learning* (1694) would run to a second edition, exacted a promise that Bentley would supply an essay on these topics. The controversy continued during the rest of the decade, with Wotton and Bentley declaring the epistles spurious on the basis of historical and linguistic anomalies, and gentleman-critics, such as Temple, Boyle, and Atterbury, triumphing over scholarship by winning 'a signal victory in "wit, taste, and breeding" '. The popular preference for taste over scholarship in this matter persisted (leaving aside such scholars as Thomas Tyrwhitt and Richard Porson) until the early years of the nineteenth century.[13] The effect of the Phalaris controversy was to lower scholarship in the estimation of polite society.

The third Earl of Shaftesbury epitomizes the views of those with pretensions to good taste; in *Advice to an Author* (1710) he declares:

[11] For an account of this controversy, see James Henry Monk, *The Life of Richard Bentley*, 2nd edn., rev. (2 vols., 1833), i. 58 ff. For a discussion principally concerned with the scholarship of the participants, see R. C. Jebb, *Bentley*, English Men of Letters (1889), chs. 4–5. For a study concerned with the history of ideas in the seventeenth century, see R. F. Jones, 'The Background of the *Battle of the Books*' (1920), repr. in *The Seventeenth Century* (Stanford: Stanford University Press, 1965), 10–40.

[12] 'Essay on Ancient and Modern Learning' (1692), quoted by Jebb, *Bentley*, p. 42.

[13] Jebb, *Bentley*, pp. 76–83, *passim*.

I AM persuaded that to be *a Virtuoso* (so far as befits Gentleman) is a higher step towards the becoming a Man of Virtue and good Sense, than the being what in this Age we call *a Scholar*. For even rude Nature itself, in its primitive Simplicity, is a better Guide to Judgment, than improv'd Sophistry, and pedantick Learning.[14]

Shaftesbury's opinions were not based on mere aristocratic prejudice, for he states that he cannot 'think it proper to call a Man *well-read* who reads *many Authors*; since he must of necessity have more ill Models, than good; 'and be more stuff'd with Bombast, ill Fancy, and wry Thought; than fill'd with solid Sense, and just Imagination'.[15] Shaftesbury's thought in this instance has an attractive simplicity, as well as an appeal to intellectual and class snobbery, and its spirit probably lies behind Pope's condescension in *The Dunciad* (1729) to Theobald's concerns with 'The Classicks of an Age that heard of none' (i. 128) as means of elucidating Shakespeare through parallel readings. Readers of Shaftesbury's *Essay on the Freedom of Wit and Humour* (1709) were, however, to have occasion to reconsider his declaration that 'A good Poet, and an honest Historian, may afford Learning enough for *a Gentleman*. And such a one, whilst he reads these Authors as his Diversion, will have a truer relish of their Sense, and understand 'em better than a *Pedant*, with all his Labours, and the assistance of his Volumes of Commentators.'[16]

When Pope issued proposals for his translation of *The Iliad* in October 1713, he had in common with other hackney writers his poverty. As Maynard Mack has said, the translation of *The Iliad* was 'a desperate gamble—which worked—by a young man who longed to cut a figure in the world, but found he lacked funds even to buy books'.[17] That he had this much in common with the hacks must have been galling. The actual translation allowed Pope to demonstrate his abilities in a task generally considered to be itself heroic. Theobald appropriately expressed the sentiments of the majority of Pope's readers when he associated the translator with Diomedes.[18] But in the

[14] Repr. in *Characteristicks*, 5th edn. (3 vols., 1732), i. 333–4.

[15] Ibid. i. 342–3.

[16] Ibid. i. 122.

[17] Introduction, *The Iliad of Homer*, trans. Pope, Twickenham Edition (London: Methuen, 1967), vol. vii, p. xlvi.

[18] *Censor*, 33 (5 Jan. 1717), ii. 19.

writing of the commentary Pope had, again, a great deal in
common with the writers of Grub Street: a sense of his dependence on others and of his consequent vulnerability, both of
which were too intimately connected with his greatest strength,
his writing. The specific nature of his problem in compiling the
commentary is set forth in an angry letter from one of his chief
helpers, William Broome, to another, Elijah Fenton: 'All the
crime that I have committed is saying he is no master of Greek;
and I am so confident of this, that if he can translate ten lines of
Eustathius I will own myself unjust and unworthy.'[19] Pope's
frustration with the sources of his commentary could only have
been made worse by a fear that this essentially secondary
matter might overshadow his success in translating the poem.
Not only was Pope's financial success threatened, but, since a
secondary part might determine judgement of the whole, his
sense of justice and propriety was also offended. Moreover, it
was pre-eminently in the commentary on Homer that he was
forced to write from external necessity rather than from any
inner need or desire: 'Notes were . . . to be provided; for the
six volumes would have been very little more than six pamphlets
without them.'[20] These aspects of his experience may well have
produced moments of extreme uneasiness for Pope at meetings
of the Scriblerus Club; they certainly have important consequences in *The Dunciad*.

In so far as Pope's Homer is an English classic, it is the first
English classic to be accompanied by extensive, systematic
commentary.[21] To this end Pope requested Broome to 'translate such notes only as concern the beauties or art of the author
—none geographical, historical or grammatical—unless some
occur very important to the sense . . . but leave out none of the
art or contrivance of the poet, or beauties, it being on account

---

[19] *Correspondence*, ii. 500 (15 June 1728). Cf. Norman Callan (ed.), *The Iliad*, trans.
Pope, ed. cit., vol. vii, p. lxxxiv: 'Broome's complaint, which Johnson echoes, that
Pope could not read Eustathius for himself, was probably just.'

[20] Johnson, 'Life of Pope', in *Lives of the Poets*, ed. G. B. Hill (3 vols., Oxford:
Clarendon Press, 1905), iii. 115.

[21] The only serious rivals to this claim for Pope's Homer are E.K.'s notes to *The
Shepheard's Calender* (1579), Thomas Speght's edition of *Chaucer* (1598), Ben Jonson's
classical references in his *Works* (1616; vol. ii, 1640), Cowley's notes to *Pindaric Odes*
and *Davideis* (*Works*, 1668), and P[atrick] H[ume]'s *Annotations on Milton's Paradise Lost*
(1695).

of those alone that I put you to this trouble'.[22] The printed work echoes these concerns. Pope begins his 'Observations on the First Book' of *The Iliad* (1715) by castigating Homer's commentators, because 'there is hardly one whose principal Design is to illustrate the Poetical Beauties of the Author'. Complaining that 'their Remarks are rather Philosophical, Historical, Geographical, Allegorical, or in short rather any thing than Critical and Poetical', he censures 'Even the Grammarians' who, 'tho' their whole Business and Use be only to render the Words of an Author intelligible, are strangely touch'd with the Pride of doing something more than they ought'. Even in the commentaries of Eustathius 'those Remarks that any way concern the Poetry or Art of the Poet, are much fewer than is imagin'd'. And he was obliged to say of Madame Dacier that although 'She has made a farther Attempt than her Predecessors to discover the Beauties of the Poet', yet 'we have often only her general Praises and Exclamations instead of Reasons'. In contrast, Pope set about the worthwhile task of commenting 'upon Homer as a Poet'.[23]

In the observations on *The Iliad* Pope appears to be the acme of Shaftesbury's gentleman-reader. There is a self-conscious effort to make scholarship the servant of critical appreciation. Johnson comments on the observations that, although 'they were undoubtedly written to swell the volumes', they 'ought not to pass without praise: commentaries which attract the reader by the pleasure of perusal have not often appeared; the notes of others are read to clear difficulties, those of Pope to vary entertainment.' Johnson's adverse criticism also has some validity: there is at times 'too much of unseasonable levity and affected gaiety . . . too many appeals are made to the ladies, and the ease which is so carefully preserved is sometimes the ease of a trifler . . . the gravity of common criticks may be tedious, but it is less despicable than childish merriment.'[24] Despite this, Pope's commentary is probably the best possible compromise between the ideals of Shaftesbury and the simple need to supply information.

A connection between Pope's commentary on Homer and

[22] *Correspondence*, i. 270 (29 Nov. 1714).
[23] *The Iliad* (quarto edn., 1715), i. 47–9.
[24] 'Life of Pope', in *Lives*, ed. Hill, iii. 240.

his approach to the editing of Shakespeare has been previously recognized.[25] It has also been thought perhaps 'an accident that Pope ever got himself involved in the business of editing'.[26] Pope's beautifully printed edition of Shakespeare was possibly intended by Jacob Tonson to celebrate the centenary of the publication of the first folio in 1623.[27] Pope may have been pleased to have his name linked with Shakespeare as well as Homer, while Tonson may have thought it appropriate that the supreme poet of the age should present the works of his great predecessor in their best possible dress. An additional attraction for Pope would have been an absence of any problems involving a knowledge of Greek. Accordingly, *The Weekly Journal, or Saturday's Post* (18 November 1721) announced: 'The celebrated Mr. Pope is preparing a correct Edition of Shakespear's Works; that of the late Mr. Rowe being very faulty.' If Pope began with an assumption that his task would be considerably easier to perform than the commentary on Homer, he was soon to discover his mistake. Commentators like Eustathius and Madame Dacier may not have given much insight into Homer as a poet, but they had provided a scholarly base from which accurate criticism might begin. As Pope discovered, no equivalent scholarship devoted to Shakespeare existed. Consequently, instead of a systematic commentary on Shakespeare comparable to that on Homer, readers of Pope's edition found only the preliminaries to such a work, that some of 'The more obsolete or unusual words are explained' and that 'Some of the most shining passages are distinguish'd by comma's in the margin; and where the beauty lay . . . in the whole, a star is prefix'd to the scene.' Pope justified this practice on the grounds that it

[25] See J. R. Sutherland, 'The Dull Duty of An Editor', *Review of English Studies*, 21 (1945), 202–15, repr. in Maynard Mack (ed.), *Essential Articles for the Study of Alexander Pope* (London: Frank Cass & Co., 1964).

[26] Ibid. 630.

[27] In a letter of 5 Nov. 1722, Pope says the edition is 'about a quarter printed' and that he thinks 'twill be a year at least before the whole work can be finished' (*Correspondence*, ii. 142). If Sherburn's date of 6 Aug. 1722 is correct for a letter from Pope to Jacob Tonson jun. (ibid. 130), both Pope and Tonson were hoping for publication in 1723. The edition finally appeared in Mar. 1725. The delay in publication seems to have been due to difficulties Pope experienced in writing the Preface and to his involvement with Francis Atterbury, who in 1723 was on trial on a charge of high treason for conspiracy in a Jacobite plot. See Sherburn, pp. 227–31, and below, ch. 8, p. 134.

seemed 'a shorter and less ostentatious method of performing the better half of Criticism (namely the pointing out an Author's excellencies) than to fill a whole paper with citations of fine passages, with *general Applauses*, or *Empty Exclamations* at the tail of them'.[28] His solution to the problem of a commentary does indeed obviate the criticisms he himself had levelled at Madam Dacier, which he echoes here,[29] but Pope's decision not to comment on particular passages in Shakespeare probably came from a fear of charges that he had misunderstood his author. He was by no means able to explain all the 'obsolete or unusual words' in his text, and thus it would have been folly to engage in commenting on Shakespeare as a poet. Johnson was mistaken in his belief that 'For this part of his task, and for this only, was Mr. Pope eminently and indisputably qualified'.[30]

The difficulty of Shakespeare for educated readers in the third decade of the eighteenth century is illustrated by a letter to Pope from Francis Atterbury in response to a plea for help:

I have found time to read some parts of Shakespear which I was least acquainted with. I protest to you, in an hundred places I cannot construe him, I dont understand him. The hardest part of Chaucer is more intillegible to me than some of those Scenes, not merely thro the faults of the Edition, but the Obscurity of the Writer: for Obscure he is, & a little (not a little) enclin'd now & then to Bombast whatever Apology you may have contriv'd on that head for him. There are Allusions in him to an hundred things, of which I knew nothing, & can guess nothing. And yet without some competent knowledge of those matters there's no understanding him. I protest Æschylus does not want a Comment to me, more than he does: so that I begin to despair of doing you any considerable Service.[31]

In a subsequent letter Atterbury provides both a comment on Pope's jottings on the text and what looks very much like the germ of Pope's stated editorial policy in his Preface: 'Shakespear shall . . . be put into your hands as clean and fair as it came out of them: tho' you, I think have been dabling here and there with the Text. I have had more Reverence for the Writer

[28] Preface, *1725*, vol. i, pp. xxii–xxiii.

[29] See above, p. 55.

[30] *Proposals for Printing . . . the Dramatick Works of William Shakespeare* (1756), Yale, vii. 57.

[31] *Correspondence*, ii. 78–9 (2 Aug. 1721).

and the Printer, and left every thing standing just as I found it.'[32] Pope also solicited help in other quarters, but not much was forthcoming. William Oldys was generally acknowledged to be learned in the older English literature, but he, according to Edmond Malone, recommended to Pope 'drastic revision of the text to achieve clarity at any cost'.[33]

The courage and pertinacity that enabled Pope triumphantly to complete the commentary on *The Iliad* were revived in his approach to Shakespeare. If a gentleman like Bishop Atterbury and a scholar like Oldys were defeated by Shakespeare, there was obviously little hope of providing an adequate commentary. Apart from the difficulties arising from Shakespeare's rude, obscure style, there were the problems arising from errors of the press. Pope began in almost complete ignorance—as late as 10 February 1722 he believed the first folio was dated 1621[34]— but, with a dedication that may have seemed excessive to his friends, he set about the business of the text. In a letter to Jacob Tonson jun. of May 1722, he is 'resolvd to pass the next whole week in London, purposely to get together Parties of my acquaintance ev'ry night, to collate the several Editions of Shakespear's single Plays, 5 of which I have ingaged to this design'.[35] Since there were no public libraries to afford him help,[36] Pope advertised in the newspapers for assistance. Eventually he had 'both paid and unpaid' assistants, among whom were Elijah Fenton, John Gay, and 'a man or two' at Oxford.[37]

In the circumstances, it is not surprising that Pope should adopt as his starting-point the edition of *Shakespear* (1709) published by his friend Nicholas Rowe. In fact, Pope had no choice: the Tonsons' claim to the copyright of Shakespeare's plays was embodied in Rowe's text, and in a literal sense Jacob Tonson jun. expected Pope to improve this particular piece of

---

[32] *Correspondence*, ii. 87–8 (15 Oct. 1721).

[33] See Lawrence Lipking, 'The Curiosity of William Oldys: An Approach to the Development of English Literary History', *Philological Quarterly*, 46 (1967), 391.

[34] *Correspondence*, ii. 102.

[35] Ibid. 118.

[36] The Revd Mr Thomas Carte, in a set of proposals (9 Nov. 1743) for a public library in the newly erected Mansion House, declared: 'There is not a great City in Europe so ill provided with Publick Libraries, as London' (British Library, Birch Coll., Add. MS 4254, fo. 6ʳ).

[37] See Sherburn, pp. 234–8.

'property'.[38] Pope based his text on the third edition of Rowe's *Shakespear* (1714), which had also benefited from being seen through the press by John Hughes, Tonson's editor of Spenser. Rowe's edition was based on the fourth folio (1685), since the Tonsons' claim to the copy stemmed from negotiations with those who had rights in this edition. Pope's view of his obligations as an editor probably resembled that of Hughes in the Dedication of Spenser's *Works* (1715): 'An Editor of the Works of a dead Author ought to consider himself as a kind of Executor of his Will; which he should endeavour to perform with the same Care, and, in every Circumstance, after the same manner he believes the Author himself wou'd have done, if living.'[39] The author should be presented in the best possible light—as determined by the taste of the editor.

Pope and his assistants went to some trouble to improve on Rowe's attempts to make Shakespeare readily intelligible to the reader. They accepted his lists of dramatis personae and his introduction of uniformity into the designation of characters in speech headings, and they followed his stage directions, especially in the notice of entrances and exits. Whereas Rowe had taken special care only with the tragedies in providing act and scene divisions and indications of locality, they gave all the plays localities and divided them all into scenes in the French manner, that is, beginning a new scene whenever a central character enters or leaves.[40] As a final touch reminiscent of *The Iliad*, a poetical index was compiled by Fenton and one of the unknown assistants.

It is in the treatment of the text itself that Pope and his assistants reveal a greater conscientiousness than Rowe's. They followed Rowe's example in improving grammar and in modernizing word forms. Since there were no manuscripts, Rowe claimed to have compared the old editions as part of his 'Care to redeem [Shakespeare] from the Injuries of former Impressions'. He continues: 'In some of the Editions, especially the last, there were many Lines (and in *Hamlet* one whole Scene)

[38] For an account of the copyright of Shakespeare's plays in this period, see Dawson, pp. 11–35, and below, ch. 8.

[39] Vol. i, pp. iii–iv. See D. Nichol Smith, *Shakespeare in the Eighteenth Century* (Oxford: Clarendon Press, 1928), 34. Pope acted as literary executor to Thomas Parnell (*Poems*, 1722) and John Sheffield, Duke of Buckinghamshire (*Works*, 1723).

[40] See McKerrow, pp. 97–103.

left out together; these are now all supply'd.'[41] In fact, Rowe collated a late quarto of *Hamlet* (probably that of 1676) with the fourth-folio text, and restored some 131 lines from the quarto of a total of 231 not found in the folio. Apart from his printing the Prologue to *Romeo and Juliet* (found in the quartos) at the *end* of the play, there is no other definite indication of his use of the early quarto texts.[42] By contrast, Pope collected twenty-nine quartos that had been published before 1623, including six first quartos, as well as the first and second folios. However, his failure to restore all the lines or 'better' readings these materials afforded has obscured his use of them.

In his role of literary executor and editor, Pope's aim was to enhance Shakespeare's reputation, rather than simply to recover what he had written. It is in this context that he was the first to declare the superiority of the quarto texts to the first folio:

The folio edition (in which all the plays we now receive as his, were first collected) was published by two Players, *Heming* and *Condell*, in 1623, seven years after his decease. They declare, that all the other editions were stolen and surreptitious, and affirm theirs to be purged from the errors of the former. This is true as to the literal errors, and no other; for in all respects else it is far worse than the Quarto's.

In asserting the superiority of the quartos, Pope was not concerned primarily with the recovery of matter omitted by the folio. In his view, the folio is inferior to certain quarto texts 'First, because the additions of trifling and bombast passages are in this edition far more numerous. For whatever had been

---

[41] *1709*, vol. i, sigs. A2^r–A2^v.

[42] McKerrow, p. 95. None the less, Rowe's activities as an editor have had enduring consequences for the text of Shakespeare. Some idea of the impact of Rowe and the other major eighteenth-century editors on the modern text of Shakespeare can be gauged from the textual notes in *Riverside*. In those plays included in the first folio, *Riverside* adopts 1,063 readings from Rowe (plus 170 lines altered from prose to verse or vice versa), 512 readings from Pope (plus 711 lines altered from prose to verse or vice versa), 744 readings from Theobald, 133 readings from Hanmer, 58 readings from Warburton, 126 readings from Johnson, 514 readings from Capell, and 71 readings from Malone (excluding alterations or additions to scene locations, stage directions, dramatis personae, and initial speech prefixes, but including emendations, significant punctuation changes, hyphenations, speech reassignments, and modernizations). Of course, these figures give no indication of the scholarship or ingenuity of the editors, and Rowe, as the first to scrutinize the text, had more occasions than his successors to make worthwhile alterations. See also below, p. 167, n. 127.

added, since those Quarto's, by the actors, or had stolen from their mouths into the written parts, were from thence conveyed into the printed text, and all stand charged upon the Author.' Shakespeare himself had 'complained of this usage in *Hamlet*, where he wishes that *those who play the Clowns wou'd speak no more than is set down for them*'. The result of this approach is that Pope is liable to prefer a bad quarto to a good quarto or the folio; for example, as proof that Shakespeare could not escape unauthorized insertion, he noted that 'in the old editions of *Romeo and Juliet* there is no hint of a great number of the mean conceits and ribaldries' to be found in the folio. Pope possessed the 'bad' quarto (Q1) of 1597 and the 'good' quarto (Q2) of 1599 of *Romeo and Juliet*. That he was far from considering Q2 authoritative is evident from his previous comment on differing quartos of the same play: 'of some of these, we meet with two or more editions by different printers, each of which has whole heaps of trash different from the other: which I should fancy was occasion'd, by their being taken from different copies, belonging to different Play-houses.'[43] Pope reveals an identical assumption in his comment on 'the latter part of the last Act' of *The Taming of a Shrew* (Q3, 1607), which he found 'manifestly better, and clear of that impertinent Prolixity which is in the common Editions'.[44]

The limitations of Pope's taste in Shakespeare dictated his assessment of his materials. A major value of the quartos for him was that they might provide authority for omission or degradation of passages he disliked. This is evident in a note on *The Two Gentlemen of Verona*, a play that exists only in the folio version:

This whole Scene, like many others in these Plays, (some of which

---

[43] Preface, *1725*, vol. i, p. xvi.

[44] 'Table of the Several Editions . . . compared in this Impression', *1725*, vol. vi, sig. Oooo^v. It is likely that Pope's mistrust of the first folio (and, by extension, of 'augmented' quartos) was in part due to Abraham Cowley. As early as 1656, Cowley had complained (Preface, *Poems* (1656), repr. in *The Works of Mr Abraham Cowley* (1668), sig. B3^v) that posthumous editions of poets' works are 'stuffed out, either with *counterfeit* pieces . . . or with such, which though of their own *Coyn*, they would have called in themselves, for the baseness of the *Allay* . . . . This has been the case with *Shakespear*, *Fletcher*, *Johnson*, and many others; part of whose *Poems* I should take the boldness to prune and lop away, if the care of replanting them in print did belong to me.' (See also Greg, *First Folio*, pp. 210–11 and n. 5.)

I believe were written by *Shakespear*, and others interpolated by the Players) is compos'd of the lowest and most trifling conceits, to be accounted for only from the gross taste of the age he liv'd in; *Populo ut placerent.* I wish I had authority to leave them out, but I have done all I could, set a mark of reprobation upon them; throughout this edition.[45]

Cowley's comments and Pope's fatigue with his editorial labours are probably sufficient to account for his rejection of the apocryphal plays. It was, however, his limited taste and his concern for his author's reputation that caused him to conjecture that, of *Love's Labour's Lost, Titus Andronicus*, and *The Winter's Tale*, 'only some characters, single scenes, or perhaps a few particular passages' were by Shakespeare.[46] As Johnson remarked, Pope 'by a very compendious criticism . . . rejected whatever he disliked, and thought more of amputation than cure'.[47]

Pope does recognize the value of 'a number of beautiful passages' that are found in quarto texts but not in the folio.[48] Whereas Rowe had restored to *Hamlet* some 131 quarto lines of the 231 omitted by the folio, Pope restored an additional 36; where the folio had omitted about 284 lines of *King Lear* found in quarto texts, none of which was restored by Rowe, Pope restored 142. Pope's failure to present everything available to him has led to a belief that he was haphazard in his collation of texts,[49] but it seems just as likely that he collated all his materials quite carefully, and that the omission or addition of lines was the result of deliberate choice, not accident. It has been plausibly argued that in his editing of *King Lear* Pope 'is very careful in his collation of this play; he constantly keeps the quarto before him and uses it to emend or augment the text, but he always reserves the right to handle his material in his own way. If he leaves out lines from the quarto edition, it is because he wishes to do so, not because he is careless or unsystematic.' In his assessment of his materials, 'the worth of a line or a passage or a quarto depends ultimately upon its conformity with what he

---

[45] *1725*, i. 157 (italics reversed).
[46] Preface, *1725*, vol. i, p. xx.
[47] Preface, *1765*, vol. i, sig. C8^r [Yale, vii. 94].
[48] Preface, *1725*, vol. i, p. xvii.
[49] McKerrow, p. 108.

feels to be good poetry'. Moreover, there is evidence that in plays where there is no quarto text, 'Pope paid the folio text as much attention as he did to any of the quarto editions he collated [with Rowe's text]'.[50]

Pope also devoted a great deal of attention to the verse of plays: he redivided according to metre lines that had been printed as prose, and relined as prose passages that had been printed roughly as verse. For example, he recognized that in *2 Henry IV* on occasion Pistol speaks blank verse while his companions speak prose (II. iv. 163–9, 181–3). He also regularized the metre by altering diction and syntax, leading Malone to declare that the editor of the second folio 'and Mr. Pope, were the two great corrupters of our poet's text'.[51] Pope's practice is consistent with his desire to present his author in the best possible light, a desire also apparent in his verbal changes in *Julius Caesar* following the Duke of Buckinghamshire's *Tragedy of Julius Caesar*, which he had seen through the press in the Duke's posthumous *Works* (1723). These changes are consistent with his removal of anachronisms, such as his substituting a dash for 'hats' in *Julius Caesar* (II. i. 73), which prompted Theobald to enquire facetiously, 'who would not suspect Mr. Pope, out of modesty, had shut out a word of bawdry here?'[52] None the less, Pope's care for his author's reputation is evident, and he justifies his procedures with his low opinion of Shakespeare's seventeenth-century 'editors':

how many faults may have been unjustly laid to his account from arbitrary Additions, Expunctions, Transpositions of scenes and lines, confusion of Characters and Persons, wrong application of Speeches, corruptions of innumerable Passages by the Ignorance, and wrong Corrections of 'em again by the Impertinence, of his first Editors? From one or other of these considerations, I am verily perswaded, that the greatest and the grossest part of what are thought his errors

[50] John A. Hart, 'Pope as Scholar-Editor', *Studies in Bibliography*, 23 (1970), 54–8, *passim*. Hart's findings are based on a study of Pope's collation of *Lear, Hamlet, Macbeth, Antony and Cleopatra, Romeo and Juliet, Othello, The Tempest, Julius Caesar*, and of individual scenes in *A Midsummer Night's Dream, As You Like It, Richard II*, and *1 Henry IV* (ibid. 59 n. 19).

[51] *1790*, vol. i, pt. i, p. xix. For Pope's regularization of Shakespeare's verse in modern texts, see Paul Bertram, *White Spaces in Shakespeare: The Development of the Modern Text* (Cleveland: Bellflower Press, 1981).

[52] Nichols, ii. 493; *1725*, v. 238; Malcolm Goldstein, 'Pope, Sheffield, and Shakespeare's *Julius Caesar*,' *Modern Language Notes*, 71 (1956), 8–10.

would vanish, and leave his character in a light very different from that disadvantageous one, in which it now appears to us.[53]

Although during the Restoration and early eighteenth century the most common solution to what was thought difficult or unsatisfactory in Shakespeare was to rewrite the plays, Pope recognized that he could not do that as an editor: 'It is impossible to repair the Injuries already done him; too much time has elaps'd, and the materials are too few. In what I have done I have rather given a proof of my willingness and desire, than of my ability, to do him justice.' In the spirit of a literary executor, he may have felt also that he should not go too far in advertising his many alterations of the text; this might be taken as excessive condescension to his author: 'I have discharg'd the dull duty of an Editor, to my best judgment, with more labour than I expect thanks, with a religious abhorrence of all Innovation, and without any indulgence to my private sense or conjecture.' Human frailty and a desire to avoid appearing a meticulous pedant are probably responsible for his failure to list completely the various readings of his materials, as he implies he has done: 'The method taken in this Edition will show it self. The various Readings are fairly put in the margin, so that every one may compare 'em; and those I have prefer'd into the Text are constantly *ex fide Codicum*, upon authority.'[54] But, by his own standards, and by the standards of Cowley, Rowe, his friends, and his publisher, Pope had acted conscientiously as an editor. By modern standards, he failed abysmally. These standards first began to be instituted when, on 5 April 1726, Theobald published in quarto (to range alongside Pope's edition) the 194 pages of *Shakespeare restored: or, A Specimen of the Many Errors, as well Committed, as Unamended, by Mr. Pope In his Late Edition of this Poet.* He also retained on his title-page part of Pope's motto to *Shakespear*:

> ------------*Laniatum Corpore toto*
> *DEIPHOBUM vidi & lacerum crudeliter Ora,*
> *Ora, manusque ambas*--------[55]

---

[53] Preface, *1725*, vol. i, p. xxi.

[54] Ibid., p. xxii.

[55] *Aeneid*, vi. 494–7, 501–2: 'And here [I] saw Deiphobus . . . his whole frame mangled, his face cruelly torn—his face and either hand—his ears wrenched from despoiled brows, and his nostrils lopped by a shameful wound. . . . Who chose to wreak a penalty so cruel? Who had power so to deal with thee?' (Loeb translation)

5. Theobald's Review of Pope: Shakespeare Restored (1726)

THEOBALD'S admiration for scholars and scholarship began with his schooling under the Reverend James Ellis. The *Censor* provides ample evidence of his early attitudes, and No. 5 (30 April 1715) is especially revealing: 'I am so profess'd an Admirer of Antiquity, that I am never better pleas'd with the Labours of my Contemporaries, than when they busy themselves in retrieving the sacred Monuments of their Fore-fathers from Obscurity and Oblivion.' Theobald conceives of textual scholarship in heroic terms:

When . . . I have discovered an uncommon Beauty and Strength of Wit in an imperfect *Paragraph*, I grieve . . . that I cannot recover the whole. . . . If upon these Occasions any of the Learned happen to [restore] a maimed Sentence to its original Life and Spirit, I pay him the same regard as the ancient *Romans* did to One who had preserv'd the Life of a *Fellow-Citizen*.[1]

Admiration for the achievements of textual scholars, especially those of Richard Bentley, seems to have been a continuing part of his outlook, and it was thus natural that his love of Shakespeare should find expression in a concern for Shakespeare's text.

Theobald is careful never to present scholarship as an end in itself. Like Pope, he is careful to make plain his aversion to pedantry. In No. 69 (30 March 1717) he maintains that 'The numerous Volumes of useless Pedantick Learning, elaborate Trifles, and tedious senseless Harangues, which infest our Press and Conversation, would be but too plain Proofs, that no small Number of the Learned World are engag'd in their Studies only by a Spirit of Curiosity, or vain Affectation of

---

[1] *Censor*, 5, i. 29, 30–1.

Knowledge'.[2] His contemporaries must have found him toler-
ably sincere in these protestations: the second volume of The
Censor was dedicated to Bentley's early antagonist, the Hon.
Charles Boyle, who had succeeded to the title of Earl of Orrery.
Like Pope, Theobald considered himself an upholder of polite
learning and by no means a pedant. Notwithstanding Pope's
subsequent representation of him in *The Dunciad Variorum*
(1729), he was able to include in the list of subscribers to his
Shakespeare (1733) 'nearly all the principal Nobility, and many
respectable Divines'.[3]

It is likely that Theobald kept his admiration for Pope as a
poet until the appearance of *The Dunciad*, and that even after
publication of *The Dunciad* he maintained a regard for his
poetry. In the Introduction to *Shakespeare Restored* Theobald is
certainly careful to distinguish between Pope as poet and as
editor, and goes out of his way to be polite:

> It was no small Satisfaction . . . to me, when I first heard Mr. *POPE*
> had taken upon him the Publication of *SHAKESPEARE*. I very reasonably
> expected, from his known Talents and Abilities, from his uncommon
> Sagacity and Discernment, and from his unwearied Diligence and
> Care of informing himself by an happy and extensive Conversation,
> we should have had our Author come out as perfect, as the want of
> *Manuscripts* and *original Copies* could give us a Possibility of hoping. I
> may dare to say, a great Number of *SHAKESPEARE*'s Admirers, and of
> Mr. *POPE*'s too, (both of which I sincerely declare myself,) concurred
> in this Expectation: For there is a certain *curiosa fælicitas*, as was said of
> an eminent *Roman* Poet, in that Gentleman's Way of working, which,
> we presum'd, would have laid itself out largely in such a Province;
> and that he would not have sate down contented with performing, as
> he calls it himself, the *dull Duty* of an EDITOR only.

Despite 'a Veneration, almost rising to Idolatry, for the
Writings' of Shakespeare, he 'would be very loth even to do
him Justice at the Expence of *that other* Gentleman's Character'.[4]

It is important to note that Theobald's veneration is for the
'Writings' of Shakespeare, and not for the myth of Shakespeare
the untutored genius (whose plays, judging from Pope's

---

2 *Censor*, 69, iii. 39–40. See also ibid. 26, i. 181–2.
3 Nichols, ii. 734.
4 pp. ii–iii.

Preface, tend to suffer from too close a scrutiny). The implicit shift in perspective apparent in Theobald's statement is fundamental to the differences between his editorial approach and Pope's. Another new element appears in Theobald's approach to Shakespeare's text: not only is Shakespeare regarded as a classic writer, but his classic status is seen in terms of the cultural history of England and of the history of the language, rather than in terms of neo-classical dramatic theory. These shifts are important because, in addition to their effect on the editor's sense of his duties, they contain in embryo a justification of the rise of English literary scholarship and a proto-Romantic regard for national cultural history:

AS *SHAKESPEARE* stands, or at least ought to stand, in the Nature of a Classic Writer, and, indeed, he is corrupt enough to pass for one of the oldest Stamp, every one, who has a Talent and Ability this Way, is at liberty to make his Comments and Emendations upon him. . . . And he, who has the Luck to be allowed any Merit in it, does not only do a Service to the Poet, but to his Country and its Language.

Theobald's following assertion, as his letters show, was not merely conventional: 'No Vein of Pedantry, or Ostentation of useless Criticism, incited me to this Work: It is a Sacrifice to the Pleasure of *SHAKESPEARE*'s Admirers. in general.'[5] As opposed to Pope's statement of his editorial principle (but not his actual practice), that he has 'discharg'd the dull duty of an Editor . . . with a religious abhorrence of all Innovation, and without any indulgence to [his] private sense or conjecture'[6], Theobald maintains that an editor,

wherever he finds the Reading suspected, manifestly corrupted, deficient in Sense, and unintelligible . . . ought to exert every Power and Faculty of the Mind to supply such a Defect, to give Light and restore Sense to the Passage, and, by a reasonable Emendation, to make that satisfactory and consistent with the Context, which before was so absurd, unintelligible, and intricate.

He continues: 'THIS is a *Task*, which . . . Mr. *POPE* has *purposely disclaim'd*, and which I (by what Fatality, or with what

5 *SR*, pp. v–vi.
6 Preface, *1725*, vol. i, p. xxii, quoted by Theobald.

Event, I know not;) have taken upon myself to prosecute.'[7] Here begins the eighteenth-century rage for emending Shakespeare; but Theobald's approach to emendation was very different from that of most of his followers.

By far the greater part of Theobald's researches into Shakespeare was to take place after the publication of *Shakespeare Restored*, but in this early work he laid the foundations of his approach in his edition. The most obvious difference between Theobald and Pope is that Theobald is much more consistent in his desire to reproduce what Shakespeare had written (as opposed to what, perhaps, he ought to have written), and that he brings to his task a recognition of the importance of Elizabethan and Jacobean English usage. Scholarship takes the place of poetic genius as the chief requirement in an editor. The earlier view is suggested by George Sewell's sanguine expectations of Pope's edition: 'When a Genius of similar Fire and Fancy, temper'd with a learned Patience, sits down to consider what SHAKESPEAR would *Think*, as well as what he could *Write*, we may then expect to see his Works answer to our Idea of the Man.'[8] Although he had attempted imitation of Shakespeare in *The Cave of Poverty*, Theobald knew he could not hope, as Pope had done, to understand (or be thought to understand) Shakespeare on the basis of shared or comparable genius. Instead, he determined to study Shakespeare as if he were a Greek or Roman classic.

The most obvious sign of Theobald's use of classical scholarship as a model is his extensive citation of parallel readings. The technique was, of course, commonplace:

> When Things appear *unnatural* or *hard*,
> Consult your *Author*, with *Himself* compar'd.[9]

The resulting lengthy lists in *Shakespeare Restored* have been ridiculed, but as the first to apply the technique to Shakespeare, Theobald initiated the study of Shakespearian grammar. For example, in *Hamlet* (I. ii. 36-7) Pope and Rowe follow the quarto of 1676:

---

[7] *SR*, p. v.

[8] Preface, *The Works of Mr. William Shakespear. The Seventh Volume* (1725), p. viii.

[9] Wentworth Dillon, Earl of Roscommon, *Essay on Translated Verse* (1684), repr. in *Critical Essays of the Seventeenth Century*, ed. Joel E. Spingarn (3 vols., Oxford: Clarendon Press, 1957), ii. 302, ll. 27-8.

> *Giving to you no further personal power*
> *OF TREATY with the King*, &c.[10]

Theobald comments: 'This is a Reading adopted, and of a modern Stamp, as I take it; either from Want of Understanding the Poet's genuine Words, or on a Supposition of their being too stiff and obsolete. All my old Copies have it, as I think it ought to be restor'd,

> *Giving to you no further personal Pow'r*
> *TO BUSINESS with the King*, &c.'[11]

On the basis of some eighteen parallel readings (after which he concludes: 'I am afraid of growing too luxuriant in Examples of this Sort, or I' could stretch out the Catalogue of them to a greater Extent') he is able to justify the restoration: 'It is a Licence in our Poet, of his own Authority, to coin new *Verbs* both out of *Substantives* and *Adjectives*; and it is, as we may call it, one of the *Quidlibet audendi's* very familiar with him.'[12] These may be elementary observations, but in 1726 they were being made for the first time.

Theobald must have felt he could scarcely adduce too much evidence for his changes. In calling into question Pope's editing, he was also challenging contemporary assumptions about absolute grammatical correctness.[13] Theobald himself found these assumptions difficult to discard. For example, despite four parallels, 'where I have observ'd the *Nominative* of *Pronouns* is used, tho' Grammar requires the *Accusative*', he congratulates Pope for correcting this solecism in Shakespeare and proceeds to do the same himself: calling it possibly 'a Liberty which *SHAKESPEARE* purposely gave himself. . . . Be this, as it will; if *Grammar* and the *Idiom* of the Tongue be directly against it, we have sufficient Warrant to make him *now*, at least, speak

---

[10] Passages quoted are as given by Theobald in *SR* (following Pope's ed., 1725).

[11] *SR*, p. 7.

[12] Ibid. 11, 8.

[13] Dryden's tendency to favour 'correctness' over historical usage is evident in 'The Defence of the Epilogue; or, An Essay on the Dramatic Poetry of the Last Age' (1672); John Dennis (with whom Theobald was now friendly—see *SR*, pp. 151, 181) seems to have been the first to state explicitly that 'Use . . . is the absolute Master of Languages', *Remarks upon Pope's Homer* (1717), *The Critical Works*, ed. E. N. Hooker (2 vols., Baltimore: Johns Hopkins Press, 1939–43), ii. 157; cf. Hooker's Introduction, vol. ii, p. cvi.

true *English*.'[14] Perhaps for Theobald the problem was not Shakespeare's grammar, but his sense of what his readers would accept from an editor. In any event, he was sufficiently like Pope to believe that a change from *we* to *us* (*Hamlet*, I. iv. 54) is trivial, and that here the interests of grammatical correctness could take precedence over historical accuracy.

In general, however, Theobald is concerned to represent accurately what he believed Shakespeare had written. The first 132 pages of *Shakespeare Restored* are devoted to *Hamlet*. At this time, Theobald possessed texts of this play in a second folio (1632), a quarto of 1637, a fourth folio (1685), a quarto of 1703, Rowe's first (1709) and third (1714) editions, John Hughes's *Hamlet* (1723), and Pope's edition (1725). R. B. McKerrow supposed that Theobald, influenced by the example of classical scholarship, collated these materials and respected their readings as if they were classical manuscripts.[15] This is a misunderstanding. Theobald does pay excessive attention (by twentieth-century standards) to his later sources, but it should be remembered that when writing *Shakespeare Restored* they were often all he had. He certainly was aware of the sequential dependence of the printed texts and that 'the more the Editions of any Book multiply, the more the Errors multiply too, and propagate out of their own Species'.[16]

Theobald continued, none the less, to pay attention to late printings. He did so for the same reasons that he consulted such Restoration adaptations of Shakespeare as Dryden's *Troilus and Cressida* (1679) and Thomas Shadwell's *Timon of Athens* (1678): he knew that there had been *some* attempts in the seventeenth century (especially with the second folio) to oversee the printing of the plays[17] and, given the almost complete ignorance in the early eighteenth century of Elizabethan and Jacobean English usage, he wished to take into account what the correctors of the press and the adapters had made of difficult passages. Of course, every modern editor, if he is to do more

[14] *SR*, pp. 40–1.

[15] McKerrow, p. 107. McKerrow's view is shared by S. K. Sen, *Capell and Malone, and Modern Critical Bibliography* (Calcutta: K. L. Mukhopadhyay, 1960), 7–8.

[16] *SR*, pp. ii–iii.

[17] Theobald frequently refers to the editors of the folios in his correspondence. See also Matthew W. Black and Matthias A. Shaaber, *Shakespeare's Seventeenth-Century Editors* (New York: Modern Language Association of America, 1937).

than reprint exactly the first edition of a work, assumes he can know better than the original compositor. As Helen Gardner observes, 'Most modern scholars would . . . entertain an emendation, proposed by a critic with bibliographical and textual expertise and familiarity with the wide range of printed discussion on particular cruces, with more respect than a compositor's untutored guess.'[18] Theobald's procedure was reasonable, since apart from their lucky guesses his predecessors seemed better placed historically to understand Shakespearian English. They too may be 'authoritative' in so far as they may have understood Shakespeare's meaning better, perhaps, than his first compositors. In fact, in his approach to emendation Theobald improved greatly on his predecessors, and brought to bear on each crux a range of considerations very similar to those of the New Bibliography.

An example of Theobald's use of later texts is found in his comment on *Hamlet* (I. ii. 132). In the seventeenth-century quartos, the folios, and Rowe's and Pope's editions, the reading is as Theobald gives it:

> *Or, that the Everlasting had not fixt*
> *His* CANNON *'gainst Self-slaughter.* —

There is a various Reading upon this Passage, as Mr. *POPE* might have observ'd, which, in my Opinion, merits a Consideration, and, possibly, may give us the Poet's own Words. If he wrote it as it now stands, his Thought is, *Or that the* Almighty *had not planted his* Artillery, *his* Resentment, *or* Arms of Vengeance *against* Self-murther: But the Quarto Edition, published in 1703. (which, indeed, has no other Authority, than its professing to be printed from the *Original Copy*;) and the Impression of *HAMLET* set out by Mr. *Hughs*, Both read,

> *Or that the Everlasting had not fixt*
> *His* CANON *'gainst Self-slaughter.*

i.e. That he had not restrain'd *Suicide* by his *express Law*, and *peremptory Prohibition*. It is a Word that *SHAKESPEARE* has used in some others of his Plays; and the Mistake of the Printers is so very easy, betwixt a double and a single *n*, in *Cannon* and *Canon*, that it has actually happen'd elsewhere in our Author upon both these very Words.

---

[18] Wilson, *New Bibliography*, ed. Helen Gardner, 98 n. 3*. Cf. John Dover Wilson (ed.), Textual Introduction, *The Tempest*, New Shakespeare (1921; repr. 1969), p. xxxii.

Theobald then discusses five other passages, carefully justifying his prolixity: 'I cannot help throwing in one Instance more, because the Error has not only obtained in the old and common Modern Editions, but has likewise got a new Sanction in Mr. *POPE*'s Edition.'[19]

If Theobald commands respect, it is not simply because he was, for his time, a remarkably conscientious collator of texts. He was in addition an extremely disciplined reader of Shakespeare. He consistently focuses his attention precisely on the meaning of his author, both in the progression of a speech and in the development of a scene. His collations and parallels are adduced as tests of his understanding of particular passages. Without established scholarly works to support him, he was forced to provide his own proofs of his proposed readings. Occasionally his citations appear unnecessarily repetitious, but he was breaking new ground, and his parallel readings had to provide the authority for his views that can now be provided by citing the *OED*. When he came to write his Preface to *Shakespeare*, he claimed to have read 'all the Plays of *B. Jonson*, *Beaumont* and *Fletcher*, and above 800 old *English* Plays, to ascertain the obsolete and uncommon Phrases'[20] in Shakespeare. This claim may be possible, if different editions of the same play were included in his reading.

Theobald's attention to meaning and his search for parallels extended beyond a concern for the meaning of individual words and historical usages to an awareness of Shakespeare's idiosyncratic habits of imagery and expression. He does, of course, use those dictionaries and lists of proverbs that were available to him. They allowed him, for example, to restore *scrimers* for *fencers* in *Hamlet* (IV. vii. 100),[21] but it is his attention to meaning and Shakespeare's patterns of imagery that produces the emendation of *bonds* to *bawds* (*Hamlet*, I. iii. 130):

OPHELIA having received the Addresses of *HAMLET*, *Polonius*, her Father, takes her to Task for Indiscretion in too lightly giving an Ear to the Prince's Protestations. He . . . cautions her to look upon

---

[19] *SR*, pp. 15–16. The modern reader may discern a play on words, but Theobald's acceptance of Hughes's emendation is rightly followed by modern editors.

[20] *1733*, vol. i, p. lxviii.

[21] *SR*, p. 118; he cites Stephen Skinner's *Etymologicon Linguæ Anglicanæ* (1671).

[Hamlet's vows] not as the real Sentiments of his Heart, but as Baits to betray her Virtue. Upon which he counsels her thus:

> --------*In few,* Ophelia,
> *Do not believe his vows; for they are brokers,*
> *Not of that die which their investments shew*
> *But meer implorers of unholy suits,*
> *Breathing like sanctified and pious* BONDS,
> *The better to beguile*------

. . . What Ideas can we form to our selves of a *breathing* BOND, or of its being *sanctified* and *pious*? Surely, so absurd a Thought could scarce come from *SHAKESPEARE*. The only tolerable Way of reconciling it to a Meaning without a Change, is to suppose that the Poet intends by the Word BONDS, *Verbal Obligations, Protestations*; and then, indeed, these Bonds may, in some Sense, be said to have *Breath*: But this is to make him guilty of overstraining the Word and Allusion; and it will hardly bear that Interpretation, at least, not without much Obscurity. As he, just before, is calling amorous Vows, *Brokers*, and *Implorers* of *unholy Suits*; I think, a Continuation of the plain and natural Sense directs us to an easy *Emendation*, which makes the whole Thought of a Piece, and gives it a Turn not unworthy of our Poet. I am, therefore, very willing to suspect it came from his Pen thus, tho' none of his *Editors* have ever been aware of it.

Theobald quotes the passage, substituting *bawds*, and continues: 'It is usual with our Poet, as his *Critical* Readers must have observed, to give those infamous Creatures the Style and Title of *Brokers*; of which it may not be amiss to subjoin a few Examples.' He provides parallels from *The Two Gentlemen of Verona* (I. ii. 41–5), *All's Well That Ends Well* (III. v. 70–2), and *King John* (II. i. 568–72) and points out that with the emendation 'a Chain of the same *Metaphors* is continued to the End'.[22]

Theobald's interest in 'a Chain of the same *Metaphors*' in his discussion of *bawds* and *brokers* in *Hamlet* and his citations of parallel imagery in other plays to support his reading anticipate Walter Whiter's suggestion in his *Attempt to Explain and Illustrate*

---

22 Ibid. 26–8. John Dover Wilson reads *bonds* in the New Shakespeare, but Theobald's emendation has been defended by Alice Walker, *Review of English Studies* (1951), 335 n. 2: 'Theobald's emendation to "bawds" is wanted; "pious bawds" is an oxymoron and the line repeats the idea of the previous line, turning it round the other way' (i.e. Theobald's 'Turn not unworthy of our Poet'). J. C. Maxwell accepts Theobald's reading in Appendix F to Wilson, *MS of 'Hamlet'*, ii. 428; Evans, *Riverside*, prints 'bonds'; Hibbard, Oxford Shakespeare, prints 'bawds,' as do *Complete Works* and Jenkins, Arden (1982).

Various Passages, on a New Principle of Criticism, Derived from Mr. Locke's Doctrine of the Association of Ideas (1794):

> If the discerning critic should discover that the train of thought, which had just occupied the attention of the writer, would naturally conduct him to the use of [a] controverted expression, we should certainly have little difficulty in admitting the reading to be genuine, even though it had before appeared to us under a questionable shape, from the singular mode in which it was applied.[23]

In *Hamlet* (III. iv. 92) Theobald again uses this technique to justify a restoration:

> *Nay, but to live*
> *In the rank sweat of an* INCESTUOUS *bed,*
> *Stew'd in corruption, honying and making love*
> *Over the nasty sty.*

He supposes that 'we have a *sophisticated* Reading palmed upon us, probably, from the Players first, who did not understand the Poet's *Epithet*' and restores 'ENSEAMED *Bed*' from the second folio (1632), observing that 'when we come to the *Etymology*, and *abstracted* Meaning of *enseam'd*, we shall have a Consonancy in the *Metaphors*, and a Reason for the Poet's calling the Bed a nasty *Sty*. In short, the Glossaries tell us, that **Seam** is properly the *Fat*, or *Grease*, of a *Hog*.' In a further note on *Seam* he carefully traces the Latin derivation of the word, using Isidore and Vossius, and says that although he recalls no other instance of Shakespeare's using the compound adjective of *seam*, the substantive form is found in *Troilus and Cressida*. He then reproduces and discusses the parallel passage in which Ulysses compares Achilles to a hog (II. iii. 184–9).[24]

Theobald's awareness of Shakespeare's imagery does not lead him to impose 'a Consonacy in the *Metaphors*' as a matter of course. Observing that the opening lines of Hamlet's soliloquy beginning 'To be, or not to be?' (III. i. 55–89) had been criticized 'for employing too great a Diversity of *Metaphors*, that have no Agreement with one another, nor any Propriety and Connexion in the Ideas', Theobald none the less rejects Pope's suggestion 'that instead of a *Sea* of Troubles, it might have been *—perhaps*, siege; *which continues the Metaphor of* slings, arrows,

---

[23] pp. 69–70.　　　[24] *SR*, pp. 104–5.

taking Arms; *and represents the being encompassed on all Sides with Troubles*'. Theobald notes that he had entertained this possibility, but that

> considering the great Liberties that this Poet is observed to take, elsewhere, in his *Diction*, and *Connexion* of *Metaphors*: And considering too, that a *Sea* (amongst the antient Writers, sacred and prophane, in the *Oriental*, as well as the *Greek* and *Latin*, Tongues;) is used to signify not only the great, collected, Body of Waters which make up the Ocean, but likewise a vast Quantity, or Multitude, of any thing else . . . So here, I conceive, *to take Arms against a Sea of Troubles*, is, *figuratively*, to bear up against the Troubles of human Life, which flow in upon us, and encompass us round, like a Sea.[25]

Theobald's discussions and defences of his proposed restorations and conjectural emendations show him to have had a taste in Shakespeare quite unlike that of Pope. His concern with the detail of Shakespeare's language is not only the result of greater scholarly care for the historical text of Shakespeare, but reflects an attitude to language that is decidedly 'modern' in its approaches and assumptions. He verges on a study of imagery for its own sake and reveals entirely novel critical preoccupations with verbal texture. In this last, he is much more advanced than Johnson. But these are not the limits of Theobald's modernity. He was also able to bring to bear on his proposed readings considerations which anticipate those of the New Bibliography. It was here that Pope, Warburton, and Johnson were least able to appreciate his methods. His approach to the text may be demonstrated in his most famous emendation, '—*for his Nose was as sharp as a Pen, and a*' babled *of green Fields*'. The emendation occurs in the Hostess's description of Falstaff's death in *Henry V* (II. iii. 16–17) and was first suggested by Theobald in his Appendix to *Shakespeare Restored*.

Fredson Bowers has written that a modern editor, in the light of recent bibliographical investigation, should concentrate

> on four main lines of endeavour: (1) to settle the nature of some few bad early texts and to establish their relation to the good line of transmission; (2) to determine the exact nature of the copy for every printed edition, especially in the cases where the entrance of new authority at a later date has complicated the problem of monogenous

---

[25] *SR*, pp. 82–3.

transmission; (3) to investigate the history of the transmission of the text in manuscript prior to the earliest printed edition deriving from a manuscript; and (4) to attempt to strip the veil of print from a text by analyzing the characteristics of identified compositors.[26]

Obviously a prime concern of the modern editor is to determine the nature of the manuscript copy from which a printed play was set. Theobald, of course, never had the slightest idea of identifying compositors, but as 'an under-strapper to the Play-house'[27] he was familiar with theatrical manuscripts and their evolution from foul papers to prompt-book. His own plays found their way into print by a process essentially unchanged from that which produced the Shakespearian quartos and first folio. As a literary antiquary, he was familiar with theatrical manuscripts dating back to the Restoration and, in all likeli-hood, much earlier;[28] as both an attorney and a literary anti-quary, he was familiar with secretary script.[29]

Although the 'bad' quartos of *Henry V*, printed in 1600, 1602, and 1619 (dated 1608) omit the passage in question, the first folio reads: 'and a Table of greene fields'. Pope's note in his edition reads:

> his nose was as sharp as a pen, and a table of green fields. *These words* and a table of green fields *are not to be found in the old editions of 1600 and 1608. This nonsense got into all the following editions by a pleasant mistake of the Stage-editors, who printed from the common piecemeal-written Parts in the Play-house. A Table was here directed to be brought in,* (it being a scene in a tavern where they drink at parting) *and this direction crept into the text from the margin.* Greenfield *was the name of the Property man in that time who furnish'd implements &c. for the actors.* A Table *of* Greenfield's.[30]

The impreciseness of Pope's thought about the printer's copy is manifest. First he asserts that the folio was set up from the parts

---

[26] Fredson Bowers, *On Editing Shakespeare and the Elizabethan Dramatists* (Philadelphia: University of Pennsylvania Library, 1955), 86–7.

[27] See above, pp. 19–20.

[28] E. K. Chambers, *William Shakespeare* (2 vols, Oxford: Clarendon Press, 1930), i. 542, in a discussion of *Double Falshood*, seems to doubt Theobald's possession of old manuscripts: 'There is no item which looks at all like them in his sale catalogue of 23 October 1744.' However, the title-page of the Catalogue refers to 'Several curious Manuscripts'. (These 'curious Manuscripts' would not, however, be those of *Double Falshood*. See Appendix C.)

[29] See Appendix A.

[30] *1725*, iii. 422.

distributed to the actors (*'the common piecemeal-written Parts'*), but then he maintains that the passage in question refers to a hypothetical property-manager, which implies that the compositor (or *'Stage-editors'*) worked from a prompt-book. Theobald's knowledge of stage-management (which Pope lacked), and his evident thought about the compositor's copy, led him to disagree with Pope. Although conscious of his superiority, Theobald is polite:

> I'll now proceed to consider a conjecture of the Editor's, which I am very free to own is *ingeniously* urg'd; But there is Something more than *Ingenuity* requir'd, to guess for the *Stage* rightly. His Conjecture is grounded upon a marginal Interpolation, that had crept into the Text of some later Editions, in Dame *Quickly*'s admirable Description of the Manner in which *Falstaffe* dy'd.

Theobald then quotes the folio reading[31] and Pope's note.

Theobald's references to 'ingenuity' should not be taken as simple exultation over Pope. Every modern editor would agree with him that what was needed 'to make these Conjectures pass current' was 'a *competent Knowledge* of the *Stage* and its *Customs*'. This Theobald proceeds to provide:

As to the History of *Greenfield* being then Property-Man, whether it was really so, or it be only a *gratis dictum*, is a Point which I shall not contend about. But allowing the marginal Direction, and supposing that a *Table* of *Greenfield*'s was wanting; I positively deny that it ever was customary (or, that there can be any Occasion for it) either in the *Promptor*'s Book, or piece-meal Parts, where any such Directions are marginally inserted for the *Properties*, or *Implements* wanted, to add the *Property-Man*'s Name whose Business it was to provide them. The Stage-Necessaries are always furnish'd between the *Property-Man* and the *Scene-Keeper*; and as the Direction is for the *Promptor*'s Use, and issued from him, there can be no Occasion, as I said, for inserting the Names either of the one, or the other.

Theobald draws further on 'that Acquaintance with Stage-Books, which it has been my Fortune to have' to provide 'a stronger Objection yet' to Pope's conjecture: 'the Directions for *Entrances*, and *Properties* wanting, are always to be mark'd in

---

[31] Theobald's vague reference to 'some later Editions' is explained by the fact, as he himself indicates elsewhere in *Shakespeare Restored*, that at this time he did not have access to a *first* folio.

the Book at about a Page in Quantity before the *Actors* quoted
are to enter, or the *Properties* be carried on. And therefore
GREENFIELD's *Table* can be of no Use to us for this Scene.'[32]
With tongue in cheek, Theobald then suggests how the words
might have functioned as a stage direction in the margin, but
insists 'they must be a Direction then for the *subsequent* Scene,
and not for the Scene *in Action*':

I suppose, with the Editor, that over-against the Words of the Text,
there might be this Marginal Quotation so close to them, that the
Ignorance of the Stage-Editors might easily give them Admittance
into the Text.

-----*his Nose was as sharp as a*   *Chairs*, and a Table off. Green
Pen.   Fields.

    The Scene in Action is part of Dame *Quickly*, the Hostess, her
House; and Chairs and Table were here necessary: The following
Scene carries us into the *French* Dominions. I therefore believe This was
intended as a Direction to the *Scene-Keepers*, to be ready to remove the
Chairs and *Table* so soon as the *Actors* went off; and to shift the Scene,
from the *Tavern*, to a Prospect of *green Fields*, representing Part of the
French Territories.[33]

Finally, drawing on his own sources and his knowledge of
secretary script and Elizabethan orthography, Theobald
provides the brilliant emendation of the passage which is found
in all modern editions:

But what if it should be thought proper to retract both Mr. POPE's
and my own Conjecture, and to allow that these Words, corrupt as
they now are, might have belong'd to the Poet's Text? I have an
Edition of *Shakespeare* by Me with some Marginal Conjectures of a
Gentleman sometime deceas'd, and he is of the Mind to correct this
Passage thus;

    for his Nose was as sharp as a Pen, and a' talked *of green Fields.*

It is certainly observable of People near Death, when they are
delirious by a Fever, that they talk of moving; as it is of Those in a
Calenture,[34] that they have their Heads run on green Fields. The
Variation from *Table* to *talked* is not of a very great Latitude; tho' we

---

[32] Cf. 'Book-Keeper's Directions', Greg, *First Folio*, p. 141 and n. 1.

[33] Here Theobald is mistakenly thinking in terms of the post-Restoration theatre.

[34] *OED*, '1. A disease incident to sailors within the tropics, characterized by deli-
rium in which the patient, it is said, fancies the sea to be green fields, and desires to
leap into it.'

may still come nearer to the Traces of the Letters, by restoring it thus;

-----*for his Nose was as sharp as a Pen, and* a' babled *of green Fields.*

To *bable*, or *babble*, is to mutter, or speak indiscriminately, like Children that cannot yet talk, or dying Persons when they are losing the Use of Speech.[35]

This discussion, of which Bentley in his prime might have been proud, exemplifies many of the virtues of Theobald: the masterly ability to weigh the evidence taking all possibilities into account; the ability to develop fully whatever hints he might find in the work of his predecessors (including possible counter-suggestions); the scrupulous acknowledgment of all sources of inspiration; and the careful attention to context (because Falstaff is described when dying, it is probable he might babble, rather than talk). But, above all, there is the effort to visualize as completely as possible the manuscript that was before the compositor when he set up his type. As is often the case with Theobald, his writing is full of implications. As a later editor has said of his own work, 'It will not always be possible, within the limits of his space, to give a complete account of the faith which is in him.'[36] Theobald's fear of charges of narrow pedantry generally makes him brief in his technical discussions, but it is evident here that he thought that in all probability the compositor read (or rather misread), not a marginal stage direction deriving from prompt-copy, but something deriving from the author's manuscript.[37] Having decided as far as possible the nature of the material misread, Theobald next proceeds to consider likely compositorial misreadings of secretary script. As will be seen, he frequently has occasion to refer to the 'Traces of the Letters'.

This conjecture, like many of Theobald's, has been accepted by modern editors[38] mainly because of its conformity with

[35] *SR*, pp. 137–8. A briefer version of the discussion appears in *1733*, iv. 30–1 n.

[36] John Dover Wilson (ed.), 'Textual Introduction', *The Tempest*, New Shakespeare (1921; repr. 1969), p. xxxv.

[37] For Theobald's discussion of the nature of the manuscripts behind individual plays, see below, ch. 8. Modern editors are inclined to believe that the folio text of *Henry V* was set up from Shakespeare's foul papers; see the New Shakespeare, ed. John Dover Wilson (1947; repr. 1968), pp. 111–13; the Arden, ed. J. H. Walter (repr. 1964), p. xl; Greg, *First Folio*, p. 287; the Oxford Shakespeare, ed. Gary Taylor (1982), pp. 18–22; *Textual Companion*, pp. 375–7.

[38] For attempts to support the folio reading, see T. H. Howard-Hill, *Shakespearian*

recent ideas about compositorial misreading of secretary script. Theobald's approach to the problem of emendation was far in advance of his time, and, indeed, his discoveries have been 'rediscovered' in the twentieth century. Thus A. W. Pollard writes:

Ninety-nine per cent. of the shots . . . of the Variorum editions are . . . off the target, and the way is prepared for a saner class of emendations, wholesomely limited by the condition that in an Elizabethan English hand they must look sufficiently like what appears in the printed texts for it to be conceivable that a scribe or printer should have mistaken the one for the other.

Pollard subsequently adds: 'It is all pioneer work and we ask for the indulgence which pioneers may fairly claim and which up to the present we gratefully acknowledge has been most generously extended to us.'[39] The reception of Theobald's discoveries in the eighteenth century was more mixed, especially after his death, and his methods were obscured. Warburton omitted the passage

Bibliography and Textual Criticism: A Bibliography (Oxford: Clarendon Press, 1971), items 937, 1310, 1321, 1323-6. E. G. Fogel provides a convenient summary of the chief arguments in favour of the folio reading, *Shakespeare Quarterly*, 9 (1958), 485-92. However, see also George Walton Williams, 'Textual Studies', *Shakespeare Survey*, 31 (1978), 195-6 nn., and Gary Taylor (ed.), Appendix B, *Henry V*, Oxford Shakespeare (1982), pp. 292-5. Theobald's emendation, in addition to being graphically plausible, has the following considerations to recommend it: (1) Falstaff's characteristic fluency is represented in appropriately pathetic terms, since he is dying; (2) the supposition that Falstaff was attempting to sing the 23rd Psalm (see John Dover Wilson's note on the passage in the New Shakespeare) is consistent with Falstaff's earlier, recurring allusions to repentance and psalm-singing in *1 Henry IV* (I. ii. 95; II. iv. 133; III. iii. 4–10; v. iv. 164–5) and in *2 Henry IV* (I. ii. 189–90; II. ii. 129; II. iv. 235) and with his deathbed repentance (it is appropriate that the Hostess should not recognize the 23rd Psalm, or any other—'Nay sure, he's not in hell; he's in *Arthur*'s [my italics] bosom, if ever man went to Arthur's bosom' (*Henry V*, II. iii. 9–10)); (3) the emendation does not force the Hostess to speak out of character; (4) the Hostess's '"How now, Sir John?" quoth I' (II. iii. 17–18) seems a response to something spoken—or babbled; (5) Falstaff's crying out 'God, God, God!' (II. iii. 19) in response to the Hostess's determined cheerfulness is an appropriate progression for one initially concerned with 'the valley of the shadow of death'; (6) 'babbling' is consistent with Falstaff's playing 'with flowers' and smiling upon 'his finger's end'; (7) the quarto's version of the Hostess's description, 'I saw him fumble with the sheetes, | And talk of floures', in its abbreviation and in its tendency to the prosaic in the use of 'talk', is consistent with what might be expected of a reported text of the fuller folio version *as emended by Theobald.*

[39] Introduction, *Shakespeare's Fight with the Pirates and the Problems of the Transmission of his Text*, 2nd edn., rev. (Cambridge: Cambridge University Press, 1920), pp. xxiv, xxviii. Pollard was over-sanguine in his claims. See below, n. 54.

containing Theobald's emendation and printed Pope's note,
which he considered 'reasonable'; according to Warburton,
Falstaff 'was now in no *babling* humour: and so far from
wanting cooling in *green fields*, that his feet were cold, and he
just expiring'.[40] Johnson accepts into his text Theobald's 'a'
babled of green fields', but, after printing Pope's and Warburton's notes on the passage, provides the following additional
comment:

> Upon this passage Mr. *Theobald* has a note that fills a page, which I
> omit in pity to my readers, since he only endeavours to prove, what I
> think every reader perceives to be true, that at this time no *table* could
> be wanted. Mr. *Pope*, in an appendix to his own edition in 12*mo* [2nd
> edn., 1728], seems to admit *Theobald*'s emendation, which we would
> have allowed to be uncommonly happy, had we not been prejudiced
> against it by a conjecture with which, as it excited merriment, we are
> loath to part.[41]

Johnson does not give his alternative emendation, but the
strange conclusion of his note seems to have been prompted by
the intrusion of some risible visual image arising from the rest
of the Hostess's account of Falstaff's death, operating in a
manner similar to those that mark his criticism of *Macbeth* in
Rambler No. 168. In any event, Johnson failed to recognize the
importance of Theobald's preoccupation with the manuscript
from which the folio version of *Henry V* was printed. Perhaps it is
Johnson's influence which leads W. W. Greg to underestimate
Theobald's understanding of the principles underlying his
emendation:

To-day all editions of Shakespeare read: 'for his nose was as sharp as
a pen, and a' babbled of green fields.' When we remember that
'babbled' would very likely be written 'babld', and that in the hands
of the time 'b' and 't', and final 'd' and 'e' are often difficult to distinguish, there need be no hesitation in accepting what many readers
feel to be a particularly Shakespearian turn of phrase. . . . Most
readers of *Henry V* feel instinctively the justness of Theobald's
emendation . . . the change from 'babld' to 'table' is perhaps more
obvious to us than it was to Theobald. . . . When we have satisfied

---

[40] *1747*, IV. 349 n.

[41] *1765*, iv. 396 n. [Yale, viii, 541]. The Yale edition makes Pope the cause of
Johnson's merriment by substituting 'Mr. Pope's first note' from edn. 1773 (? George
Steevens's alteration) for 'a conjecture' (*1765*).

ourselves that an emendation is acceptable, the next question we ought to ask is what it implies with respect to the history and origin of the text. We may find that it implies something that . . . conflicts with the implications of other emendations, or with evidence from some different source. Thus Theobald's emendation, though he may not have realized it, implies that the folio text of *Henry V* was set up from a manuscript written in the ordinary English hand of the period. In the circumstances this is, of course, what we should expect.[42]

It is, admittedly, difficult to be sure whether Theobald takes his readers' knowledge of secretary script for granted,[43] or whether he wishes merely to avoid labouring technicalities. But there can be no doubt of his own knowledge when he says in his edition that 'Every knowing Reader will agree' with a proposed emendation 'as far as the Traces of the Letters are concern'd; especially, in the old Secretary Handwriting, the universal Character in our Author's Time'.[44] Indeed, in his discussion of 'a' babled of green Fields' in *Shakespeare Restored*, Theobald refers not only to 'the Traces of the Letters' but reveals a concern with Elizabethan orthography: 'To *bable*, or *babble*, is to mutter.' The same approach is found elsewhere in *Shakespeare Restored*, when he promises to

Endeavour to restore Sense to Passages, in which, thro' the Corruption of successive Editions, no Sense has hitherto been found: Or to restore, to the best of my Power, the Poet's true Text, where I suspect it to be mistaken thro' the Error of the *Press* or the *Manuscripts*. The utmost Liberty that I shall take in this Attempt, shall generally confine it self to the minute Alteration of a *single* Letter or *two*.[45]

That his procedure implies an attempt 'to strip the veil of print from a text'[46] is frequently apparent. In proposing an

---

[42] 'Principles of Emendation in Shakespeare', Annual Shakespeare Lecture of the British Academy (1928), repr. in *Aspects of Shakespeare*, ed. J. W. Mackail (Oxford: Clarendon Press, 1933), 129, 130–1, 132, *passim*. Cf. Wilson, *New Bibliography*, p. 118; 'The effective use of *ductus literarum*, known to classical scholars for centuries, only became possible in Shakespeare after the recent study of Elizabethan palaeography. It is true that Theobald preferred "a' babbled" to "a' talked" as an emendation of the Folio's "a Table of greene fields" on the ground that it came nearer to "the traces of the Letters", but he applied the test very seldom, and he did not make it clear that the letters which he had in mind were those of the Elizabethan secretary hand.'

[43] See Appendix A.

[44] *1733*, v. 273 n.

[45] p. 165.

[46] See Bowers, op. cit., above p. 76.

emendation of *Julius Caesar* (II. ii. 46), when confronted with 'WE HEARD *two Lions litter'd in one .day*', he remarks: 'The Copies, indeed, are all corrupt; and the Passage, of Course, Nonsense and unintelligible, till we look nearer, and see thro' the Disguise of the bad Text.' He then suggests: 'WE WERE *two Lions litter'd in one Day*'.[47] A knowledge of Elizabethan manuscript conventions appears in his emendation of *1 Henry VI* (I. iii. 29), which in Pope's edition reads: 'How now, ambitious UMPIRE, what means This?' Theobald was 'persuaded the Duke's Christian Name lurks under this Corruption, and the very Traces of the Letters convince me that our Poet wrote, as it ought certainly to be restor'd . . . "*How now, ambitious* HUMPHREY*, what means This?*"'[48] For once, Theobald expands his reasoning in his edition: '"*How now, ambitious* umpire, *what means this?*"] This Reading has obtain'd in all the Editions since the 2d *Folio*. The first *Folio* has it, *Umpheir*. It is observable that, in both, the Word is distinguish'd in *Italicks*. . . . The Traces of the Letters, and the Word being printed originally in *Italicks*, convince me, that the Duke's Christian Name lurk'd under this Corruption.'[49] In the Prologue to *Troilus and Cressida* (1. 19) Pope had 'STIR *up the Sons of* Troy.' Theobald comments:

The second *Folio* Edition reads it thus;

STIRRE up the Sons of Troy.

This odd Manner of Spelling the Word both gave me a Suspicion of the Place being corrupt, and administer'd to my Conjecture for restoring it. The Author, I take it, means no more than This; that the *Greeks* have pitch'd their Tents upon the Plains before *Troy*; and that the *Trojans* are securely barricaded within the Walls of their City. I have no Doubt therefore but we ought to read;

SPERRE up the Sons of Troy.

For, to *sperre*, or *spar*, (from the old *Teutonick* Word, 𝔰𝔭𝔢𝔯𝔯𝔢𝔫,) signifies to *shut up, defend* by *Bars*, &c. And in this very Sense I remember CHAUCER uses the Term in the fifth Book of his *Troilus and Cressida*.[50]

[47] *SR*, p. 183; the generally accepted modern reading, *are*, does not seem preferable. See Sisson, ii. 186, and *Textual Companion*, p. 389.

[48] *SR*, p. 161.

[49] *1733*, iv. 122 n.; cf. Greg, *Editorial Problem*, p. 34: 'As a rule the text was written in an English "secretary" hand, proper names and directions in Italian script.'

[50] *SR*, p. 187.

Perhaps Theobald's happiest emendation occurs in *Romeo and Juliet* (I. i. 153), where again, as part of his justification, he takes into account the manuscript before the compositor. Pope's edition (following all the quartos and folios) reads:

> *As is the Bud bit with an envious Worm,*
> *E're he can spread his sweet Leaves to the Air,*
> *Or dedicate his Beauty to the* SAME.

Theobald observes:

Sure all the Lovers of *Shakespeare* and Poetry will agree with me that —*to the same*—is here a very idle, dragging *Parapleromatick*, as the Grammarians style it. I do not think the Author was any ways necessitated to it, since he might by an additional *Epithet* in the foregoing Verse have avoided the Fault objected, and express'd his Thought with more Elegance: As thus,

> *E're he can spread his sweet* and infant *Leaves,*
> *Or dedicate his Beauty to the* Air.

This would have been the Natural Way of conveying his Idea, without those unpleasing *Expletives*: but SHAKESPEARE generally in his *Similies* is accurate in the *Cloathing* of them; and therefore, I believe, would not have over-charg'd This so *insipidly*. When we come to consider that there is some Power else besides *balmy Air*, that brings forth, and makes the tender Buds spread Themselves, I do not think it improbable that the Poet wrote thus;

> *E're He can spread his sweet Leaves to the* Air,
> *Or dedicate his Beauty to the* SUN.*

Or Sunne, *according to the old Spelling, which brings it nearer to the Traces of the corrupted Text.*[51]

Theobald was an indifferent poet, but he had an extremely well-cultivated taste in Shakespeare. His sensitivity to Shakespeare's style was greatly increased by his habit of providing parallel readings. In addition he was concerned, as he said in the Preface to his edition, that his emendations should be 'establish'd with a very high Degree of moral Certainty'.[52] His use of the *ductus litterarum* was, however, only one of his tests; in *Shakespeare Restored* he speculates on one occasion that half a line in *Hamlet* (IV. i. 40) 'fell out in the *printing*, or was so blind in the *Copy* as not to be guess'd at, and therefore necessarily came

to be omitted'.[53] Degrees of 'blindness' in the copy are pre-
supposed in most of his emendations, and the *ductus litterarum*
could not always be of help when attempting to determine what
lay behind a compositor's guess—as opposed to his misreading. It was, of course, impossible to distinguish with certainty
when a compositor might have guessed his author's word and
when he might have misread it.[54]

Theobald's taste and his knowledge of Shakespeare's style
and usage ultimately determine his treatment of the text.
Parallel readings and the *ductus litterarum* are only potentially
helpful in providing him with 'moral Certainty' in his emendations. He seems to have recognized early that, in the absence of
good dictionaries and other philological studies, his greatest
liability to error came from unfamiliarity with Shakespeare's
more unusual words and phrases. For example, in the main
body of *Shakespeare Restored* he suggests the reading (*Hamlet*, IV.
vii. 138) '*A Sword* IMBAITED' for '*A sword* UNBATED',[55]
but in the Appendix he declares: 'I should reckon it very disingenuous, as well as ridiculous, in . . . the Restoration of
SHAKESPEARE, if I should be asham'd to own myself mistaken, and retract the Error. . . . Since my Beginning this
Appendix, I have chang'd my Opinion, and begin to think the
Text may rather be *explain'd*, than *disturb'd* or *alter'd*.' He then
suggests that Shakespeare 'may mean a Sword *unabated*, or not
robb'd of its Point'.[56] As his knowledge increased, he was glad
to be able to explain difficult passages, rather than alter them.
Of course, since his time the combined efforts of scholars have
made possible the discovery of satisfactory sense in many passages he believed to be corrupt. Theobald was the pioneer in all
this subsequent activity, and it cannot be surprising that he was
frequently mistaken. But it remains to his credit that he
initiated disciplined, close reading of Shakespeare's plays and
was the first to bring to bear on his texts a refined critical taste
tempered by wide-ranging scholarship.

Theobald had reason to be proud of his performance in

[53] *SR*, p. 107.
[54] Cf. Wilson, *New Bibliography*, p. 120: 'The vagaries of Elizabethan orthography
enlarge the boundaries of conjecture', etc.
[55] p. 119.
[56] pp. 191–2. Item 444 of Theobald's *Sale Catalogue* (1744) is the classic on rapier-
and-dagger play, *Vincentio Saviolo his Practise* (2 pts., 1595).

Shakespeare Restored. At the same time, he was aware of the novelty of his efforts and knew that he was running a risk, both with the public and with Pope. In self-defence he intimated his general indebtedness to Bentley's example in the classics:

> I ought to be in some Pain for the Figure that these Sheets may make, this being the *first Essay* of *literal Criticism* upon any Author in the ENGLISH Tongue. The Alteration of a *Letter*, when it restores Sense to a corrupted Passage, in a *learned Language*, is an Atchievement that brings Honour to the *Critick* who advances it: and Dr. BENTLEY will be remembered to Posterity for his Performances of this Sort, as long as the World shall have any Esteem for the Remains of *Menander* and *Philemon*.[57]

Theobald expected that his services to Shakespeare would not be appreciated in all quarters:

> I must expect some Attacks of Wit, upon being engag'd in an Undertaking of so much *Novelty*: The Assaults that are meerly *idle*, or meerly *splenatick*, I shall have the Resolution to despise: And, I hope, I need be under no great Concern for Those, which can proceed from a *generous Antagonist*. Wherever I am mistaken, it will be a Pleasure to me to be *corrected*, since the Publick will at the same Time be *undeceiv'd*: And wherever I have the Luck to be right in any Observation, I flatter my self, Mr. POPE himself will be pleas'd, that SHAKESPEARE receives some Benefit.[58]

Short of bungling *Shakespeare Restored*, there was little more that Theobald could have done to salve Pope's wounded pride as an editor.

[57] *SR*, p. 193. For a detailed account of Bentley's influence on Theobald, see Jones, pp. 31–99.

[58] *SR*, p. 194; cf. ibid. 133–4.

6. The Hero of The Dunciad

POPE'S first printed reaction to *Shakespeare Restored* occurs in lines that initially appeared in March 1728. Here are the essence of Pope's subsequent aspersions upon Theobald's abilities and the foundations of the later eighteenth-century misunderstanding of his work:

> Pains, Reading, Study, are their just Pretence,
> And all they want is Spirit, Taste, and Sense.
> *Commas* and *Points* they set exactly right;
> And 'twere a Sin to rob them of their *Mite*.
> In future Ages how their Fame will spread,
> For routing *Triplets*, and restoring *ed*.
> Yet ne'er one Sprig of Laurel grac'd those Ribbalds,
> From sanguine *Sew[ell]*[1] down to pidling *Tibbalds*:[2]
> Who thinks he *reads* when he but *scans* and *spells*,
> A Word-catcher, that lives on Syllables.[3]

In fact, Theobald had maintained that 'too nice a Regard must not be had to the Numbers of *SHAKESPEARE*',[4] but one of Pope's chief concerns as an editor of Shakespeare was adjustment of the metre of the plays. Thus the final couplet is actually self-descriptive. (The epithet 'pidling' that Pope applied to Theobald was also associated in Pope's mind with his own activity as a translator of Homer.) However, Pope's chief tactic was to emphasize Theobald's inferiority as a poet, and accordingly Pope teased him in *Peri Bathous*,[5] by including him in the ranks of the swallows and eels. Theobald replied with a letter to *Mist's Journal* (27 April 1728) in which he promised

---

[1] 'slashing *Bentley*' in the *Epistle to Arbuthnot*, l. 164.

[2] Theobald's name was properly pronounced trisyllabically (as the name is still pronounced in Sittingbourne). See J. R. Sutherland's note, *Dunciad*, i. 106.

[3] 'Fragment of a Satire', ll. 9–16; first published in *Miscellanies. The Last Volume* [Mar. 1728]; in *Minor Poems*, ed. Norman Ault and John Butt, Twickenham Edition, vi, 2nd edn., rev. (London: Methuen, 1964), 283 and n.

[4] *SR*, p. 2; cf. ibid. 20: 'Mr *POPE* . . . who in so many Passages has a particular Regard to the Numbers'.

[5] Published in *Miscellanies. The Last Volume* [Mar. 1728].

'above *five hundred* more fair *Emendations*' of Pope's forthcoming second edition of *Shakespear*. In May, Pope published the first edition of *The Dunciad*.

Pope also adopted the posture of one who has been thwarted in his attempts to serve the public. In an Appendix to his second edition of *Shakespear* (7 November 1728), in which he listed emendations by Theobald under the heading 'Various Readings or Conjectures,' he charged Theobald with withholding help, 'when we, by publick Advertisements, did request the assistance of all Lovers of this Author'.[6] Theobald replied in a letter to *The Daily Journal* (26 November 1728): 'I must own, I consider'd the Labour of Twelve Years Study upon this Author of too much Value, rashly to give either the Profit of it to a *Bookseller*, whom I had no Obligations to; or the Credit of it to an *Editor* so likely to be thankless.'[7] This remark suggests that Theobald may have contemplated assisting Pope in his edition, but had decided not to. However, Tonson had advertised on Pope's behalf for the loan of 'old editions', and at this time Theobald had yet to form his collection.[8] With publication of *The Dunciad Variorum* in April 1729, Pope renewed and elaborated his charge that Theobald withheld assistance:

During the space of two years, while Mr. *Pope* was preparing his Edition of *Shakespear*, and published Advertisements, requesting all lovers of the Author to contribute to a more perfect one; this Restorer (who had then some correspondence with him, and was solliciting favours by Letters) did wholly conceal his design, 'till after its publication. . . . Probably that proceeding elevated him to the Dignity he holds in this Poem.[9]

The point of Pope's charge is that Theobald was withholding

----

[6] Vol. viii, sig. Aa2^r.

[7] No. 2460. In 1722, Pope may have been instrumental in the suppression of Edmund Curll's proposed edition of 'The Works of the late Right Honourable John Sheffield Duke of Buckinghamshire, in Prose and Verse with his Life (compleated from a Plan drawn up by his Grace) by Mr. Theobald'. George Sherburn conjectures that Theobald may have resented Pope's possible role in this action, especially since in Jan. 1723 Pope, now the 'official' editor, published his own edition of the Duke's *Works*. This dispute was essentially between Pope and Curll, not Pope and Theobald, although the episode may also help to account 'for the fact that Theobald, who had been Pope's admirer, did not offer any aid on Pope's edition of Shakespeare' (Sherburn, pp. 222-3).

[8] See Appendix E.

[9] i. 106 n. See also J. R. Sutherland's commentary.

assistance from Pope's edition of *Shakespear* and planning *Shakespeare Restored*, when he was also soliciting favours. In a letter printed in *The Daily Journal* (17 April 1729) Theobald qualifies Pope's assertion: 'To say I concealed my Design, is a slight Mistake: for I had no such certain Design, till I saw how *incorrect* an Edition Mr. *Pope* had given the Publick.' Publication of the edition prompted Theobald to undertake his work, but he does say he had 'no such *certain* design' (my italics) until Pope's edition was published, which suggests that earlier he had considered writing on Shakespeare's text.

In his letter Theobald also indicates the extent of his demands on Pope: 'I think, I dare securely charge my Memory with all the *Favours* that ever I ventur'd to ask of Mr. *Pope*; and I challenge him to produce my Letters against me, if he thinks there is any Room for it.' Theobald had solicited Pope for two favours. The first was the usual request of a playwright for support on his benefit night, in this case 12 December 1719, for a performance of Theobald's adaptation of *Richard II*. Theobald asked 'that [Pope] would assist me in a few Tickets towards my Benefit. In about a Month after this Request, I received my Packet back, with this civil Excuse, that he had been all the while from Home, and had not my Parcel till it was too late to do any thing with it.' Initially Theobald must have accepted Pope's excuse completely, since it preceded publication of *The Grove* (1721) with its lavish praise of Pope's *Iliad*. Theobald's second request was understandably distasteful to Pope:

This, I confess, induced me, when I put out my Proposals for *Æschylus*, to sollicit Mr. *Pope* for this *Second Favour*, that he would please to recommend *that* my *Design*, if it did not interfere with his own Affair of the *Odyssey*.[10] To this Mr. *Pope* reply'd by Letter, 'that *he was glad I had undertaken this Work, and should be as glad to promote my Interest, notwithstanding his own Subscription to the* Odyssey: *That his own Awkwardness, and indeed Inability, of sollicting in any Kind, made him quite useless to his own Interest; but that he might not be intirely so to mine, he would ask those of his Friends for me, with whom he was familiar enough to ask any*

---

[10] Proposals for *The Odyssey* were published in *The Daily Courant* (25 Jan. 1725) but had been privately circulated earlier (Sherburn, p. 242). In Richard Savage's *A Collection of Pieces in Verse and Prose, Which have been publish'd on Occasion of the Dunciad* (1732), a letter attributed to Leonard Welsted dates Theobald's *Proposals* for *Aeschylus* Nov. 1723 (p. [40]).

thing.'—But, from that Day to the Publication of my *Shakespeare Restored*, (an interval of above Two Years) I never received one Line more from Mr *Pope*, no intimation of *one* Subscriber by his Interest, not even an Order that I should put his *own* Name down in my List. Upon this naked Fact, I submit the Censure both of my *Obligations* and *Ingratitude*.[11]

In his failure to assist Theobald with his subscription to Aeschylus, Pope wished to avoid drawing attention to the similarity of his and Theobald's endeavours as translators publishing by subscription. Pope's translation of *The Odyssey* in concealed collaboration with Fenton and Broome was already a cause of discomfort for him, and he had no desire to engage in any activity that might suggest that he and Theobald were on a comparable footing.

It is not known when Pope was 'So humble, he has knock'd at *Tibbald*'s door',[12] but the visit was surely before publication of the first edition of *The Dunciad* in 1728 and most likely before publication of *Shakespeare Restored* (1726). Pope might well have resented feeling that he was expected to engage in a quid pro quo for Theobald's public praise of his translation of Homer, and probably Pope's courtesy in making his visit was sufficiently delayed for Theobald himself to feel uncomfortable. If the meeting took place after publication of Pope's *Shakespear* (1725), when *Shakespeare Restored* was definitely planned or begun, it might well have been extremely awkward. At that stage, Theobald would have been aware of Pope's unwillingness to be of assistance in the matter of Aeschylus, and probably he would not have felt obliged to reveal his intentions. Publication of *Shakespeare Restored* after Pope's courtesy (however much delayed) would have increased Pope's resentment of Theobald's exposure of the shortcomings of his edition. Possibly Pope's partial recognition of these circumstances sharpened his attack in *The Dunciad*, and accounts for his charge that Theobald concealed his design. By the time he planned *Shakespeare Restored*, Theobald realized he had been snubbed by Pope, but there is no evidence to suggest that he was moved by personal animus

---

[11] No. 2582. Also repr. in Nichols, ii. 221–2, and [Matthew Concanen], *A Miscellany on Taste* (1732), 31–41.

[12] *Epistle to Dr Arbuthnot*, l. 372; for Warburton's letter (12 Jan. 1757) to Hurd (repr. in Nichols, ii. 741 n.) referring to Pope's visit, see Appendix D, below, n. 7.

to write. However, to the extent that he felt inferior to Pope as
a translator and poet, he must have been gratified by an awareness of his own superior understanding of Shakespeare's
text—although this satisfaction would have been undercut by
the knowledge that Pope had been chosen to edit Shakespeare.
Perhaps Pope's description of Theobald in *The Dunciad*
captures ambivalent feelings that surfaced in the course of their
meeting:

> Great Tibbald sate: The Proud Parnassian sneer,
> The conscious simper, and the jealous leer,
> Mix on his look.   (ii. 5–7)

It must have been evident to Pope that Theobald had made
Shakespeare's works his study and delight, reading them by
day and meditating by night. It must also have been evident to
him that Theobald had ambitions of being a professional editor
of Shakespeare. Why, then, did Pope not take refuge gracefully
in his amateurism? Certainly *The Dunciad* and the other pieces
by Pope associated with it are out of all proportion to *Shakespeare
Restored*, even taking into account Theobald's query whether
Pope, as editor, had read his proofs.[13] Theobald, of course,
was not the cause of *The Dunciad*, but merely a catalyst in its
production. He was, however, an important catalyst, and it is
worth considering his role in Pope's thought and feeling.

The chief cause of Pope's resentment may have been a belief
that 'pidling' Theobald was using him as a means of raising
himself from relative obscurity: after courting his friendship,
Theobald changed tactics and counted on Pope's fame to draw
attention to *Shakespeare Restored* and to himself. If this was
perceived as Theobald's meditated stratagem, *The Dunciad* may
have been designed both to fulfil and to exceed his expectations.
In a letter to Swift (14 December 1725) on the subject of slan-
derous scribblers Pope observed: 'It would vexe one more to be
knockt o' the Head by a Pisspot, than by a Thunderbolt. . . .
But to be Squirted to death . . . by the under Strappers of
Under Secretaries . . . this would provoke as dull a dog as
Ph[ilip]s himself.'[14] The publication in early April 1726 of

---

[13] *SR*, pp. 75, 97.

[14] *Correspondence*, ii. 350. Pope's imagery (cf. Dennis's description of Theobald,
above, p. 20) suggests that by this time he had received intimations that Theobald was
at work on Shakespeare.

Shakespeare Restored, if not a bolt from the blue, was certainly vexing. To have survived the perils of translating *The Iliad* with his reputation enhanced only to be exposed as an editor of Shakespeare must have seemed to Pope a ludicrous irony. His sense of the absurdity of this reversal could only have been intensified by his remembrance of the acuteness of his suffering as a translator.

Pope's position in relation to *Shakespeare Restored* (as he may have sensed, thanks to Theobald's concluding reference to Bentley) was not unlike that of the party of Temple and Boyle in relation to Bentley's first *Dissertation on Phalaris.* Given the nature of their activities, the antagonists were interested (if only for a time) in essentially the same things. One of the responses of Boyle and his friends to Bentley was to adopt a posture of scorn towards the matters which so recently had engrossed their attention. Their supposed concern with higher things is well represented by their sympathizer, Shaftesbury.[15] The coming together of these complexities of attitude, whereby a man may ridicule another for having concerns related to his own interests, is nicely illustrated by lines in *The Dunciad,* where Pope enjoys his own punning wit while ridiculing Theobald for rescuing puns and resolving cruces in Shakespeare:

> Here studious I unlucky moderns save,
> Nor sleeps one error in its father's grave,
> Old puns restore, lost blunders nicely seek,
> And crucify poor Shakespear once a week.   (i. 161–4)

Both men violated their formal positions in their different concerns with puns. Pope would not have wished his own pun to pass unnoticed, while Theobald shared Pope's condemnation of punning humour, when he said of Hamlet's pun on 'country matters' (III. ii. 116) that 'if ever the Poet deserved Whipping for low and indecent Ribaldry, it was for this Passage', and apologized for his scholarly duty when drawing attention to

---

[15] It was Shaftesbury who also gave ridicule quasi-respectability as a test of truth. For this controversy, see Shaftesbury, 'A Letter concerning Enthusiasm', *Characteristicks*, 5th edn. (3 vols., 1732), i. 10–14; *'Sensus Communis*: An Essay on the Freedom of Wit and Humour', ibid. i. 59 ff.; 'Advice to an Author', ibid. i. 259–60; Anthony Collins, *A Discourse concerning Ridicule and Irony* (1729); John Brown, *Essays on the Characteristicks* (1751); Johnson, 'Life of Akenside', *Lives of the English Poets*, ed. G. B. Hill (3 vols., Oxford: Clarendon Press, 1905) iii. 413.

what he felt were Shakespeare's misdemeanours.[16] Ridicule often presupposes some sharing of values, and, on the other side, Pope was not indifferent to Theobald's criticism of his editing. Probably each man saw his own failed aspirations in the other's success.

Pope certainly cared more about his performance as an editor than Boyle did about his role in the Phalaris controversy. As an aristocrat, Boyle had no difficulty asserting that he had better things to do than to worry himself with either Phalaris or Bentley, and he wished '*to avoid being thought to have thrown away any considerable part of my life upon so trifling a subject: which, as idle a man as I am, is an Imputation I would not willingly lye under*'.[17] Indeed, it was left to Atterbury to write most of the examination of Bentley's first dissertation. Pope, on the other hand, had devoted too much of his life to pursuits related to scholarship to take such an easy view. Although he found aristocratic loftiness attractive, he could not adopt Boyle's pose completely. His experience was too close to that of Theobald, and he could not afford simply to dismiss Shakespeare, as Boyle had Phalaris, even if his critical doubts about his author were intensified by resentment of Theobald's review of the edition.

The Dunciad of 1729 was Pope's means of redress for the years of suffering, beginning with his commentary on *The Iliad*, that the tribulations of scholarship had caused him. His solution was brilliant. His trials when supplying Homer with notes and commentary had been acute, in part because of the insecurity and fear he had had to endure arising from his difficulties with Greek. Having turned his attention to what he may well have expected to be the easier problem of Shakespeare, his inadequacies were unexpectedly exposed; but as author and commentator of his own poem, nobody could fault his scholarly abilities. The experience of translating Homer and of providing a commentary had a more direct impact on *The Dunciad* and, in particular, on Pope's portrait of Theobald than has hitherto been recognized. That his suffering in the early part of his translation was great and that he felt its effects for the rest of his life are known from his conversations with Joseph Spence:

[16] *SR*, pp. 87, 135–6.
[17] Preface, *Dr Bentley's Dissertations . . . Examin'd*, 2nd edn. (1698), sig. A3[r].

The *Iliad* took me up six years, and during that time, and particularly the first part of it, I was often under great pain and apprehensions. Though I conquered the thoughts of it in the day, they would frighten me in the night. I dreamed often of being engaged in a long journey and that I should never get to the end of it. This made so strong an impression upon me that I sometimes dream of it still: of being engaged in that translation and got about half way through it, and being embarrassed and under dreads of never completing it.

This account was related to Spence in March 1743; in August 1739 he had said: 'In the beginning of my translating the *Iliad* I wished anybody would hang me, a hundred times. It sat so heavily on my mind at first that I often used to dream of it, and so do sometimes still.'[18] Surely, the agony responsible for these recurring nightmares produced those gloriously comic lines in *The Dunciad* describing—Theobald:

> Studious he sate, with all his books around,
> Sinking from thought to thought, a vast profound!
> Plung'd for his sense, but found no bottom there;
> Then writ, and flounder'd on, in mere despair.
>
> (i. 111–14)

The translation of *The Iliad* itself was not Pope's greatest problem—'When I fell into the method of translating thirty or forty verses before I got up, and *piddled* with it the rest of the morning, it went on easily enough, and when I was thoroughly got into the way of it, I did the rest with pleasure.'[19] Far worse was the trouble he experienced with his commentary. Hence his cry to Thomas Parnell:

The minute I lost you Eustathius with nine hundred pages, and nine thousand Contractions of the Greek Character Arose to my View—Spondanus with all his Auxiliaries in Number a thousand pages (Value three Shillings) & Dacier's three Volumes, Barnes's two, Valterie's three, Cuperus half in Greek, Leo Allatius three parts in Greek, Scaliger, Macrobius, & (worse than 'em all) Aulus Gellius: All these Rushd upon my Soul at once & whelm'd me under a Fitt of the Head Ach, I curs'd them all Religiously, Damn'd my best friends among the rest, & even blasphem'd Homer himself. Dear Sir not only as you are a friend & as you are a Goodnatur'd Man, but as you are a Christian & a Divine come back Speedily & prevent the

---

[18] Spence, Nos. 193, 197.   [19] Ibid., No. 198 (Aug. 1739). My italics.

Encrease of my Sins: For at the Rate I have begun to Rave, I shall not only Damn all the Poets & Commentators who have gone before me, but be damned my Self by all who come after me—[20]

In addition to the general similarity of circumstance common to Pope's self-description in his letter and his description of Theobald in *The Dunciad*, the joke about the monetary value of scholarly books is given a further turn, and, through an allusion to *Paradise Lost*, the theme of damnation is also maintained:

> He roll'd his eyes that witness'd huge dismay,[21]
> Where yet unpawn'd, much learned lumber lay,
> Volumes, whose size the space exactly fill'd;
> Or which fond authors were so good to gild. . . .
>
>   (i. 115–18)

In a note to l. 115 Pope suggests: 'The progress of a bad Poet in his thoughts being (like the progress of the Devil in *Milton*) thro' a Chaos, might probably suggest this imitation.' However, the endless journeys of his nightmares, as related to Spence, provide a telling gloss on his note. Pope's own experience is ultimately responsible for the comic greatness of the lines describing Theobald. Pope continues his letter to Parnell: 'To be Serious you have not only left me to the last degree Impatient for your Return'—but, even as he intensifies his ironic mode, when making his appeal for further assistance, the underlying concern of his jesting is apparent—'You are a Generous Author, I a Hackney Scribler, You are a Grecian & bred at a University, I a poor Englishman of my own Educating.'[22]

It is likely that Pope's lack of a formal education often caused him to take refuge behind a mask of deliberately ambiguous irony when he was confronted with the forms of scholarship. The obvious joke of *The Dunciad* of 1729 was that the apparatus of scholarship was turned against the scholar who had successfully exposed Pope's scholarly shortcomings: the whole paraphernalia of the *apparatus criticus* was completely perverted to Pope's personal ends. But it is also possible that he took pride in the scholarly appearance of *The Dunciad*, as if it indeed embodied

[20] *Correspondence*, i. 225 (25 May or 1 June 1714).

[21] Cf. *Paradise Lost*, i. 56–7: 'round he throws his baleful eyes | That witness'd huge affliction and dismay.'

[22] *Correspondence*, i. 225, 226.

serious scholarship.[23] Bentley's edition of *Paradise Lost* appeared in 1732, and Theobald's *Shakespeare* in January 1734. When Pope heard of the official proposals for the latter work, he was very distressed, and after various manœuvres, including pro- posals for commentaries on popular English poets, he wrote to Jacob Tonson sen.:

> I think I should congratulate your Cosen [*i.e. nephew*] on the new Trade he is commencing, of publishing English classicks with huge Commentaries. Tibbalds will be the Follower of Bentley, & Bentley of Scriblerus. What a Glory will it be to the Dunciad, that it was the First Modern Work publish'd in this manner? In truth I think myself happier in my Commentator than either Milton or Shakespear; & shall be very well content if the same hands proceed to any other mans work, but my owne, and in this I depend upon your Friendship, & your Interest with your Cosen, that you will not let the Tibbalds ever publish notes upon such things of mine, as are your Property yet, or shall be hereafter—*Oh shade those Laurels which descend to you!*[24]

At the obvious level, Pope is merely being ironic, but there is no reason to believe that he intended any irony when he con- tinued the process of annotation of his works and finally be- queathed the task to Warburton.

Pope's awareness of the informality of his education probably encouraged him to emphasize, after the manner of Shaftesbury, the importance of inherent taste, as he publicly adopted a pose of condescension to scholars and scholarship. When he allowed Theobald 'Pains, Reading, Study', but denied him 'Spirit, Taste, and Sense', he was concerned with the rivalry between them as poets and translators; this explains the otherwise ir- relevant 'Yet ne'er one Sprig of Laurel grac'd those Ribbalds | From sanguine *Sew[ell]* down to pidling *Tibbalds*'. He was also probably intent on suggesting a general superiority of poets to scholars. In a note to *The Dunciad* he assumes, however, that

[23] For accounts of the seriousness with which Pope took his self-annotation, see John Butt, 'Pope's Poetical Manuscripts', *Proceedings of the British Academy*, 40 (1954), repr. in *Essential Articles for the Study of Alexander Pope*, ed. Maynard Mack (London: Frank Cass, 1964), 507–9, and William Kinsley, 'The *Dunciad* as Mock-Book', *Huntington Library Quarterly*, 35 (1971), repr. in Maynard Mack and James A. Winn (eds.), *Pope: Recent Essays by Several Hands* (Hamden, Conn.: Archon Books, 1980), 717.

[24] *Correspondence*, iii. 243–4 (14 Nov. 1731); the quotation is from Dryden's 'To my Dear Friend Mr. Congreve', l. 75.

pure good taste is the sole basis of verbal criticism as a scholarly textual criticism:

> TWO things there are, upon which the very Basis of all verbal Criticism is founded and supported: The first, that the Author could never fail to use the very best word, on every occasion: The second, that the Critick cannot chuse but know, which it is. This being granted, whenever any doth not fully content us, we take upon us to conclude, first that the author could never have us'd it, And secondly, that he must have used That very one which we conjecture in its stead.[25]

The note is satirical, but it is clear that Pope could not provide any alternative mode of proceeding. Theobald, it will be remembered, had referred to *Shakespeare Restored* as the '*first Essay* of *literal Criticism* upon any Author in the ENGLISH Tongue', because he recognized the importance of the *ductus litterarum* as a potential guide to taste. Probably his point was missed. It is not known whether Pope read through *Shakespeare Restored* marking *rectè, benè, pulchrè* in the margin as he did with Bentley's *Paradise Lost*, but the second edition of his *Shakespear* (1728) incorporated some 106 alterations based on Theobald's work.[26]

That there were alternatives to unsupported taste as a guide to emendation was made evident in a letter from Theobald to his friend, Matthew Concanen, published in *Mist's Journal* (16 March 1728). The letter entreats Concanen 'that no partiality in opinion, to my attempts upon this beloved Author, may over-sway you to be convinced, contrary to your own private judgment'. He then proceeds to a consideration of four suspect passages in Pope's edition, of which the first and the last are especially worth noting:

> Your first question is upon the following passage of Coriolanus [I. iv. 56–60].

[25] ii. 1 n.

[26] In his Appendix to his second edition of Shakespeare (1728), entitled 'Various Readings or Conjectures on Passages in Shakespear', Pope does print 'rectè' by a couple of Theobald's proposed readings (vol. viii, sig. Aa3^r–Aa3^v). He was prepared to acknowledge changes deriving from *SR* in his second edition 'amounting to about twenty five *words*' (sig. Aa2^r). Theobald suggested (*The Daily Journal*, 2460 (26 Nov. 1728)) that alterations including '*material Pointings*' came to '*about* an *Hundred*'. He slightly under-estimated the number.

> Thou wast a Soldier
> Even to *Calvus'* wish, not fierce and terrible
> Only in *strokes*, but with thy *grim looks*, and
> The thunder-like percussion of thy *sounds*,
> Thou mad'st thine enemies shake.

Observing that 'Greek and Roman History will be at a loss to account for such a man' as *Calvus* and that 'many of the principal speeches [in the play are] copied from the Life of Coriolanus in Plutarch', Theobald substitutes '*Cato's* wish' because 'Plutarch, in his Life of Coriolanus, speaking of this Hero, says, "He was a man (that which Cato required in a Warrior) not only dreadful to meet with in the field, by reason of his hand and stroke; but insupportable to an enemy for the very tone and accent of his voice, and the sole terror of his aspect."' As he says, 'The error probably arose from the similitude in the manuscript of *to* to *lv*; and so this unknown wight Calvus sprung up.'[27] Theobald's discussion of this crux, in addition to drawing on his knowledge of secretary script when applying the *ductus litterarum*, is interesting as an example of his use of multiple proofs for the support of an emendation, and as an example of his attention to Shakespeare's classical sources.

If Theobald's attention to Shakespeare's classical sources has important textual results, the same is true of his attention to what Pope called 'The Classicks of an Age that heard of none' (*Dunciad*, i. 128). His discussion of the last crux in his letter to Concanen is significant on two counts: first, there is the recognition of the importance of Shakespeare's reading in *English* texts; second, Theobald is concerned to explain a passage in the light of his knowledge, rather than to emend it:

I come now, to your last question, upon a passage in Troilus and Cressida [V. v. 14–15], which requires an explication, no correction.

> The dreadful Sagittary
> Appals our Numbers.

Mr. Pope, as you observe, thinks, by *Sagittary*, that our Poet means *Teucer*; who, indeed, was famous for his bow. But, when Teucer is not once mentioned by name throughout the whole Play, would Shakespeare decypher him by so dark and precarious a description? I dare

---

[27] Nichols, ii. 199–201. Nichols misdates the letter 1729. See Sisson, ii. 123: 'Theobald's emendation . . . is certain, and plausible graphically.'

be positive, he had no thought of that Archer here. This passage contains a piece of private history, which, perhaps, Mr. Pope never met with, unless he consulted the old Chronicle, containing the Three Destructions of Troy, printed by Caxton in 1471, and Wynken de Werde in 1503; from which Book, as I shall hereafter shew, our Poet obtained this circumstance.

'Beyonde the royalme of Amazonue came an auncient kynge, wysse and disscreete, named Epystrophus, and brought a M. knyghtes, and a mervayllouse beste that was called *Sagittarye*, that behynde the myddes was an horse, and to fore, a man; this beste was heery like an horse, and had his eyen rede as a cole, and shotte [right] well with a bowe: *this beste made the Grekes sore afrede, and slew many of them with his bowe.*' [28]

Pope was particularly irritated by Theobald's exposure of his false surmise; however, his appeal to classic taste and his ridicule of Theobald's antiquarianism, because 'he laboured to prove *Shakespear* . . . conversant in such authors as *Caxton* and *Wynkin*, rather than in *Homer*', now seem merely the consequence of another variety of literary parochialism. [29] Theobald's concern in his explication of Shakespeare with 'all such reading as was never read' (*Dunciad*, i. 166) marks the beginning of modern scholarship devoted to Renaissance English literature.

Theobald's initial response to the first edition of *The Dunciad* (May 1728) appeared in a letter to *Mist's Journal* in late June of that year, and it is evident from his confident, cheerful tone that he was receiving substantial support from his friends and from the public. After rejecting Pope's charge that he was '*cackling to the Tories*', [30] he comments on *The Dunciad* as a whole: 'The Extravagance of *wanton* Wit, perhaps, may transport People to an *involuntary* Neglect of Truth: and let *Inspiration* answer for it. I speak this merely from Conjecture; for I have no Fear of ever being so *unhappily* actuated.' Throughout his letter Theobald maintains an air of genial indifference to Pope's lampoon:

---

[28] Nichols, ii. 203–4. Lot 465 of *A Sale Catalogue of the Library of Lewis Theobald, Deceas'd* [1744] is 'The Siege of Troy, printed by Wynken de Werde, *a very fair copy* (1503)'.

[29] *Dunciad*, i. 162–3 n. See Sutherland's note, *Dunciad*, i. 129.

[30] *Dunciad* (1728), i. 182; *Dunciad Variorum* (1729), i. 192.

In short, I believe, I may speak it in the Name of a Number, if Mr. *Pope* will please to tye up his Satyre from *moral* Character, and such *Flirts* as may affect us as *meer* Inhabitants of the *lower* Earth; we'll give him Leave to divert Himself with our *poetical* Reputations, and Claims to *Parnassus*: And if the Publick will be so partial to him, to take every Thing implicitly upon his *Ipse dixit*; we must submit to be registred *Dunces*, and *Scoundrels*, and Sons of *Dullness*, and to divide the genuine Inheritance of *Grubstreet* amongst Us.

After these offhand comments he arrives at what is the real point of his letter, the formal announcement of 'Proposals for Printing, by Subscription, Notes and Remarks, critical and explanatory, on all the Comedies, Histories, and Tragedies of *Shakespeare*' in three volumes.[31]

If Pope had hoped to crush Theobald, *The Dunciad* was not a success. When *The Dunciad Variorum* was published in April 1729, Theobald again replied in a tone of genial indifference: ''Tis certain, I ought to be very well satisfied with my Share of *Honours* in his Kingdom of *Dullness*, since the Preamble to my Patent is, that *He could not find One more fit to wear them.*' He declares that he 'would not willingly act like the Favourite, whom *Shakespeare* somewhere describes, who being made Proud by his Prince, advanc'd his Pride against the Power that bred it [*Much Ado about Nothing* (!), III. i. 9–11]'. Instead, he would rather assert 'the Legality of my Master's Title to those Dominions, in which he exercises so free a Sway, and from whence he so unsparingly dispenses his *Promotions*'.[32] There follow eight corrections of Pope's second edition of *Shakespear* (1728), by way of proving the legality of Pope's prerogatives. The outcome of these skirmishes was that Theobald was subsequently encouraged by friends and patrons to abandon his proposed three volumes of commentary in the manner of *Shakespeare Restored* and, after protracted negotiations with Jacob

---

[31] *Mist's Journal* (22 June 1728). See also the Preface to *Double Falshood*, 2nd edn. (1728), sig. A5ᵛ: 'I am honour'd with so many powerful Sollicitations, pressing Me to the Prosecution of an Attempt, which I have begun with some little Success, of *restoring* SHAKESPEARE from the numerous Corruptions of his Text: that I can neither in Gratitude, nor good Manners, longer resist them. I therefore think it not amiss here to promise, that, tho' *private Property* should so far stand in my Way, as to prevent me from putting out an *Edition* of *Shakespeare*, yet, some Way or other, if I live, the Publick shall receive from my Hand his *whole* WORKS corrected, with my best Care and Ability.'

[32] *The Daily Journal*, 2582 (17 Apr. 1729), repr. in Nichols, ii. 214–15.

Tonson, the owner of the copyright, to provide a new edition of Shakespeare. That he must have had powerful support is evident, when it is remembered that Tonson effectively prevented Johnson from editing Shakespeare in 1745. Indeed, the choice of Theobald as the hero of *The Dunciad* proved to be an embarrassment, and Pope had good reason to depose him in favour of Colley Cibber in the revised *Dunciad* of 1743. But although Theobald surmounted Pope's ridicule, he was now facing in the person of William Warburton an even greater threat to his reputation.

7. Theobald's Correspondence with Warburton

Early in life, Bishop then Mr. Warburton was introduced to the celebrated Critic Dr. Bentley, the Master of Trinity College. When he had left the room a friend asked Dr. Bentley, What he thought of Mr. Warburton? 'He appears to me,' replied the Master, 'to have a great appetite for learning, but no digestion.'[1]

THE Shakespearian correspondence of Theobald and William Warburton has survived only in part.[2] Nichol Smith rightly says that 'we cannot, in estimating [Theobald's] capacity, ignore the evidence of his correspondence with Warburton'. Observing that by far the greater part of the correspondence, as it has survived, consists of Theobald's letters to Warburton, he maintains: 'it would have been more fortunate for Theobald's reputation had they perished.' Nichol Smith concludes:

A considerable share of the merit of Theobald's edition—though the share is mostly negative—belongs to Warburton, for Theobald had not taste enough to keep him right when he stepped beyond collation of the older editions or explanation by parallel passages. Indeed, the letters to Warburton, besides helping to explain his reputation in the

---

[1] William Seward, *European Magazine*, 21 (1792), 260. Cf. James Henry Monk, *The Life of Richard Bentley*, 2nd edn., enlarged (2 vols., 1833), ii. 410.

[2] Theobald received most of his letters back from Warburton when he was preparing his *Shakespeare* for the press (publication was in Jan. 1734); Warburton's letters were returned after the two men quarrelled, around 4 May 1736. Warburton presumably destroyed his letters; 65 of Theobald's letters to Warburton were preserved by Theobald's son and were presented to a Mr Edward Roberts of Ealing in gratitude for favours received. Roberts made the collection available to John Nichols, who printed Theobald's letters (with 5 from Warburton to Theobald that Theobald had overlooked) in the 2nd volume of *Illustrations of the Literary History of the Eighteenth Century* (1817) (see p. [189] n. *). The originals, bound in 2 volumes, are now in the Folger Library (MSS W.6.74, W.6.75). Forty additional letters from Theobald, which Warburton had neglected to return, were discovered by R. F. Jones in the British Library (Egerton MS 1956) and were printed by him in an Appendix to *Lewis Theobald: His Contribution to English Scholarship*.

eighteenth century, would in themselves be sufficient to justify his place in the *Dunciad*.[3]

These judgements, which have been quoted approvingly by A. W. Evans in his *Warburton and the Warburtonians*,[4] seem the result of compounded misunderstandings. And, notwithstanding Nichol Smith and Evans, it is apparent that Warburton lost his reputation as a Shakespearian when he ventured to publish an edition independently of Theobald. Actually, the evidence indicates that the success enjoyed by Warburton as a textual critic was due to Theobald.

In the Preface to his *Shakespear* (1747), Warburton suggested it was his 'ill Fortune to have some accidental Connexions' with Theobald.[5] The connections were, however, of Warburton's own making, and began a few months after publication of *Shakespeare Restored* (1726). Apparently Warburton met the members of the Concanen Club for the first time in December 1726. Warburton was almost ten years younger than Theobald and without claims to fame.[6] He was visiting London, probably in order to make arrangements for his ordination as an Anglican priest. Previously he had been an attorney's clerk, a schoolmaster, and a deacon in Newark, Nottinghamshire. There, about 1718, he had met Dr William Stukeley, the antiquary, who was probably his oldest friend. In later years, after Warburton had quarrelled with Theobald, had contracted his friendship with Pope, had married Ralph Allen's niece, and had thereby 'effectually made his fortune', Stukeley recorded the consequences of Warburton's progress:

alas, I soon found, a change of fortune had chang'd his manners. a hundred [let]ters I have rec[eive]d from him with infinite address & love, & friendship. but all now chang'd to bare civility. his natural conceit of his own sup[er]iority is so great, y^t in his indigent estate, when I first knew him, he w^d bear no equal. but *now* fortune has

---

[3] Smith, Introduction, pp. xxx, xlv–xlvi.

[4] (Oxford: Clarendon Press, 1932), 143–4. See also Maynard Mack, *Alexander Pope: A Life* (New York: Norton, 1985), 888 n.

[5] Vol. i, p. x.

[6] Prior to meeting Theobald he had published *Miscellaneous Translations in Prose and Verse from Roman Poets, Orators, and Historians* (1724). According to Samuel Parr, *Bibliotheca Parriana* (1827), 227, 'This was Warburton's first publication. It is very scarce, having been bought up by his order, as often as it appeared for sale.' There were errors in the Latin dedication (see Evans, op. cit., p. 13).

advanc'd it to an imp[er]ial pitch: & he looks down upon the whole world.

Stukeley observed that Warburton is 'fickle in his friendships; haughty in his carriage: excessively greedy of flattery'. Most pronounced was Warburton's ambition: 'I have heard him say, he w[oul]d give his eyes to be a Milton. & his love for fame and reputation prevails above all his passions. 'tis the incentive of his unwearied endeavours.'[7] Stukeley's portrait is the product of hurt feelings, but it is consistent with Warburton's relations with Theobald.

Warburton's first steps towards fame and reputation began with his assiduous cultivation of Theobald, initially by taking advantage of Theobald's friendship with Matthew Concanen, founder of the Concanen Club and subsequently Attorney-General of Jamaica. In a letter to Concanen of 2 January 1727, Warburton gives his 'thanks for all your favours when in town, particularly for introducing me to the knowledge of those worthy and ingenious Gentlemen that made up our last night's conversation'. The chief purpose of his letter was to engage Theobald's attention. He begins with an apology: 'Dear Sir, having no more regard for those papers which I spoke of and promis'd to Mr. Theobald, than just what they deserv'd, I in vain sought for them thro' a number of loose papers that had the same kind of abortive birth.' To make amends for this loss, Warburton accuses Pope of borrowing 'for want of genius' and engages in a comparison of Addison and Shakespeare. Towards the end of this letter he again attempts to capture Theobald's interest: 'My paper fails me, or I should now offer to Mr. Theobald an objection ag^t. Shakespear's acquaintance with the ancients. As it appears to me of great weight, and as it is necessary he shou'd be prepared to obviate all that occur on that head. But some other opportu[n]ity will presente itselfe.'[8] In this period of his life, when he was attempting to ingratiate himself with those who might assist his advancement, Warburton was capable of abject humility, although in later

---

[7] Bodleian MS Eng. Misc. e. 260, fos. 108^v–111^v, *passim*. Selections from Stukeley's papers are published in *The Family Memoirs of the Rev. William Stukeley, M.D.*, ed. W. C. Lukis (Surtees Society), lxxiii (1882), lxxvi (1883), and lxxx (1887).

[8] Nichols, ii. 195–8, *passim*.

years he would habitually misrepresent the nature of his early relationships.[9]

In 1727, opportunities for Warburton to ingratiate himself with Theobald were limited, and the next indication of any contact occurs just over a year later, when Warburton was again in London.[10] He eventually decided to align himself with Theobald and about a year later attacked Pope in three numbers of *The Doily Journal*.[11] His involving himself in a

[9] For example, on 12 Aug. 1732 Concanen wrote informing him of his appointment as Attorney-General of Jamaica, and Warburton replied (16 Aug. 1732): 'I have just now had the very great pleasure of hearing an article of the public news, in your favour, confirmed by your selfe. But you have unkindly taken care that it should not be excessive by warning me in pretty plain terms of an approaching period to the effects of our mutual friendship. I suppose on pretence of removing to a greater distance from me. I call this correspondence the effects of my friendship, both, for that in reality it was so, even of the most sincere: but principally because penurious fate has made me so unhappy as never to be able to give you any other proofe. But I do not know whether I ought to complain of this, when I reflect that I must needs have blushed had capricious fortune so jumbled and confounded matters as to have subjected so much merit to the dishonour of owing anything but good wishes, to one of my insignificancy' (British Library, Egerton MS 1955, fos. 1ᵛ–2ʳ).
   When he had achieved his goals, Warburton gave a radically different account of his relations with Concanen in a letter (3 Jan. 1757) to Richard Hurd: 'I met many years ago with an ingenious Irishman at a coffee-house near Gray's Inn, where I lodged. He studied the law, and was very poor. I had given him money for many a dinner; and, at last, I gave him those papers [Warburton refers to *A Critical and Philosophical Enquiry into the Causes of Prodigies and Miracles* (1727)], which he sold to the booksellers for more money than you would think, much more than they were worth. But I must finish the history of both the Irishman and the papers. Soon after, he got acquainted with Sir William Younge, wrote for Sir Robert [Walpole], and was made Attorney-General of Jamaica: he married there an opulent widow, and died very rich a few years ago here in England; but of so scoundrel a temper, that he avoided ever coming into my sight: so that the memory of all this intercourse between us has been buried in silence till this moment. And who should this man be but one of the Heroes of the *Dunciad*, *Concannen* [*sic*] by name!' (*Letters from a Late Eminent Prelate to One of his Friends*, ed. Richard Hurd, 2nd edn. (1809), 218–19; see also Evans, op. cit., pp. 24–6).

[10] In *Mist's Journal* (8 June 1728), under Domestic News, it is reported that the 'KNIGHTS of the BATHOS' resolved 'Nemine contradicente, that a Committee of the whole Lower House, do consult on Ways and Means for reducing the *current Sense* of this Kingdom, and the exorbitant Power of the *Pope*'. It was subsequently 'Ordered, That a Committee of Secrecy be appointed to draw up a *Report* against the said *Pope*. And that Mr. *M.* Mr. *A.H.* Mr. *W.* Mr. *D.* and the Rev. Mr. *W.* do prepare and bring in the same.' The Rev. Mr. *W.* petitioned to be excused 'on Account of an ancient Friendship between his *best Patron* [Sir Robert Sutton] and the *Pope*'. The Concanen Club, as a whole, seem to have been amused by Pope's *Peri Bathous*, published in *Miscellanies: The Last Volume* (8 Mar. 1728). Warburton was presumably visiting London at this time.

[11] 22 March (No. 2560), 8 April (No. 2574), 22 April 1729 (No. 2586). T. R. Lounsbury, *The Text of Shakespeare* (New York: Scribner, 1906), 353–61, first attributed

printed controversy prior to cementing a friendship was a pattern to be repeated in his subsequent courting of Pope with an unsolicited defence of *An Essay on Man* against Crousaz. In 1729, however, the most striking feature of Warburton's style in controversy is the coarseness of his abuse.[12]

In the beginning of their third year of acquaintance, anticipation of Theobald's rising fortunes prompted Warburton to promote a Shakespearian correspondence with great persistence. In what appears to be Theobald's first letter to him, dated 18 March 1729, Theobald thanks Warburton for a second paper of criticisms which he has received via Concanen. He comments: 'it comes attended not only with the pleasure it brings in itself, but with that of an information that you have read over all Shakespeare.' Assured that this preliminary to a critic's work had been fulfilled, Theobald began to entertain the possibility of a correspondence. He proceeds to obviate any possible embarrassment on Warburton's part arising from a discrepancy between his earlier preparations and his pretensions as a critic. Referring to a previous solicitation by Warburton and to his own subsequent silence, Theobald writes:

You may wonder, doubtless, when I promised to follow you so closely with my troublesome enquiries, that no catalogue of *loci desperati* has yet reached you. It has happened, unluckily, that I have been fatigued with more Law business than the present crisis of my affairs made desirable: and I hope you will forgive an avocation that has been so disagreeable to myself. I wish it may not prove now your misfortune to find me too diligent and importunate.[13]

Warburton certainly had no grounds for complaint concerning this last possibility. He promptly replied to Theobald's first letter, so that Theobald, when he wrote to him again on 8 April 1729, acknowledging this 'last most obliging Epistle', was

these attacks to Warburton, and Evans, op. cit., pp. 73–4, accepts his evidence (although he misdates them 172*8*). See also Robert M. Ryley, 'Warburton's Copy of Theobald's *Shakespeare*', *Transactions of the Cambridge Bibliographical Society*, 7 (1980), 451. Theobald subsequently had occasion to refer to these attacks (Nichols, ii. 621 (18 Nov. 1731)), which are not listed by J. V. Guerinot, *Pamphlet Attacks on Alexander Pope, 1711–1744: A Descriptive Bibliography* (London: Methuen, 1969).

[12] See especially *The Daily Journal*, 2586 (22 Apr. 1729) and Mack, *Pope: A Life*, 744.
[13] Nichols, ii. 204.

reduced to apologizing for not having replied sooner.[14] Theobald's next letter is dated 20 May 1729, and begins with another half-apology: 'Since the pleasure of your last (for not answering to which sooner I will attempt no apology, as you have given me so free an indulgence;) I have received your pamphlet.'[15] A week later Theobald again replied to Warburton, and yet again two days later, on 29 May. In this letter there is more evidence that Warburton was pressing Theobald to correspond, and that Theobald, although pleased by the prospect, by no means solicited Warburton's help: 'I have received the pleasure of your last, and very zealously embrace the encouragement you give me of corresponding; which I shall always be fond of continuing, so long as you indulge me in it, and I am capable of desiring self-improvement.'[16]

Theobald's elaborate politeness, which carefully ensured complete freedom for either one should he wish to discontinue the correspondence, should not be interpreted as a confession of weakness and incapacity. As it happened, he did not take advantage of Warburton's invitation immediately, and five months later (25 October 1729) he is again responding to Warburton's renewed importunities: 'The cessation of my correspondence was indeed occasioned by the hope of seeing you in town, from the letter which you mention; and by the intervention of the summer months, which have obliged me to be too much a flyer.'[17] He was, however, finally convinced that Warburton had a genuine interest in Shakespeare, and in a letter of 20 November 1729 writes: 'Upon the most obliging encouragement given me, you may depend nothing but the most pressing interposition of hated business shall break into my promised uninterrupted correspondence.'[18] So began the pattern of a letter every two or three days, until 26 September 1730, when there were other developments. Warburton's persistence paid off, and his ambitions began to be fulfilled. It is merely typical of him that in the Preface to his own edition of *Shakespear* (1747) he preferred to forget his first obligations and

---

[14] Ibid. 209, 212.
[15] Ibid. 230.
[16] Ibid. 242.
[17] Ibid. 248.
[18] Ibid. 282.

suggested that Theobald had been 'recommended to me as a poor Man'.[19]

Warburton did play a useful part in the years Theobald devoted to Shakespeare. Like many researchers, Theobald had a great need for another's interest in the various matters that came to hand, and his love of Shakespeare, combined with Pope's attacks in *The Dunciad Variorum* (1729), probably made his desire to discuss his work as it progressed irresistible. Theobald's enjoyment of his work must have been infectious—even if, in Warburton's case, his sensitivity to Shakespeare's style, usage, and meaning was not. But then Warburton's part in the correspondence was essentially that of devil's advocate. His kind of learning made him eminently suited to this role, and his function was to anticipate the reactions of potential critics of the edition. While Warburton indulged either in flights of imagination or in cavilling criticism, Theobald exercised critical and scholarly judgement. At the same time, as will be seen, it was a measure of Theobald's skill and diplomacy that he managed, at least until the edition appeared, to refute about ninety per cent of Warburton's proposed emendations of the text and yet keep the friendship of a man so sensitive about his own talents. But for reasons that will become apparent, he was occasionally forced to accept an emendation and a note against his better judgement. By way of further compensation, he fostered Warburton's pretensions to being an aesthetic critic, but reveals his own real abilities in that area in his treatment of the text.

There are many instances in his letters of the pleasure Theobald experienced in his work: 'as Hamlet says [II. ii. 429–30], "We'll e'en to't like friendly faulconers, fly at any thing. . . ." '[20] Indeed, he was dismayed by the thought of the work's being concluded and frequently expresses his enjoyment of it: 'The series of Plays to come will furnish such continued delight, that, spite of the necessity for finishing, I shall regret my task being finished'; 'I am drawing so near the end of my task, that, like a boy with a dear sweet morsel, I am afraid of eating it quite up; and am for extending my pleasure in spite of

[19] *1747*, vol. i, p. x.
[20] Nichols, ii. 205 (18 Mar. 1729); *Friendly*, rather than *French*, is the Q2 reading.

gluttony.'[21] After wondering whether to pursue the laureate-
ship, since 'I would fain sit down to my little studies with an
easy competency', he dismisses the matter because 'Dear
Shakespeare ought always to have a place in my correspondence with you'.[22] In the light of these expressions, it is not
surprising that he took advantage of the delay in publishing his
edition of Shakespeare (the result of a scarcity of compositors)
to continue his researches.[23] His delight, however, was qualified by his need to combat what Johnson called Warburton's
'rage for saying something, when there's nothing to be said'.[24]

Very early in their correspondence, Theobald responds to
Warburton's cogitations on *Lear* (III. vii. 61) simply by writing,

As to the passage in Lear . . .

And quench'd the *steeled* fires.

I had always suspected it of corruption, and had attempted to cure it
in this manner:

And quench'd the *stelled* fires,

i.e. stellati, vel stellei ignes.[25]

Warburton was liable to let his imagination run wild whenever
the topic touched on astronomy, and the brevity of Theobald's
correction is probably in deliberate contrast to a longer dis-
quisition. (As with a number of other cruces, Warburton expressed his gratitude, when he came to prepare his own edition,
by subjoining 'spelt right by Mr. *Theobald*' to the passage.)[26] In
any event, Theobald did think it necessary to add the following
very important corrective:

I scarce need to observe to you, Sir, that *I ever labour to make the smallest
deviations that I can possibly from the text; never to alter at all, where I can by
any means explain a passage into sense; nor ever by any emendations to make the
Author better when it is probable the text came from his own hands.*[27]

This statement of principles characterizes Theobald's approach

[21] Nichols, ii. 464 (31 Jan. 1730); ibid. 557 (10 Mar. 1730).

[22] Ibid. 617 (Dec. 1730).

[23] Jones, p. 314.

[24] Boswell, *Life*, i. 329.

[25] Nichols, ii. 209 (8 Apr. 1729); the reading is accepted.

[26] *1747*, vi. 94 n.

[27] Nichols, ii. 209–10 (8 Apr. 1729); in his letter, Theobald underlined the italicized
passage with red ink (Folger MS W.6.74, fo. 63ʳ). Cf. Preface, *1733*, vol. i, p. xl.

to the text of Shakespeare, but his essential conservatism was tempered by recognition of the need for emendation governed by scholarly and critical tact. Thus he next adduces an example 'in which I may seem to have transgressed my own rule':

Where Cleopatra is characterizing Mark Anthony, after his death, to Dolabella, she says, among other fine things: Anthony [V. ii. 86–8]

> For his Bounty,
> There was no *Winter* in't. An *Antony* it was,
> That grew the more by reaping.

Surely, there is no consonance of ideas betwixt a Winter and an Anthony; nor, I am afraid, any common sense in an Anthony growing by reaping. I shrewdly suspect, our Author wrote:

> For his Bounty,
> There was no Winter in't. An *Autumne* 'twas,
> That grew, &c.

I appeal to you with some diffidence in it; though certainly this restores an uniformity of metaphor, and conveys some meaning in an Autumn still growing by reaping: *nor is the variation from the traces of the letters very great, especially if we consider the old way of spelling the* two words *Antonie* and *Automne.*[28]

Theobald is careful to support the possibility of compositorial misreading (in this case, of minims) as the source of corruption with additional arguments deriving from his knowledge of secretary script and Elizabethan orthography, in addition to critical considerations. He was not, however, content to stop here, and it is interesting to follow this note through to his edition, observing his care to do justice to his friends (and how he himself has been deprived of credit for a discovery):

There was certainly a Contrast, both in the Thought and Terms, design'd here, which is lost in an accidental Corruption. How could an *Antony* grow the more by reaping? I'll venture, by a very easy Change, to restore an exquisite fine Allusion: and which carries its Reason with it too, why there was no *Winter* (i.e. no Want, Bareness,) in his Bounty.

> *For his Bounty,*
> *There was no* Winter *in't: an* Autumn *'twas,*
> *That grew the more by reaping.*

---

[28] Nichols, ii. 210; Theobald again underlined the italicized passage with red ink.

I ought to take Notice, that the ingenious Dr. *Thirlby*[29] likewise started this very Emendation, and had mark'd it in the Margin of his Book. The Reason of the Depravation might easily arise from the great Similitude of the two Words in the old way of spelling, *Antonie* and *Automne*. Our Author has employ'd this Thought again in a Poem, call'd, *True Admiration* [Sonnet 53].

> *Speak of the* Spring *and* Foyzen *of the Year,*
> *The* One *doth shadow of your* Beauty *shew;*
> *The* other *as your* Bounty *doth appear;*
> *And you in ev'ry blessed shape we know.*

For 'tis plain, that *Foyzen* means *Autumn* here, which pours out its Profusion of Fruits bountifully; in Opposition to *Spring*, which only shews the youthful Beauty, and Promise of that future Bounty.[30]

The Arden *Antony and Cleopatra*[31] ascribes the discovery of the parallel imagery of Sonnet 53 to Malone, who apparently went no further than Johnson's version of Theobald's note, which ended (typically) at the 'margin of his book'. But Johnson was always loath to allow Theobald the merit of parallel readings.

In this emendation, Theobald follows the four main principles that governed his alterations of the text: that the proposed reading should make sense, where previously there was none; that, if possible, the reading should follow the *ductus litterarum* and Elizabethan orthography; that the rhetorical context (in this case, of schemes and tropes) should be taken into account; and that, if possible, the reading should be supported by a parallel reading. This scene of *Antony and Cleopatra* is representative of the differences between Theobald's reasoned caution in changing the received text and Warburton's procedure, which was based on his infatuation with his own aesthetic sense. The proximity of the passages also suggests why Theobald found

---

[29] Styan Thirlby, a fellow of Jesus College, communicated a number of emendations to Theobald (see Nichols, ii. 222–30) and saw him in Cambridge (Preface, *1733*, vol. i, p. lxv). See Christopher Spencer and John W. Velz, 'Styan Thirlby: A Forgotten "Editor" of Shakespeare', *Shakespeare Studies*, ed. J. Leeds Barroll, 6 (1970), 327–33. (The authors occasionally accept Thirlby's claims uncritically; e.g., on p. 330 they appear to accept as Thirlby's the emendation of *The Merchant of Venice* (ii. i. 35) of 'page' for 'rage' in 'So is Alcides beaten by his *page*', apparently unaware that Theobald had originally proposed the emendation in *SR* (1726), pp. 166–7. See also John Hazel Smith, 'Styan Thirlby's Shakespearean Commentaries: A Corrective Analysis', *Shakespeare Studies*, 11 (1978).)

[30] *1733*, vi. 324 n. The emendation is generally accepted, although Emrys Jones (ed.), New Penguin Shakespeare (1977), reads *Anthony*.

[31] Ed. M. R. Ridley (repr. 1964), p. 214 n.

himself in the position of having to compromise with his assist-ant. Within twelve lines of Theobald's emendation (that is, on the facing page of the edition) an emendation of Warburton's appears:

> Nature wants stuff
> To vye strange Forms with Fancy; yet t'imagine
> An Antony were Nature's piece, 'gainst Fancy,
> Condemning Shadows quite.]   [V. ii. 97–100]

According to Warburton, 'This is a fine Sentiment, but unin-telligible in the present false Reading'; he substitutes 'Prize' for 'piece' and asserts that 'The Word *Prize*, which I have restored, is the prettiest Word in the World in this place; as, figuring a Contention between *Nature* and *Imagination* about the larger Extent of their Powers; and Nature gaining the Prize by producing *Antony*.'[32]

Although Theobald printed Warburton's emendation and note, in his correspondence he observed that 'piece' is a favour-ite Shakespearian word and expressed doubt about Warburton's emendation.[33] None the less, although the emendation is quite unnecessary, this is one of Warburton's better notes and has the merit, frequently lacking in those that appear in his own edition (1747), of explicating the passage correctly. Warburton tended to become too enamoured of his substitutions, or the ingenuity or fancy which suggested them, to consider what Shakespeare might actually have written. What is worse, he seemed unable to appreciate that what Shakespeare had written was actually more interesting and more important. He was inclined to condescend to Shakespeare, as Theobald evidently realized in a deliberately ambiguous answer to a question concerning his proposed edition of the poems: 'I had like to have forgot answering your ques-tion, as to Shakespeare's poems, whether they are so good as to engage in your thorough Attention in Reading.'[34]

Theobald never indulged in direct rebuke—let alone personal attack—as a means of maintaining his point of view. Even when writing *The Censor* behind the persona of 'Ben Johnson',

[32] *1733*, vi. 324–5 n.
[33] Nichols, ii. 369. In *1765*, vii. 241–2 n., Johnson rejected Warburton's emendation and pointed out that 'The word *piece*, is a term appropriated to works of art' (as in 'masterpiece').
[34] Jones, p. 325 (5 Mar. 1734).

despite attempts to approximate to the received character of his namesake, he remained consistently amiable. Typical of the man is a stray sentence in No. 34: 'I could not be so ill-natur'd as to shock him with a direct Reproof, but chose to insinuate my Dislike of his Proceedings by an oblique Reproach.'[35] He apparently came to realize early in their correspondence that Warburton was a potentially dangerous ally, but, none the less, he attempted to educate his assistant. Warburton, unfortunately, was not the man to benefit from Theobald's manner of oblique reproach. This Theobald must have also suspected, but he persisted. Once the correspondence was established, he probably felt he had no choice because, in the midst of his controversy with Pope, he could not afford to risk Warburton's becoming disaffected. Theobald is always polite in correcting Warburton, but as the work progressed, he found it necessary to maintain extreme care.

In the emendation of *Antony and Cleopatra* above, Theobald instructed Warburton in the subtlety and disinterestedness necessary in the art of emendation by his own example. Occasionally, he was a little less painstaking, as in the following comment on lines in *King John* (III. iv. 1–3):

> So, by a roaring tempest on the flood,
> A whole Armado of collected sail
> Is scatter'd and disjoin'd from fellowship.[36]

You take this for a flat, absurd, and ill-timed simile. I confess, I never thought it a simile; nor, on a nearer view, do I believe you will. The French King begins the scene abruptly, as Virgil has done his fourth Æneid:—*AT Regina gravi*, &c.—and the 'So,' here, is but a connective particle to what is supposed to have preceded the opening of the scene in discourse.

Thus in Hamlet:

> So Rosencraus[37] and Guildenstern go to 't.

And thus the French King here seems to mean—'So, as you tell me, [or, as our accounts are,] this *Armado* of ships is scattered by stress of weather.'[38]

Notwithstanding Theobald's defence of Shakespeare and his

---

[35] ii. 21 (8 Jan. 1717).

[36] *Collected* is Pope's substitution for *convicted*.

[37] The spelling of Q2.

[38] Nichols, ii. 410 (15 Jan. 1730).

comparison with Virgil, Warburton persisted in his view, as appears from his note in his edition (1747). The note also indicates why he was eager to maintain that there is a simile in the passage; despite the anachronism, *Armado* is to be taken as a direct reference to the occurrences of 1588:

> *A whole Armado*, &c,] This similitude, as little as it makes for the purpose in hand, was, I do not question, a very taking one when the play was first represented; which was a winter or two at most, after the *Spanish* invasion in 1588.[39]

Warburton was so eager to remind his readers of this historical event that Shakespeare must be thought to have committed an obviously anachronistic simile requiring editorial comment and condescension. Theobald printed the passage without comment.

When it became apparent that Warburton could not accept straightforward, reasoned rejection of his notes and emendations, Theobald encouraged impartial criticism of his own readings in an attempt to foster disinterestedness in his correspondent:

> Pursuant to promise in my last, of the 27th instant, I open this with my conjecture on the hemistich, as you desire. But I beg you will not be so partial as to give it any weight it has not in your real opinion; for I have no fondness for any thing in this work, any farther than as it bears the appearance of being right, or probable.[40]

The passage is from *1 Henry VI* (I. i. 55–6):

> A farre more glorious Starre thy Soule will make,
> Then *Iulius Cæsar*, or bright—

The first problem presented by the lines, as they appear in the first folio, is whether the break was intended by Shakespeare to emphasize the messenger's news that immediately follows, or whether it is merely the result of a compositor's inability to decipher the manuscript before him. Pope, who evidently had not considered the nature of Shakespeare's anachronisms, suggested that the gap might be filled by 'Francis Drake', probably, as Theobald remarked, 'for Rhyme-sake'.[41] Like

[39] *1747*, iii. 434 n.

[40] Nichols, ii. 451 (29 Jan. 1730).

[41] *1725*, iv. 7 n.: '*I can't guess the occasion of the Hemystic, and imperfect sense, in this place; 'tis not impossible it might have been fill'd up with*—Francis Drake—*tho' that were a terrible*

Pope, Theobald was prepared in his letter to Warburton to believe that the hiatus was accidental. But he was not prepared to accept 'or bright Francis Drake', because he rightly refused to accept the kind of anachronism such a reading entails. In his opinion, 'Some hard name . . . filled up this chasm, which, either from the badness of the transcript, or their own ignorance, the first Editors could not make out; and so chose to leave a blank for it.' He continues: 'The utmost we can pretend to is conjecture; but that conjecture has the best chance to be espoused, which is backed with the best shew of reason, or probability.' Instead of Pope's reading, he proposes 'or bright CASSIOPEIA', and argues that this reading would have been complimentary to Queen Elizabeth.[42]

Warburton, having been invited to criticize the critic, was faced with three choices: to accept Theobald's conjecture, to propose another in its place, or to maintain that the break was intentional. He apparently chose the last, for on 12 February 1730 Theobald writes: 'I have received the pleasure of yours . . . with a kind and judicious refutation of *Cassiopeia*; and, with a just deference to your most convincing reasons, I shall with great cheerfulness banish it as a bad and unsupported conjecture.'[43] Theobald, who considered that the evidence supported both interpretations equally, omitted mention of his conjecture when the play was printed, but contented himself with a short essay on Shakespeare's anachronisms, which indisputably refuted Pope's conjecture as a matter of course.[44]

Anachronism (as bad as Hector's quoting Aristotle in Troil. and Cress.) yet perhaps, at the time that brave Englishman was in his glory, to an English-hearted audience, and pronounced by some favourite Actor, the thing might be popular, though not judicious; and therefore by some Critick, in favour of the author, afterwards struck out. But this is meer slight conjecture.' Theobald's comment appears *1733*, iv. 112 n.

[42] Nichols, ii. 452–3. John Dover Wilson (ed.), *The First Part of King Henry VI*, New Shakespeare (1952; repr. 1968), 114 n., writes: ' "Bright Cassiopey", found in *Selimus* (2216), seems a good candidate.' Andrew Cairncross, Arden (1962), p. xxiii, believes that 'a long name, with many minims, may have baffled the reader'. Sisson, ii. 69 asserts that 'this is a genuine interruption, and not due to illegible copy'; *Textual Companion*, p. 219, comments: 'a dramatic interruption is almost certainly intended.'

[43] Nichols, ii. 477–8.

[44] *1733*, iv. 112. See below, p. 192. Johnson misses the point of Theobald's discussion. Instead, he prints Pope's note, only to remark, 'To confute the *slight* conjecture of *Pope* a whole page of vehement position is annexed to this passage by *Theobald*' (*1765*, iv. 494 n.) [Yale, viii. 567].

(Dover Wilson graces Pope's reading with a bracketed exclamation-mark.) But the matter does not end here: in his edition (1747) Warburton subjoins to the passage Pope's note suggesting 'Francis Drake'.[45] It seems that Warburton's rejection of Theobald's conjecture, both in his letter to him and in his own edition, was prompted simply by captiousness, rather than by any belief in what Shakespeare might actually have written. Theobald's example of disinterestedness was to no purpose.

To no purpose, that is, until Nichol Smith interpreted Theobald's reply to Warburton as a representative example of incapacity and general dependence on his assistant:

> Theobald submits his conjectures anxiously to the judgement of Warburton, and again and again Warburton saves him from himself. In one of the letters Theobald rightly condemns Pope's proposed insertion of 'Francis Drake' in the incomplete line at the end of the first scene of *Henry VI, Part I*; but not content with this flawless piece of destructive criticism he argues for inserting the words 'and Cassiopeia'. The probability is that if Warburton had not condemned the proposal it would have appeared in Theobald's edition.[46] 'With a just deference to your most convincing reasons,' says Theobald, 'I shall with great cheerfulness banish it as a bad and unsupported conjecture' (id. ii, p. 477); and this remark is typical of the whole correspondence.[47]

Nichol Smith has entirely missed the point of Theobald's letter: by his own example he was attempting to teach Warburton a cheerfully disinterested approach to emendation.[48]

At times, Theobald went to extraordinary lengths in correcting Warburton in a manner least harmful to his correspondent's self-esteem. His use of self-deprecating French phrases in remarks leading up to a refutation is amusing, and his rejection of Warburton's proposed alteration of *Henry V* (IV. vii. 62) is a particularly good example of the gentleness of the arts of persuasion that he practised against Warburton's predilections. His letter is especially pleasing because it takes fully into account Warburton's love of the show of learning, the army of

---

[45] *1747*, iv. 435 n.

[46] Cf. above, n. 42.

[47] Smith, p. xlv.

[48] However, Smith's misunderstanding shapes the rest of his account of Theobald, and further reference will have to be made to his argument. See below, p. 127.

quotations adding to its delicate ambivalence of seriousness and teasing:

Before I proceed to the remaining two Acts of Henry the Eighth, give me leave to trouble you with *une petite dissertation*, a few lines concerning a most ingenious conjecture you lately favoured me with on this passage of Henry the Fifth [IV. vii. 62]:

------old ASSYRIAN slings.

I own, I was charmed with your guess of BALEARIAN; it struck me with so strong an appearance of its being right. But, though I could easily fill this sheet with a parade of collected learning, in proof that the Balearick Islanders were not only most expert at the *sling*, but by many Authors have been called the inventors of it; yet I have some doubts, with regard to the certainty of the latter assertion, hanging about me; which you, or nobody, will be able to clear me of: and I have likewise a few passages to submit to your consideration, which as yet seem to me strong in support of our Author's text as we found it.[49]

There follow almost a page and half of quotations and references to Salmasius, Isidore, Strabo, Pliny, Xenophon, and finally (most relevant of all) the Bible, along with Greek and Hebrew etymologies, all tending to justify 'Assyrian slings', as found in the first folio. After which, Theobald concludes with studied politeness:

From these loose hints I submit to your judgment, dear Sir, what I am to determine on this point: whether to conclude, that *Assyrian slings* might be the term used by our Author, or the corruption of his unknowing Editors.
And now I return to order.[50]

But this out-warburtoning Warburton was to no avail, for in a subsequent letter Theobald writes, not without a trace of impatience:

I have received, dear Sir, the satisfaction of yours . . . in which you very finely vindicate your emendation of *Balearian*, upon the just observation of the poetical rule of characterizing nations for something *for which they are eminent far* above others. It is doubtless an argument that ought to have all its weight on the side of your conjecture, as it shall have in my consideration: and, I hope, it will go some way towards accounting for an emendation, that some readers

[49] Nichols, ii. 465 (3 Feb. 1730).   [50] Ibid. 467.

might be apt to think too wide from the traces of the corrupted text.[51]

Unlike Warburton, Theobald had reached that point where learning is the servant of truth, not its master. As was his wont, he printed '*Assyrian* slings' without comment in his edition.[52] There can be little doubt that he was trying to instil in Warburton a sense of editorial principle. At any rate, this much is clear: in his earlier letter he showed that learning might reveal a second possibility and deduce a probability. When Warburton countered with his literary critical preconceptions (the kind of preconceptions that Theobald consistently attempted to undermine, when determining what Shakespeare had written, by reasoned probabilities based on a knowledge of his author's historical background), Theobald, like a schoolmaster, abandons the irrelevancies that constituted half the set problem and returns to fundamentals—the manuscript behind the print. In this instance, he managed to save Warburton from himself, for in 1747 the passage remained unaltered.

Although Theobald frequently softened his corrections of Warburton by inviting impartial criticism of his own conjectures, inevitably Warburton was displeased by the reception of the great majority of his proposed notes and readings, and Theobald found himself having to apologize for his rejections: 'I did not design peremptorily to object to.'[53] However, their letters continued without intermission until 31 March 1730, when there was a slight pause, Theobald writing on 11 April that 'Business has obliged me to intermit a few posts, as the want, I suppose, of materials sufficient for your reply has occasioned the silence on your part'. Shakespeare maintained his pre-eminence in a letter of early May, in which Theobald also refers to the return of his letters.[54] Between 12 May and 3 September there was again an interval in their correspondence, when, apart from the interruption of the summer vacation, Theobald was consolidating his work on Shakespeare and was preparing his *Orestes: A Dramatic Opera* (1731) for the press. During this period Warburton also paid a visit to London.

---

[51] Nichols, ii. 490 (12 Feb. 1730).
[52] *1733*, iv. 84.
[53] Nichols, ii. 582 (26 Mar. 1730).
[54] Ibid. 597, 603.

After his return to Newark on 11 June, their exchange was hampered because Theobald broke his right arm.[55] Shakespearian cruces reappear, however, in a letter of 3 September 1730, which Theobald begins with references both to his accident and to a silence on Warburton's part. By 15 September he was again writing to Warburton, thanking him for a letter and expecting a renewal of their correspondence. But it appears that Warburton was now either beginning to tire, since Theobald refers to his 'occasional second perusal' of the major cruces, or that he was temporarily doubtful about the value of his contributions. Concerning this second possibility, Theobald writes:

I would by no means wish you to restrain your genius, or the scope of your suspicions, so long as you are pleased to indulge me in such a labour; for, though every conjecture should not upon trial prove standard, give me leave to say, without flattery, there is something so extremely ingenious in all you start, that I would with great regret be defrauded of such a fund either of entertainment, or erudition.[56]

Theobald probably felt that the vindication of his reputation after the onslaught of *The Dunciad* might be in jeopardy if Warburton embarked on a separate course. It is significant that there immediately follows in his letter an example of his accepting a reading of Warburton's, apparently against his better judgement. Warburton's reading of *gemell* for *jewell* in *A Midsummer Night's Dream* (IV. i. 191):

> And I have found Demetrius like a jewel,
> Mine own, and not mine own

has not been accepted.[57] Theobald also seems more than half inclined to reject the proposed reading. Having just said that he would greatly regret the loss of the correspondence, he continues: 'It has not been yet in my power fully to weigh every emendation in your last: but to some of them I am prepared to speak in present.' He then addresses Warburton's emendation:

---

[55] See letters of 11 June and 2 July 1730, Jones, pp. 272–3.

[56] Nichols, ii. 607.

[57] In a set of Theobald's *Shakespeare* (1733) in my possession that belonged to John Upton, author of *Critical Observations on Shakespeare* (1746), there is a MS note by Upton on *jewel* (which anticipates Malone's generally accepted explanation): 'i.e. as if I found w^t was not my own really but anothers' (i. 131).

This is so finely guessed, and gives so natural a sense where before there was none at all, that I wish heartily the word had ever been used again by Shakespeare; or that I could meet with it either in Spenser, Chaucer, or any of the old Glossaries. Our Author, you know, once has *jimmold*, or *gimmald* [*Henry V* (IV. ii. 49)]], a *ring of two rounds*, from *gemellus*; and *gemells*, Skinner tells us, is a word in Heraldry, to signify a *pair of bars*. But neither of these, I am afraid, will sort with our allusion. But then again, on your side, Blunt and Phillips both acknowledge such a word as GEMINELS to signify *twins*. I have no exception to the derivation of the term; I only wish, they had subjoined an authority by whom it had been adopted into English.[58]

After these objections, Theobald seems inconsistent when he writes: 'Upon the whole, I cannot but embrace your emendation'—even when he justifies it by remarking that 'though the word should be an ἄπαξ λεγόμενον, yet the appositeness of its usage may well excuse Shakespeare for coining it'.[59] Since Theobald retains Warburton's reading and note in his second edition of *Shakespeare* (1740), it seems he had not been able to make sense of the passage in its original form. Some further explanation of Theobald's inability to grasp its meaning is found in his first edition. Warburton's note reads:

Hermia had said, Things appear'd double to her. *Helena* says, So, methinks; and then subjoins, *Demetrius* was like a *Jewel*, her own and not her own. According to common Sense and Construction, *Demetrius* is here compar'd to something that has the Property of *appearing* the same, and yet not *being* the same: and this was a Thought natural enough, upon her declaring her Approbation of what *Hermia* had said, that every thing seems *double*. But now, how has a Jewel, or any precious Thing, the Property, rather than a more worthless one, of appearing to be the same and yet not the same? This, I believe, won't be easily found out. I make no doubt therefore, but the true Reading is;

> *And I have found* Demetrius *like a* Gemell,
> *Mine own, and not mine own.*

from *Gemellus*, a *Twin*. For *Demetrius* acted that Night two such different Parts, that she could hardly think him one and the same *Demetrius*: but that there were two Twin-*Demetrius*'s to the acting this Farce, like the two *Socia*'s.[60]

58 Nichols, ii. 607–8.
59 *OED* cites Drayton's *Barons War* (1603) for contemporary use of *gemell*.
60 *1733*, i. 131 n.

Joseph Ritson believed that, in suppressing the comparison of the circumstances of *finding*, Warburton 'wilfully misstates Helena's words to found his *ingenious emendation*'.[61] Theobald's difficulty, however, probably arose because Warburton (apparently) justified his misguided ingenuity by referring to 'the similar Trace of the Letters, and the Difficulty of the Transcribers understanding the true Word'.[62] For Theobald to have rejected Warburton's reading would also have required either what might have been construed as an attack on his own general principles (since the emendation was susceptible to a defence based on the *ductus litterarum*) or worse, making explicit the need for taste and tact in the applying of those principles. Either course would have been highly complicated and probably offensive. In his letter, Theobald went so far as to voice his doubts as well as his acceptance of the reading. Perhaps at this juncture he felt he could go no further. On the other hand, it is possible that in his approach to *jewel* Theobald's own understanding was clouded by Warburton's arguments—quite apart from the probability that he was aware he could hardly hope, when writing to Warburton, that Warburton would accept the sincerity of his letter's preliminary remarks if they were accompanied by an immediate rejection of his emendation. This kind of problem was inescapable in the relations between the two men, and Theobald's edition suffered accordingly. Johnson printed *jewel*—his sole comment on Warburton's emendation and note, as they appeared in his edition (1747), being 'This emendation is ingenious enough to deserve to be true'.[63]

The remainder of Theobald's letter is as impartial as ever, which is to say that it refutes a series of Warburton's conjectures. Perhaps as a consequence he found himself beginning his next letter (26 September 1730) as follows: 'I have received the great pleasure of yours . . . though I am to regret the notice given in your Postscript, that I am not to expect above two or three letters more, as the fruits of your *new view*.'[64] There is no sign of either resentment or distress. Theobald merely notes

---

[61] *Remarks, Critical and Illustrative, on the Text and Notes . . . of Shakespeare* (1783), 46.

[62] *1733*, loc. cit. It is possible that this further justification was added by Theobald, when editing Warburton's contributions (see below, p. 129), since the passage does not appear in *1747*, i. 154 n.

[63] *1765*, i. 157 n. [Yale, vii. 156].

[64] Nichols, ii. 612.

those emendations which he intends to print and then proceeds with his reasons for rejecting others. Finally, he subscribes himself as 'dearest Sir, Your most affectionate and obliged humble servant'. Their Shakespearian correspondence was not resumed for little over a year, the intervening silence being broken once by a Christmas letter from Theobald.

When Warburton ceased corresponding, in addition to feeling irritation at Theobald's rejections of his conjectures, he probably had come to believe that Theobald's hopes for publication would never be realized after all. In the early days of their correspondence, Theobald had intended to publish by subscription, in three volumes, notes and emendations in the manner of *Shakespeare Restored* (1726), because the Tonsons' ownership of the copyright of the plays effectively prevented his undertaking an edition. The Tonsons were, of course, also Pope's friends and publishers. How successful Theobald was in gaining subscriptions for the three volumes is not clear, but it is evident that the real demand was for a new edition.[65] In particular, Lady de la Warr[66] was drumming up support among the nobility, and on 6 November 1729 Theobald confided to Warburton 'perhaps I may venture to join the *Text* to my *Remarks*'.[67] However, not until 10 March 1730 did he feel ready to announce his intentions of publishing an edition.[68] The following month Theobald wrote to Warburton that Jacob Tonson jun. 'has been wth my friend, the Lady De la Warre, & submitts to make her the Arbitratress of Termes betwix us for my publishing an edition of Shakespeare'.[69] He expected to know the outcome of these negotiations within a fortnight, but there were delays. Lady de la Warr again met Tonson in July 1730, but at this time Tonson had little reason to hurry: he had glutted the trade with the second edition of Pope's *Shakespear* (1728) and was only interested in terms highly favourable to

[65] Preface, *1733*, vol. i, pp. lxiii–lxiv.

[66] Charlotte, the first wife of John West, Baron de la Warr. Her father was Donogh MacCarthy, 4th Earl of Clancarty, and her mother was the daughter of Robert Spencer, 2nd Earl of Sunderland. Her husband was Lord of the Bedchamber, 1725–7, and Treasurer of the Household, 1731–7.

[67] Nichols, ii. 254.

[68] Ibid. 551.

[69] Jones, p. 266 (25 Apr. 1730).

himself. Lady de la Warr counselled Theobald to delay, and no agreement was reached by the end of the summer. Warburton, perhaps also convinced that Pope would use all his influence to prevent Theobald's edition from ever being published, ceased corresponding.[70]

The stand-off with Tonson jun. placed Theobald in a quandary: he could not publish an edition of Shakespeare without the Tonsons' agreement, and he did not wish to jeopardize an agreement by publishing his commentary. To add to his difficulties, it was being suggested that he was taking money from subscribers 'without ever designing to give them any Thing for it'.[71] He was also in the depths of financial distress, 'the Severity of a rich Creditor' having stripped him 'so bare, that I never was acquainted with such Wants, since I knew the Use of Money'.[72] This trying state of affairs continued until the summer of 1731, when he was approached by rivals of the Tonsons who were eager to publish his edition as part of a scheme to break the Tonsons' hold on the copyright of Shakespeare.[73] In a final attempt to gain Theobald's co-operation, the rival booksellers also contacted Warburton in the late summer of 1731, in the hope that he would influence Theobald in their favour. But, having entrusted his interests to Lady de la Warr, Theobald was unable to make any commitments. Jacob Tonson jun. was now faced with a choice between defending his perpetual copyright in Shakespeare by bringing a suit against his rivals in the Court of Chancery (if they should succeed with Theobald and proceed with their plans) or signing articles with Theobald himself. He prudently chose the second course, and an agreement was concluded on Thursday, 26 October 1731 which was to result in Theobald's becoming the best paid of the early editors of Shakespeare.[74] Lady de la

[70] For Pope's attempts to dissuade the Tonsons from publishing Theobald's *Shakespeare*, see *Correspondence*, iii. 241–45.

[71] Preface, *1733*, vol. i, p. lxiv.

[72] Jones, p. 280.

[73] See Dawson, pp. 11–35, and Terry Belanger, 'Tonson, Wellington and the Shakespeare Copyrights', *Studies in the Book Trade in Honour of Graham Pollard* (Oxford: Bibliographical Society, 1975), 195–209.

[74] A draft of the agreement is in the Bodleian Library (MS Rawl. D. 729). See Appendix B. Theobald was allowed 400 sets printed on Demy 'Free and Clear' and a further 100 sets on a fine Royal paper, free of all charges save the cost of the paper. He estimated these would bring him 1,100 guineas (Jones, p. 278). According to a

Warr had not stinted in her efforts on his behalf, either in her bargaining with Tonson jun. or in her recommendations to the aristocracy, and Theobald was able to write: 'my Lady Delawarr has befriended me with such a list of Quality as were well worth waiting for.'[75]

When Warburton was apprised by the rival booksellers of their interest in publishing an edition by Theobald, he wrote to Theobald urging him to take up their offer, but in terms that may have been offensive. This letter Theobald did not immediately answer. Warburton thereupon became alarmed that he might not receive any of the credit and honour that might attach to those associated with the edition, and a slightly later recanting letter (10 November 1731) to Dr William Stukeley shows that he set about calumniating Theobald:

> Mr. *Theobald* has entered into articles for publishing Shakespeare with Tonson. It is to appear by next March; and he is to have for it *eleven hundred guineas*, and your humble servant for his pains one copy of the royal paper books.[76] But, *as he has given me full satisfaction for his late conduct*, and appears to be willing to perform the part of a man of honour, I absolve him from all hard thoughts, and am disposed to serve him all I can. This I thought proper, for good reasons, to let you know, whom I had acquainted with my (groundless as I am glad to find it) suspicions and complaints.[77]

memorandum (Folger MS S. a. 163) by Somerset Draper, a servant of Tonson and a witness to Theobald's agreement, the value (to Tonson) of Theobald's sets was about £600. The same memorandum indicates that Rowe received £36 10*s.* Pope's agreement with Tonson (Folger MS S. a. 161) allowed him £100; Warburton's agreement (Folger MS S. a. 165) allowed him £500. Johnson earned about 1,000 guineas. His price to subscribers was 2 guineas; he was allowed 250 sets free of charge and any additional sets at a cost of 1 guinea each. See Appendix G, Boswell, *Life*, i. 545. Thomas Birch understood there were about 750 subscribers in all (letter (5 Oct. 1765) to Lord Hardwicke (British Library, Add. MS 35400, fo. 316ᵛ), quoted by Arthur Sherbo, *Samuel Johnson, Editor of Shakespeare*, Illinois Studies in Language and Literature, 42 (Urbana: University of Illinois Press, 1956), 10). According to an anonymous notation added to Somerset Draper's memorandum (Folger MS S. a. 163), Edward Capell was paid £300.

[75] Nichols, ii. 254.

[76] This evidently rankled with Warburton. See Theobald's letter to him after they finally quarrelled (18 May 1736, Jones, pp. 343–4): 'I am sure, I never dreamt to this day, but that the Assistance of my Friends were design'd gratuitous, & if I misunderstood this Point, I should have been set right by some Hints before the Publication.'

[77] Nichols, ii. 13–14. A letter from Theobald to Stukeley in the Bodleian (MS Eng. Misc. c. 114, fos. 240–1) indicates that they were acquainted by 14 June 1728.

Before this last was written, Warburton had written a second, ingratiating letter to Theobald and had received a reply. Something of the tone and substance of his letters can be surmised from Theobald's answer (30 October 1731):[78]

> I hope I shall yet have so much Credit with you that you will believe, tho' I had not yesterday rece[ive]d the Pleasure of yours, I was fully determin'd this Evening to salute you by letter: & I am convinced presently you will believe me.
>
> You may, perhaps, imagine from my late Silence, that I really took y^r. last kind Letter, as you there hinted, for the rudest I ever received; but I assure you by my Honesty (if I have any) I prize it as a most cordial Testimony of a Friendship, that shall ever be dear to me; & tho' for reasons yet unknown to You, I have seemed to slumber over Gratitude, & postpon'd my Acknowledgments till now; yet I dare assure You, yor. Counsel has not lost its Effects.

Theobald subsequently explains that his delay in answering Warburton's first letter was owing to a determination to remain silent until negotiations with Tonson were complete; but it seems that he is also responding to a charge of duplicity in Warburton's first letter, and also that his initial silence might well have been interpreted as a response to rudeness. A further assurance 'that neither awkward Disgust, Disregard, nor Indolence, have kept me dumb' suggests there were grounds for disgust and disregard, if he had chosen to respond in those ways. Warburton's charges apparently had to do with complaints made to him by the rival booksellers. Theobald's reply makes clear that they were outbid by Tonson: 'As to the Booksellers, Dear S^r., who once made some Overtures to me, you hinted that they complain'd I had not dealt so honourably wth. them: I fancy, you will be satisfied I can turn the Tables upon them, when I tell you, Tonson has acceded to double the Terms they offer'd me. . . .' In his protracted negotiations with Tonson, Theobald had, as he said, 'at last fix'd the Proteus'.[79]

[78] Jones quotes this letter in his text (pp. 157–8), but gives the date as 30 Oct. 1730, although a check of the British Library, Egerton MS 1956, fo. 16^v, confirms the date given in his Appendix C, 30 Oct. 1731 (p. 279). Theobald was engaged in intermittent negotiations with Tonson over a year and a half, and not, as Jones thought, only during the summer of 1730. The duration of the negotiations is significant in the relations of Theobald and Warburton.

[79] Jones, p. 277.

With publication of the edition assured, Warburton wasted no time in re-establishing the correspondence on its old footing. He had, indeed, included emendations in his latest letter, and Theobald writes: 'I thank you, Dearest S^r. for yor Conjectures last communicated'—although it is significant that Theobald immediately adds: 'but indeed I have not yet had time to weigh them sufficiently.'[80] After receiving Theobald's good news, Warburton was especially friendly, and Theobald acknowledges 'the pleasure of yours, wch. comes fraught wth. Kindness even beyond my own Prepossessions'.[81] Theobald, of course, had little choice but to accept Warburton's renewed overtures, even if, as seems certain, he realized that his friend's revived interest in Shakespeare was scarcely disinterested. Warburton would now be either for him or against him, and it would have been foolish not to avoid a controversy. His tactic in this situation was to gloss over potential disputes by adopting a tone of high compliment.[82]

Warburton's 'Kindness' was accompanied by the promise of further notes and emendations, and Theobald replies: 'I have great Satisfaction in the News you tell me, that you have a fresh Fund of Entertainment for Me upon 6 of our Author's Traged-ies: & I shall live in a sweet Expectation of their Arrival.' But his flattery of Warburton serves to make palatable his deter-mination to be most careful in deciding what should be printed:

Tonson has sent me in a Shakespeare interleav'd;[83] & I am now

[80] Ibid. 278.

[81] Ibid. 279.

[82] This habit remained with him. Thomas Seward, the father of Anna Seward and a co-editor with Theobald of *The Works of Mr. Francis Beaumont, and Mr. John Fletcher* (10 vols., 1750), records in a Postscript, apropos of an editorial disagreement: 'Mr. *Theobald*'s high-flown Compliments to me here, should certainly be expung'd, could I take such a liberty with the Part which Mr. *Theobald* printed. . . . This Note was printed just after a slight Disagreement between us was compromis'd, and must be look'd on as the Effect of mere Complaisance' (i. 375–6). Theobald had written: 'If I have made some tolerable Emendations thro' the Work, I would give the Merit of them all up, to have been the Master of that Correction which the Sagacity of Mr. *Seward* has shewn in restoring the undisputed Sense of our Authors' (ibid. 187). Warburton's love of flattery, as noted by Stukeley, has already been observed, and Theobald's tactics worked well with him.

[83] A copy of part of vol. vii (*Antony and Cleopatra*) of Pope's 2nd edn. (1728) with MS notes by Theobald bound in at the end is in the British Library (c.45.b.11). Nine other plays bound in three volumes are in the Fellows' Library, Winchester College. See Richard Corballis, 'Copy-Text for Theobald's "Shakespeare"', *The Library*, 6th Series, 7 (June 1986).

extracting such notes & Emendations, as upon the Maturest Deliberation, I am certain will stand the Test. For the Censures, that may succeed [publication of the edition], make me reflect in Time, that I had much better smother uncertain Suspicions than appear too boldly peremptory. There are some Passages in wch. I shall be obliged to retract my own Emendations; & even where they have met with your Concurrence.[84]

Now that the edition was definitely to be published, Warburton was not in the least abashed by Theobald's critical caution, and countered by proposing that plausible conjectures should then be printed in the notes. To this suggestion Theobald replied (18 November 1731): 'I agree with you perfectly as to such conjectures that bear the face of probability, and yet upon which I must not venture to tamper with the text, that they should however be submitted to judgment in a note. I mean to follow the form of Bentley's Amsterdam Horace, in subjoining the notes to the place controverted.'

Theobald had also been reminded by Warburton of the emendations Warburton had printed in *The Daily Journal* as part of his attacks upon Pope in 1729. His enthusiasm for these conjectures may be gauged from the fact that, when the edition was published, only one was included. In his letter to Warburton, however, he observed: 'As to the *three printed criticisms* with which you obliged me and the publick, it is a very reasonable caution that what is gleaned from them should come out anonymous; for I should be loth to have a valued friend subjected, on my account, to the outrages of Pope, virulent though impotent.'[85] But Warburton's most successful manœuvre—it is central to Nichol Smith's argument that Theobald was almost totally dependent on him—was to suggest that, apart from notes and emendations, he might be of assistance when the Preface to the edition came to be written.

After misinterpreting Theobald's attempts to instil in Warburton a disinterested approach to the text, Nichol Smith considers Warburton's role in the writing of Theobald's Preface: 'Warburton had undoubtedly given Theobald ungrudging assistance and was plainly interested in the success of the edition. But as he had gauged Theobald's ability, he had some

[84] Jones, p. 280.   [85] Nichols, ii. 621.

fears for the Preface.'[86] In fact, Theobald did not need Warburton's assistance: his concerns, once publication was assured, were to prevent Warburton from disfiguring the text and to avoid open conflict with him. When Warburton expressed an interest in the Preface, Theobald took advantage of the opportunity to divert his attention from the text and commentary.

Theobald begins his reply to Warburton's enquiries in a style of grateful compliment: 'I am extremely obliged for the tender concern you have for my reputation in what I am *to prefix to my Edition*: and this part, as it will come last in play, I shall certainly be so kind to myself to communicate in due time to your perusal.'[87] As early as 11 November 1729, Theobald had planned a *Prolegomena* to his work on Shakespeare; he now changed his mind: 'The whole affair of *Prolegomena* I have determined to soften into *Preface*.'[88] It is unfortunate that in his desire to avoid parallels with Martinus Scriblerus' *Prolegomena* to *The Dunciad* Theobald abandoned his *Prolegomena* to *Shakespeare*, since that was exactly what was needed at the time and would have helped ensure that he received credit for his editorial principles. In his letter to Warburton he returns to Warburton's interest in the preliminaries: 'But, dear Sir, will you, at your leisure hours, think over for me upon the contents, topics, orders, &c. of this branch of my labour? You have a comprehensive memory, and a happiness of digesting the matter joined to it, which my head is often too much embarassed to perform; let that be the excuse for my inability.' In these compliments Theobald went too far and played into Warburton's hands. His further qualifying statement (which implicitly recognizes Warburton's thirst for recognition, while at the same time admitting that any assistance in the Preface cannot be publicly acknowledged) seems to place him in a worse light: 'But how unreasonable is it to expect this labour, when it is the only part in which I shall not be able to be just to my friends: for, to confess assistance in a *Preface* will, I am afraid, make me appear too naked.'[89]

Out of context, the section of Theobald's letter dealing with

[86] Smith, p. xlvi. See above, p. 116.
[87] Nichols, ii. 621.
[88] Ibid. 258, 621.
[89] Ibid. 621–2.

his Preface could only be damaging to his reputation, and Warburton, before he returned Theobald's letter with others of this period in June 1732, made an almost verbatim transcript of these complimentary passages, except that 'friends' becomes 'friend' and 'in a *Preface*' is omitted. The transcript is headed: 'Tibbald's Word in a letter to me, of 18th Novr. 1731.'[90] The adoption of Pope's spelling in *The Dunciad* of his friend's name suggests animosity; Warburton was already preparing the way for his later claims to have been the guiding light of the edition. These claims were accepted by Nichol Smith, and in his Introduction to *Eighteenth Century Essays on Shakespeare* Smith quotes all of Theobald's letter that deals with the Preface and concludes: 'This confession of weakness is valuable in the light of Warburton's Preface to his own edition of 1747.'[91]

Neither Warburton, in his transcription of Theobald's letter, nor Nichol Smith, in his Introduction, chose to transcribe the next paragraph of Theobald's letter. This paragraph (to which Theobald referred, when the two men finally quarrelled) is, however, the most important in the letter. Indeed, all Theobald's flattery preceding it was designed to ensure that Warburton would accept the proposals contained in it. The paragraph is brief and casually introduced, but it is, for Theobald, the letter's central point: 'What you mention of your own negligence in expression during this correspondence, literally written *currente calamo*; wherever casually there be any such, if you dare trust me with the re-modeling; be assured, in this office, your reputation shall be as sacred to me as my own.'[92]

---

[90] Jones, pp. 344–5.

[91] Smith, p. xlvi.

[92] Nichols, ii. 622. That Theobald had a very real need after the renewal of their correspondence to check Warburton's textual licentiousness is apparent from the history of a metaphysical note to *Love's Labour's Lost* (iv. iii. 317–20):

> For when would you, my liege, or you, or you,
> In leaden contemplation have found out
> Such fiery numbers, as the prompting eyes
> Of beauty's tutors have enrich'd you with?

(quoted from *1733*, ii. 143)

In a letter written in Dec. 1731 Theobald comments: 'You call these obscure lines, and imagine they contain an allusion I cannot possibly discover in them. On the strength of this supposition, you have given me a very ingenious note. . . . But, indeed, I cannot think the lines are in any degree obscure; and I can but wonder as yet how my dear Friend is become so metaphysical to fancy *fiery numbers* have any relation to the

Obviously Theobald's self-deprecation and flattery of Warburton in the matter of the Preface are designed to ensure that he will have a free hand in the editing of the text and commentary. There were, of course, latent ironies in Theobald's concluding line to the paragraph far beyond that of which he was aware. But he has explained the otherwise inexplicable difference in the quality of those notes attributed to Warburton in Theobald's edition of 1733 and those that appeared for the first time in Warburton's own edition of 1747. When the two men finally quarrelled, it was over notes and conjectures of Warburton's that Theobald had omitted from his edition.[93] Theobald, however, had his editorial priorities right and safeguarded the standards of his text and commentary.[94]

---

stars.' Theobald then explains that 'fiery numbers' means 'such verses of fire and spirit . . . as the sight of your fair mistress's eyes have inspired you with' (Nichols, ii. 627–8). Having once written a note, Warburton was extremely reluctant to abandon it. Whereas Theobald printed the passage without comment, Warburton, in *1747*, first omitted the lines (iv. iii. 298–300):

> From womens eyes this doctrine I derive;
> They are the ground, the book, the academies,
> From whence doth spring the true *Promethean* fire
>
> (quoted from Warburton's copy-text,
> Theobald's *1740*, ii. 223–4)

—by mere oversight, Johnson supposed (*1765*, ii. 176 n. Warburton would have to have indicated deletion). He then subjoined a version of the note Theobald had rejected: '*In leaden contemplation have found out* | *Such fiery numbers . . .*'. 'Alluding to the discoveries in modern astronomy; at that time greatly improving, in which the ladies eyes are compared, as usual to *stars*. He calls them *numbers*, alluding to the *Pythagorean* principles of astronomy, which were founded on the laws of harmony' (*1747*, ii. 246 n.) Johnson's comment suffices: 'The Astronomer, by looking too much aloft, falls into a ditch' (*1765*, ii. 177 n.).

[93] See Jones, pp. 343–4 (18 May 1736): 'I used, you say, what Notes, I thought fit; & the remaining Ones are your Property. I own as Editor, I believ'd I had a discretionary Power of picking & chusing my Materials; & I am certain during the Affair, you conceded this Liberty to Me.'

[94] For Warburton's claims to have written substantial parts of Theobald's Preface and Nichol Smith's assessment of those claims, see below, Appendix D.

8. Theobald's Edition: Establishment of the Text and Principles of Emendation

IN their simplest terms, the tasks of an editor of Shakespeare are to reproduce as accurately as possible what Shakespeare wrote and then to elucidate his texts. That Theobald under-stood the essential purpose and order of these duties is clear, not only from his correspondence with Warburton, but also from the Preface to his edition. In the first half of the eighteenth century literary-critical predilections tended, however, to inter-fere with the concern to discover what Shakespeare had actually written. Pope and Warburton both claimed to have made avail-able Shakespeare's genuine texts, but Pope deliberately altered, relegated to the bottom of the page, or omitted passages he felt might diminish Shakespeare's reputation. Warburton's editing was primarily an excuse for displaying his own cleverness, and he did not hesitate to make the texts conform to his philosoph-ical, historical, and literary-critical fancies.

Theobald realized that meaningful criticism of Shakespeare had to be preceded by some certainty as to what he had written. He insisted that, as far as possible, the tasks of the editor must be distinguished from those of the literary critic. This distinc-tion is one of his major contributions to the study of English literature. Consequently, Theobald's *Shakespeare* also marks the beginning of a consistently historical approach to English texts. His aims are stated in that part of his Preface, presumably derived from his proposed *Prolegomena* to *Shakespeare*,[1] where he rightly claims to 'have ventur'd on a Labour, that is the first Assay of the kind on any modern Author whatsoever'. Whereas 'the chief Turn' of Bentley's edition of *Paradise Lost* (1732) 'is plainly to shew the World, that if *Milton* did not write as He

[1] First mentioned in a letter (11 Nov. 1729) to Warburton (Nichols, ii. 258).

[Bentley] would have him, he ought to have wrote so', his own editing 'is of a quite different Kind'. Shakespeare's 'genuine Text is religiously adher'd to, and the numerous Faults and Blemishes, purely his own, are left as they were found. Nothing is alter'd, but what by the clearest Reasoning can be proved a Corruption of the true Text; and the Alteration, a real Restoration of the genuine Reading.' Theobald acknowledges that his ̄zeal 'to give the true Reading, tho' sometimes not to the Advantage of my Author' has exposed him to the ridicule of those 'who either were iniquitously for turning every thing to my Disadvantage; or else were totally ignorant of the true Duty of an Editor'. In contrast to the examples of Pope and Bentley, he asserts:

The Science of Criticism, as far as it affects an Editor, seems to be reduced to these three Classes; the Emendation of corrupt Passages; the Explanation of obscure and difficult ones; and an Inquiry into the Beauties and Defects of Composition. This Work is principally confin'd to the two former Parts: tho' there are some Specimens interspers'd of the latter Kind, as several of the Emendations were best supported, and several of the Difficulties best explain'd, by taking notice of the Beauties and Defects of the Composition peculiar to this Immortal Poet. But This was but occasional, and for the sake only of perfecting the two other Parts, which were the proper Objects of the Editor's Labour. The third lies open for every willing Undertaker: and I shall be pleas'd to see it the Employment of a masterly Pen.[2]

Obviously Theobald supposes the chief function of an editor to be emendation of corrupt passages. The first concern of a modern editor of a Shakespearian play is to select the text which will form the basis of his own edition. This means choosing (when there is a choice) between either a first good quarto or the first folio text of the play. The choice depends upon a determination of the nature of the copy behind the quarto and folio versions of the play. An editor will usually wish to base his edition on the text that is closest to Shakespeare's autograph. Theobald's *Shakespeare* is based on Pope's second edition

---

[2] *1733*, vol. i, pp. xxxix–xli. Warburton wished these passages to be thought his, and marked them accordingly in his set of Theobald's edition now in the library of Trinity College, Cambridge. They were retained by Theobald in his revised Preface to *1740*, vol. i, sigs. a5ᵛ–a6ʳ, and may be safely attributed to him. See below, Appendix D.

(1728), which was based on Rowe's third edition (1714), which in turn was based on the fourth folio (1685). That is to say, instead of basing his edition on the printed texts closest to Shakespeare's manuscripts, he based it on a text eight printings removed from the first folio, which itself, in the case of a number of plays, was printed from quarto copy. Theobald's use of Pope's edition as the basis for printer's copy is primarily responsible for the reservations about his editorial judgement felt by modern textual critics.[3] His judgement seems most confused in this fundamental decision, especially since he himself lists Rowe's and Pope's editions as 'Editions of no Authority' in his 'Table of The several Editions of Shakespeare's Plays Collected by the Editor'.[4] Of course, the slur on Pope was deliberate, but the decision to use Pope's second edition as the basis of his own was not, in fact, a matter in which Theobald was free to exercise choice.

Theobald originally intended to publish a continuation of his work in *Shakespeare Restored*, because he could not publish the texts of the plays without Tonson's consent. Under the terms of the first English copyright statute,[5] which came into effect on 10 April 1710, the owners of copyrights in old books had the sole right to publish these works for the next twenty-one years. By two assignments of 20 May 1707 and 22 October 1709,[6] Tonson purchased the copyright of twenty-three Shakespearian plays from the descendants of those who had rights in the text of the fourth folio (1685). Subsequently, he owned the copyright for all but three or four of the plays. Tonson established his rights with the publication of Rowe's edition (1709) and, under the terms of the Act, had nothing to fear from his competitors until April 1731.[7] After this date, Tonson's legal

---

[3] See Alfred W. Pollard, *Shakespeare's Fight with the Pirates and the Problems of the Transmission of his Text*, 2nd edn. rev. (1920; repr. Cambridge: Cambridge University Press, 1967), 82–4; McKerrow, pp. 106–7; R. B. McKerrow, *Prolegomena for the Oxford Shakespeare: A Study in Editorial Method* (1939; repr. Oxford: Clarendon Press, 1969), 36–8; Wilson, *New Bibliography*, pp. 97–9.

[4] *1733*, vol. vii, sig. Hh8[r]. *Collected* is corrected to *Collated* in the final erratum of the edition.

[5] Entitled *An Act for the Encouragement of Learning, by Vesting the Copies of Printed Books in the Authors or Purchasers of such Copies, during the Times therein mentioned* (8 Anne, c. 19).

[6] Bodleian MS Charters Surrey 84 and Folger MS S.a.160 respectively. I am indebted in the following paragraphs to Dawson, pp. 11–35.

[7] Richard Wellington (d. 1715) and his descendants owned the copyright of *Hamlet*, *Othello*, and *King Lear* and an interest in *Julius Caesar* and possibly in *Macbeth* and

claims to perpetual copyright in Shakespeare were very doubt-ful, although it was not until 1774, in the case of *Donaldson* v. *Becket*, that the House of Lords decided that the Act of 1709 had ended perpetual copyright in books. Tonson's awareness that the legality of his claims was precarious[8] played a role in his willingness to come to terms with Theobald in October 1731 by outbidding the rival booksellers.[9]

The Copyright Act also provided for the protection of new material for a period of fourteen years. Tonson maintained that the emendations and other textual matter of his editors came under this head, and in his letter to Edward Cave, to prevent Johnson from publishing an edition of Shakespeare in 1745, he wrote: 'I doubt not I can shew you such a title as will satisfy you, not only as to the original copy, but likewise to all the emendations to this time.'[10] Tonson attempted to reinforce his claims to perpetual copyright in the original material by claim-ing successively the fourteen-year copyrights in the work of each of his editors: hence Pope's first edition, based on Rowe's (first published in 1709), was planned for publication in 1723,[11] and hence he sent Theobald Pope's second (that is, latest) edition to use as the basis of his own edition.[12] Fourteen years after Theobald's edition (dated 1733, but published in January 1734), Warburton's edition (1747), based on Theobald's, was published. If the need had arisen, Tonson could have argued his case in court in terms of the current legal view of copyright, which founded the right to copy on the labour, judgement, and expense involved in preparing a work for publication.[13]

1 Henry IV (see Dawson, pp. 28–9). Until 1731, the Wellingtons presumably co-operated fully with Tonson in allowing him to publish editions of Shakespeare's plays. According to the title-page, Theobald's edition was printed for A. Bettesworth, C. Hitch, J. Tonson, F. Clay, W. Feales, and R. Wellington.

[8] See Dawson, p. 29.

[9] These rival booksellers may have been the Wellingtons or their agents. See above, p. 123.

[10] Quoted by Dawson, p. 32.

[11] Although the title-page of Pope's edition is dated 1725, corresponding to the actual year of publication owing to Pope's difficulties with his Preface, sig. f4^r, the last leaf of the preliminaries (following the list of subscribers), prints a second title and is pre-dated 1723 to coincide with the dates of the title-pages of vols. ii–vi. Pope's agreement with Tonson (Folger MS S.a.161) is dated 22 May 1721, and Pope committed himself to completing his duties 'within Two years from the date hereof'.

[12] See above, p. 126.

[13] See William J. Howard, 'Literature in the Law Courts, 1770–1800', in D.I.B.

Apart from Tonson's claims to perpetual copyright in the text, it is conceivable that if Theobald had chosen not to comply with Tonson's wishes, Tonson could have threatened to prevent Theobald's using material related to Pope's editing (for example, the dramatis personae, scene locations, emendations, regulations of prose and verse passages). As it was, Tonson usually succeeded in preventing publication of Shakespeare by his rivals simply by applying—or threatening to apply—to the Court of Chancery for an interim injunction to stay publication until his claims to all the material had been determined. The Court of Chancery was notoriously slow in its proceedings, and Theobald was in no position financially to wish delay in the publication of his edition or to contest Tonson's claims in a suit. His title-page reflects Tonson's manœuvres to maintain control over the copyright of Shakespeare: 'The Works of Shakespeare . . . Collated with the Oldest Copies, and Corrected'—the 'Works' refers specifically to Pope's edition. Consequently, *Pericles* and *The Two Noble Kinsmen*, which were not included in Pope's edition, as well as *Double Falshood*, were omitted from Theobald's.[14] The reference to 'the Oldest Copies' also makes it plain that their textual authority was recognized.[15] Thus it was as a consequence of legal and commercial considerations and in defiance of editorial logic that Theobald's edition was based on Pope's. Theobald's choice of copy must be attributed to circumstances of publishing history and not to ignorance.

Smith (ed.), *Editing Eighteenth-Century Texts* (Toronto: University of Toronto Press, 1968), 78–91, esp. pp. 80–1, 86–7. Tonson was careful to ensure that he owned the copyright to Theobald's editorial work. See below, Appendix B., p. 217.

[14] Theobald refers to *Double Falshood* in *1733*, iv. 188 n., as 'a *posthumous* Play of our Author's which I brought upon the Stage'. See also below, Appendix C. In his correspondence, he refers to *Two Noble Kinsmen* as a play in which Shakespeare assisted (Nichols, ii. 623); in *1733*, iv. 20 n., Theobald refers to *Pericles* as 'a Play, which has been attributed to our Author; and, indeed, some Part of it is certainly of his Writing'. He also notes the attribution of *Locrine* to Shakespeare (*1733*, vi. 9 n.) and appears to accept the ascription (*1733*, v. 350 n.). Tonson published in separate editions with ascriptions to Shakespeare *The Tragedy of Locrine* (1734), *The London Prodigal* (1734), *The History of Sir John Oldcastle* (1734), *Pericles* (1734), *The Puritan: Or, the Widow of Watling-Street* (1734), and *A Yorkshire Tragedy* (1735) the plays, without ascriptions on their title-pages, had appeared in a ninth volume published with Pope's 2nd edn. (1728).

[15] It will be apparent from the following discussion that *the Oldest Copies* refers to Theobald's collection of quartos and the first folio.

In addition to questions surrounding his use of Pope's edition
as the basis of his own, Theobald's understanding of the textual
relationships of the different editions has been doubted because
he lists in his table of editions the second folio (1632) as an
edition of authority and the third folio (1664) as being of middle
authority. His statement in *Shakespeare Restored* that successive
editions of the plays multiplied errors because the press was set
to work from *printed* precedents[16] has been overlooked, and
Johnson has been given credit for being the first to recognize the
absolute authority of the first folio over its successors. Actually,
Johnson is partly responsible for the assumption that Theobald
did not grasp the relationship of the folios. In his Preface to
Shakespeare he remarks of Theobald: 'In his enumeration of
editions, he mentions the two first folios as of high, and the
third folio as of middle authority; but the truth is, that the first
is equivalent to all others, and that the rest only deviate from it
by the printer's negligence.'[17] The latter part of this statement
is not accurate; the second folio in particular was subjected to a
great deal of attention by an 'editor' who, without reference to
any manuscript authority, made a large number of alterations
in the texts of the plays.[18] Theobald's collation of the folios was
such that he was aware of later editorial interference. He consistently assumes, however, that no reference was made to
manuscripts by those in charge of printing the later folios. For
example, in *Troilus and Cressida* he comments on the first folio
reading '*Time*, orce *and Death*' (IV. ii. 101) that

When the Second Impression came to be publish'd, the Editors, I
presume, were at a Loss, and so sunk the Word upon us which they
could not make out. There is no Doubt, but the Poet wrote;

Time, Force, *and Death*,

i.e. The Compulsion of Fate; That, which the Latines call'd *Sæva
Necessitas*.[19]

On the other hand, Theobald knew that the seventeenth-
century editors were capable of engaging in conjectural emenda-

---

[16] See above, p. 70.

[17] *1765*, vol. i, sig. D1ᵛ [Yale, vii. 96].

[18] See Matthew W. Black and Matthias A. Shaaber, *Shakespeare's Seventeenth-Century
Editors, 1632–1685* (New York: Modern Language Association of America, 1937);
Greg, *Editorial Problem*, p. 155 n. 2.

[19] *1733*, vii. 82 n.

tion. Thus, when emending Pope's reading of *2 Henry VI* (IV. ix. 33), 'Is straitway *claim'd* and boarded with a pirate', to *calm'd*, he observes: 'The Oldest *folio* Edition led me to this Emendation, where we find it—*Is strait way* calme:—and the 3d *Fol.* Impression, as I have observ'd since, anticipates my Correction.'[20] These examples are representative of Theobald's *use* of post-1623 texts in his edition; his classification in his 'Table' reflects primarily his sense of their importance to him when he was engaged in forming his collection. It must be remembered that he was working before there were great public libraries in London, and that, for example, he had difficulty in acquiring a first folio. To a lesser degree, his classification also reflects his sense of the ability of the 'editors' of these texts to engage in successful conjectural emendation.

Theobald's habit of collating the texts that he acquired revealed to him that the texts of certain plays in the first folio were based on previously published quartos. When emending *Richard III* (V. iii. 147), '*Let us be* laid *within thy Bosom*, Richard', he comments:

This is a poor feeble Reading, which has obtain'd by Corruption, ever since the first Edition put out by the Players: and, indeed, up as high as the *Quarto* in 1602. But I have restor'd from the elder *Quarto*, publish'd in 1597, which Mr. *Pope* does not pretend to have seen;

Let us be Lead *within thy Bosom*, Richard,

This corresponds with what is said in the Line immediately following,

And weigh *thee* down *to Ruin, Shame, and Death!*

And likewise with what the Generality of the Ghosts say threateningly to *Richard*;

Let me sit heavy *on thy Soul to morrow*![21]

If the change from *lead* to *laid* is the result of simple compositorial error (as Theobald says, the reading 'has obtain'd by Corruption'), other changes, he supposed, were the result of the editors of the first folio being unfamiliar with Shakespeare's language as found in a quarto. In *Othello* (IV. ii. 188–90), when confronted with '*You have told me, she hath receiv'd them, and return'd me Expectations and Comforts of sudden Respect and* Acquaintance', he argues: 'This was, first, the Reading of the Player-Editors,

---

[20] *1733*, iv. 283 n. The reading is accepted.   [21] Ibid. 503 n.

who, I presume, did not understand the Reading of the old
Quarto [*acquintance*], which I take to have been the Poet's Word,
Acquittance; i.e. a Requital, a proper Return of her Favours.'[22]
Further examples of Theobald's working assumption that
certain plays in the first folio were set up from quartos will be
found in the discussion of his principles of emendation. It
should be remarked, however, that hitherto Johnson has been
incorrectly supposed to have been the first to detect the use of
quarto copy in 1623.[23]

Because circumstances dictated that Theobald base his *Shake-*
speare on Pope's edition, he was forced to consider the status of
passages in the quartos and folios omitted or degraded by
Pope. After collating the quarto and folio texts with Pope's
edition, Theobald had to determine the authority of the earliest
texts in his possession before he could decide whether or not to
reinstate the passages in question. This requirement led him to
form theories about the nature of the manuscript copy from
which the compositors worked. The general accounts of the
manuscripts underlying the quarto and folio texts given by
Theobald in his Preface and by Johnson in his *Proposals* (1756)
for his edition were greatly influenced by Pope. Pope begins
his summary of the texts and their copy with considerable
optimism: he is inclined to believe that the printing of the
quarto versions of the two parts of *Henry IV* and *A Midsummer*
Night's Dream may have been supervised by Shakespeare himself.[24] However, this happy view soon gives way to despair,
when he is struck by Heminge and Condell's address 'To the
Great Variety of Readers' in the first folio, and as a consequence he shifts his ground and appears to believe that all (as
opposed to 'diuerse') quartos were surreptitiously printed. The
folio texts give him no comfort either, because he believes that
any additional matter found in the folio is due to the players.[25]
It seems that Pope had seen a quarto that may have played
some part in providing copy for the folio, having first served as
a prompt-book after collation with a manuscript—although his

[22] *1733*, vii. 470 n.
[23] See Robert E. Scholes, 'Dr. Johnson and the Bibliographical Criticism of Shakespeare', *Shakespeare Quarterly*, 11 (1960), 169.
[24] *1725*, vol. i, p. xv.
[25] Ibid., p. xvi.

dislike of Shakespeare's prolixity leads him to assume that he has further evidence of actors' interpolations: 'And I have seen one [quarto] in particular (which seems to have belonged to the playhouse, by having the parts divided with lines, and the Actors names in the margin) where several of those very passages were added in a written hand, which are since to be found in the folio.'[26]

In Pope's opinion the impertinence of the players is responsible for all the differences between the quarto and folio texts. This despondent view resulted in part from the allurements of classical allusion: the players, as 'was said of *Procrustes*', were given to 'either lopping, or stretching an Author, to make him just fit for their Stage'.[27] Although the evidence was before him, Pope did not conclude that sometimes the folio derives its text from a quarto. Instead, he remarks that the folio

is said to be printed from the *Original Copies*; I believe they meant those which had lain ever since the Author's days in the play-house, and had from time to time been cut, or added to, arbitrarily. It appears that this edition, as well as the Quarto's, was printed (at least partly) from no better copies than the *Prompter*'s *Book*, or *Piece-meal Parts* written out for the use of the actors: For in some places their very names are thro' carelessness set down instead of the *Personæ Dramatis*: And in others the notes of direction to the *Property-men* for their *Moveables*, and to the *Players* for their *Entries*,* are inserted into the Text, thro' the ignorance of the Transcribers.

*Such as,
—My Queen is murder'd! *Ring the little Bell*—[28]
—His nose grew [sic] as sharp as a pen, and *a table of Greenfield's*, &c.[29]

The idea of piecemeal parts conjures up (and is made to justify) Pope's vision of large-scale confusion, resulting in transposition of scenes, alterations, and interpolations. Reading the bibliographical section of Pope's Preface produces a curious sense of fragmentation: the individual paragraphs seem to ignore the implications of their fellows. Probably the account of the manu-

26 Ibid., p. xvii. Of course, the quarto in question may have been collated with the folio later in the seventeenth century in preparation for use as a prompt-book.
27 Ibid.
28 Malone remarked, *1790*, vol. I. pt. i. p. 93 n.: 'There is no such line in any play of Shakespeare, as that quoted . . . by Mr. Pope.'
29 *1725*, vol. i, pp. xvii–xviii and nn.

script sources of the quartos and folio was intended to excuse the unsatisfactoriness of Pope's own text.

The account of the manuscript copy for the printed plays in Theobald's Preface seems designed to accentuate his success in providing an orderly, readable text. However, he confidently states his belief that 'The Nature of any Distemper once found has generally been the immediate Step to a Cure'.[30] Theobald's collection of pre-1623 quartos included eight first 'good' quartos, three quartos deriving from first 'good' quartos, one 'intermediate' quarto (a reprint), and six 'bad' quartos (excluding his reprints).[31] When describing the derivation of the quartos, he seems to have had in mind only his six 'bad' quartos and Pope's Preface. His assertion in his Preface, that 'We are to consider [Shakespeare] as a Writer, of whom no authentic Manuscript was extant', is not supported by his commentary, where there is evidence he thought certain plays were printed from 'foul papers'. Theobald adds a considerable amount of theatrical history to what may be found in Pope, but he was not aware of Shakespeare's close ties to his company and considers him 'a Writer, whose Pieces were dispersedly perform'd on the several *Stages* then in Being'. But he is essentially correct in his belief that the acting companies wished to prevent publication of their plays: 'As it was the Interest of the *Companies* to keep their Plays unpublish'd, when any one succeeded, there was a Contest betwixt the Curiosity of the Town, who demanded to see it in Print, and the Policy of the *Stagers*, who wish'd to secrete it within their own Walls.' This policy of the companies leads him to suggest that shorthand was used to provide copy for a number of the quartos published in Shakespeare's lifetime:

Hence, many Pieces were taken down in Short-hand, and imperfectly copied by Ear, from a *Representation*: Others were printed from piece-meal Parts surreptitiously obtain'd from the Theatres, uncorrect, and without the Poet's Knowledge. To some of these Causes we owe the train of Blemishes, that deform those Pieces which stole singly into the World in our Author's Life-time.[32]

Theobald unfortunately does not specify which of the 'many

[30] *1733*, vol. i, p. xxxix.
[31] See below, Appendix E.
[32] *1733*, vol. i, pp. xxxvii–xxxviii.

Pieces', in his view, were 'taken down in Short-hand'.[33] There is no other reference to the use of shorthand, either in the notes to his edition or in his correspondence, although he does occasionally attempt to explain a reading in terms of phonetic spelling. Theobald may well have been acquainted with Thomas Heywood's statement in a late prologue (*c.*1630) to *If you Know not Me you know Nobody: Or, The troubles of Queen Elizabeth* (first printed in a pirated edition, 1605) 'that some by Stenography drew | The plot, put it in print: (scarce one word trew . . .').[34]

Theobald's reference to the use of shorthand in his Preface seems designed primarily to add to the list of possible causes of corruption in the texts of certain quartos. His picture is, however, no happier when he turns to the folio:

There are still other Reasons, which may be suppos'd to have affected the whole Set. When the *Players* took upon them to publish his Works intire, every Theatre was ransack'd to supply the Copy; and *Parts* collected which had gone thro' as many Changes as Performers, either from Mutilations or Additions made to them. Hence we derive many Chasms and Incoherences in the Sense and Matter. Scenes were frequently transposed, and shuffled out of their true Place, to humour the Caprice or suppos'd Convenience of some particular Actor.[35] Hence much Confusion and Impropriety has attended, and embarras'd, the Business and Fable. For there ever have been, and ever will be in Playhouses, a Set of assuming Directors, who know better than the Poet himself the Connexion and Dependance of his Scenes; where Matter is defective, or Superfluities

33 It will be apparent, however, that W. W. Greg is mistaken when he says Theobald 'was, of course, speaking of the quartos in general' (Greg, *Editorial Problem*, p. 57 n. 2).

34 *Pleasant Dialogues and Dramma's* (1637), p. 248. See Greg, Appendix, *Bibliography*, iii. 1202, and Greg No. 215I(a) n. Greg believed Heywood's statement to be 'presumptive evidence' of the use of shorthand. Helen Gardner (ed.) says that 'The shorthand hypothesis received its death-blow with the publication of G. I. Duthie's *Elizabethan Shorthand and the First Quarto of "King Lear"* (1949). He showed conclusively that the available contemporary systems of shorthand were inadequate to report acted plays' (Wilson, *New Bibliography*, p. 88 n.). Other scholars are not so convinced; see, for example, J. K. Walton, *The Quarto Copy for the First Folio* (Dublin: Dublin University Press, 1971), 270 n. 5. Theobald's copy of *If you Know not Me* (pt. 2, 1623) (Greg 224(c)) survives in the Garrick Collection, British Library (C.34.c.48(2)).

35 Nowhere in his edition does Theobald object to the location of a scene in the first folio or early quartos. He strongly objects (*1733*, ii. 328 n.) to Pope's shifting Act IV, Scene ii of *The Taming of the Shrew* to the first scene of Act V and tells his readers: 'I have replac'd the Scenes in that Order, in which I found them in the Old Books.' He also objects to Pope's transposition of a scene in *Cymbeline* (*1733*, vi. 416 n.).

to be retrench'd; Persons, that have the Fountain of *Inspiration* as peremptorily in them, as Kings have That of *Honour*.[36] To these obvious Causes of Corruption it must be added, that our Author has lain under the Disadvantage of having his Errors propagated and multiplied by Time: because, for near a Century, his Works were republish'd from the faulty Copies without the assistance of any intelligent Editor: which has been the Case likewise of many a *Classic* Writer.

If '*Shakespeare*'s Case has in a great Measure resembled That of a corrupt *Classic*', in Theobald's view 'the Method of Cure was likewise to bear a Resemblance'.[37] However, between them, Pope in his Preface and Text and Theobald in his Preface created a tradition of despair in their accounts of Shakespeare's manuscripts and of the copy used for the printing of his plays. Although Johnson scarcely added any detail to Pope's and Theobald's representations of the textual tradition of Shakespeare, he did give these representations their most trenchant expression.[38]

In his Preface Theobald avoided detailed discussion of the evidence afforded by printed texts of the nature of their manuscript copy. He feared giving his enemies further opportunities to ridicule him for scholarship, 'Which nor to taste, nor genius has pretence, | And if 'tis learning, is not common sense'.[39] His views on the derivations of some quarto and folio texts appear in his notes incidentally, when he gives his reasons for reinstating passages degraded or omitted by Pope, or in the course of justifying an emendation. In these instances it may be said of him, as W. W. Greg has said of the exponents of the New Bibliography, that he attempts to bring criticism 'down from the fascinating but too often barren heights of aesthetic and philosophic speculation to the concrete familiarities of the theatre, the scrivener's shop, and the printing house'.[40] This kind of approach has been seen in his discussion of 'a Table of

[36] For a modern account of such interference, see Hardin Craig, 'Textual Degeneration of Elizabethan and Stuart Plays: An Examination of Plays in Manuscript', *The Rice Institute Pamphlet*, 46(4) (1960), 71–84. See also General Introduction, *Textual Companion*, pp. 15–23 and nn.

[37] *1733*, vol. i, pp. xxxviii–xxxix.

[38] See Johnson's *Proposals for Printing . . . the Dramatick Works of William Shakespeare* (1756), Yale, vii. 52.

[39] David Mallet, *Of Verbal Criticism: An Epistle to Mr. Pope* (1733), ll. 13–14.

[40] Greg, *Editorial Problem*, p. 3.

greene fields' (*Henry V*, II. iii. 16–17) in *Shakespeare Restored* (1726), where he gives an extensive summary of his reasoning. After publication of *The Dunciad Variorum* (1729), he was more circumspect in his discussion of such matters because he wished to avoid further ridicule, and in his edition he was also restricted by the space available for his footnotes. Although in his Preface he repeats and expands Pope's despairing account of the textual history of the plays, in his notes he frequently implies that compositors worked from manuscripts that were in the main reliable witnesses of Shakespeare's plays.

For example, Pope conjectured in his Preface (1725) that 'only some characters, single scenes, or perhaps a few particular passages' of *Love's Labour's Lost* were by Shakespeare,[41] and in his editing of the text he degraded some 222 lines, omitted others entirely, and signified his general disapprobation of four complete scenes by marking them with triple daggers. Presumably Pope expected that his account of the textual history of the plays in his Preface would justify this treatment. The unrelenting word-play of *Love's Labour's Lost* did not appeal to eighteenth-century sensibilities, and Theobald sympathized with Pope's implicit critical assessment. None the less, he felt obliged to restore from the first folio (the oldest text of the play in his possession) the passages omitted or degraded by Pope:

I have made it a Rule throughout this Edition, to replace all those Passages, which Mr. *Pope* in his Impressions thought fit to *degrade*. As We have no Authority to call them in Question for not being genuine; I confess, as an Editor, I thought I had no Authority to displace them. Tho, I must own freely at the same time, there are some Scenes (particularly, in this Play;) so very mean and contemptible, that One would heartily wish for the Liberty of expunging them. Whether they were really written by our Author, whether he penn'd them in his boyish Age, or whether he purposely comply'd with the prevailing Vice of the Times, when *Puns, Conundrum,* and *quibbling* Conceits were as much in Vogue, as *Grimace* and *Arlequinades* are at this wise Period, I dare not take upon me to determine.[42]

Theobald could, of course, also sympathize with what he considered Shakespeare's compliance with the literary vices of his times, as his allusion to eighteenth-century pantomime

---

[41] See above, p. 62.   [42] *1733*, ii. 109–10 n.

(and, by implication, his own practice) shows. His assessment of the textual authority of the play was hampered by his not possessing the first quarto (1598), to which he knew Pope had had access.[43] However, in his notes on the play he frequently refers to the author's thought and intentions, and it is evident he considers the folio text to be derived from an essentially reliable manuscript.[44] Theobald visited Styan Thirlby in Cambridge early in 1729; something of their conversation can be surmised from Theobald's recognition, after Thirlby, that certain lines in *Love's Labour's Lost* (V. ii. 817–22) represent Shakespeare's first draft of matter that receives its final expression further on in the scene (ll. 837–54). In his edition Theobald places the lines 'between Crochets: Not that they were an Interpolation . . . but as the Author's first Draught, which he afterwards rejected; and executed the same Thought a little lower with much more Spirit and Elegance'.[45] Theobald does not use the now generally accepted term 'foul papers.' in his discussion, but it is clear that he believed the printed text of *Love's Labour's Lost* derived from a manuscript of Shakespeare's that had not reached its final form in a fair copy.

Theobald possessed the 'good' quarto of *Much Ado about Nothing* (Q1, 1600), and in his first note on the play he observes that

Innogen, (the Mother of *Hero*) in the oldest *Quarto* that I have seen of this Play, printed in 1600, is mention'd to enter in two several Scenes [I. ii; II. i]. The succeeding Editions have all continued her Name in the *Dramatis Personæ*.[46] But I have ventur'd to expunge it; there being no mention of her thro' the Play, no one Speech address'd to her, nor one Syllable spoken by her. Neither is there any one

---

[43] The quarto is listed in Pope's 'Table', *1725*, vol. vi, sig. Oooo[r].

[44] The folio text is a reprint of the quarto (which is now believed to have been set up from 'foul papers').

[45] *1733*, ii. 179 n. Theobald adds: 'Mr *Warburton* conjectures, that *Shakespeare* is not to answer for the present absurd Repetition, but his Actor-Editors.' That Theobald agreed with Thirlby is evident from the first part of his note and from his correspondence. See Nichols, ii. 226, 328.

[46] Rowe first compiled a list of characters for *Much Ado*, which was copied by Pope, and which included Innogen, whose name is found, as Theobald observes, in the opening stage directions for Act I, Scene i, and Act II, Scene i. In Theobald's usage, *Dramatis Personae* is not always confined to a list of characters found at the beginning of a play, but may include (as here) opening stage directions which name the characters that are to appear in the following scene, or simply the characters in the play, whether or not they have been brought together in a list.

Passage, from which we have any Reason to determine that *Hero*'s Mother was living. It seems, as if the Poet had in his first Plan design'd such a Character; which, on a Survey of it, he found would be superfluous; and therefore he left it out.[47]

Again, Theobald assumes the quarto text to be derived from an authorial manuscript that had not been finally tidied up (and that the quarto is the copy from which the folios derive).

As a playwright himself, Theobald was familiar with the possible kinds of manuscript associated with the evolution of a play. In addition to contemplating his own 'foul papers' he had, for example, prepared in conjunction with his friend John Stede, the prompter in John Rich's company at Lincoln's Inn Fields, the prompt-books of his *Perfidious Brother* (1715) and of Elkanah Settle's *The Lady's Triumph* (to which he added 'Entertainments'). The texts of these plays and the majority of the prompt-notes are in Theobald's handwriting.[48] The prompt-book and the printed version of *The Perfidious Brother* reflect differences in the treatment of the text: some passages common to both are marked for deletion in the prompt-book, and a passage found in the printed text is added vertically in the margin of the manuscript.[49] Inevitably, Theobald must have learned that as a general rule authors tend to write plays that actors consider too long. Of course, he would have been intimately acquainted with the textual history of his own play. He would have known what served as copy for the printer and what served as copy for the prompt-book, and he could have accounted for the states of the two texts. In addition to his 'Acquaintance with Stage-books',[50] he was familiar with 'literary' versions of dramatic pieces. For instance, by command of Frederick Prince of Wales he had made a fair copy of his *Orestes* (1731) for presentation.[51] It seems very likely that

---

[47] *1733*, i. [403] n.

[48] Bodleian MS Rawl. poet. 136. For a descriptive account, see Edward A. Langhans, 'Three Early Eighteenth-Century Manuscript Promptbooks', *Modern Philology*, 65 (1967), 114–29. Langhans, pp. 114, 117–18, supposes that the texts and most of the prompt-notes are 'probably' in John Stede's hand. A comparison of the manuscripts with other documents known to be in Theobald's hand indicates, however, that Theobald was responsible.

[49] See Langhans, op. cit., p. 117.

[50] See *SR*, quoted above, pp. 77–8.

[51] See Theobald's letter (10 Feb. 1730), Jones, p. 264.

Theobald's own experience would encourage him to speculate on the kinds of copy potentially available to the printers of Shakespeare's plays and would help him to recognize in the texts of the quartos and folio some of the general characteristics of different kinds of manuscripts, despite the veil of print. One thing is certain: in his notes he envisages for *Love's Labour's Lost* and *Much Ado about Nothing* a manuscript authority very much superior to that of the printer's copy he describes in his Preface.

There are other instances where Theobald appears confident that the compositors of quarto texts worked from authoritative manuscripts. In *A Midsummer Night's Dream* (V. i. 44–60) the folio alternates the text between Theseus and Lysander. Theobald follows Q1 (1600) in his edition and assigns the speeches to Theseus with the comment: 'this, I dare say, was the Poet's own Design and Distribution.'[52] When restoring from his quarto (Q2, 1598) a passage in *Richard II* (I. iii. 268–74), he observes that despite the low imagery 'there is no Doubt of the Passage being genuine'; subsequently he refers to 'the genuine old Copies' and to 'the good old *Quarto*'.[53] Of a stage direction in *Titus Andronicus* (IV. iv. 61), '*Enter* Nuntius Æmilius', he remarks: 'Thus the old Books have describ'd this Character: and I believe, I can account for the Formality, from the Ignorance of the Editors. In the Author's Manuscript, I presume, 'twas writ, *Enter* Nuntius; and they observing, that he is immediately call'd *Æmilius*, thought proper to give him his whole Title, and so clapp'd in *Enter* Nuntius Æmilius.'[54] Later in the same play (V. iii. 124), he has occasion to suggest that 'The Manuscript must have been obscure and blindly writ, so that the first Editors could not make out the Word which I have ventur'd to restore.'[55] Theobald's willingness to account for a difficulty in the text in terms of the manuscript's being 'obscure and blindly writ' and his earlier references to 'the Author's Manuscript' suggest that he may again have supposed the compositors worked from 'foul papers'. He does not usually explain textual difficulties in these terms. Rather, he prefers, as in his comment on *Twelfth Night* (V. i. 256), to account for

---

[52] *1733*, i. 136 n.
[53] *1733*, iii. 271 n., 283 n., 330 n.
[54] *1733*, v. 366 n.
[55] Ibid. 382 n.

supposed errors and omissions by suggesting that 'the Copyists, or Men at Press, committed a slight Mistake'.[56]

Theobald possessed the 'good' quarto of *Hamlet* (Q2, 1604–5), and he believed the quarto to be closer to what Shakespeare had originally written than the first folio. Judging by the omissions in his edition, Pope thought the quarto to be contaminated by actors' interpolations, but Theobald argued that the folio was set up from a prompt-book that had shortened the play.[57] In a note on Pope's omissions in Hamlet's speech to Gertrude (III. iv. 53–88), Theobald writes that he has replaced the verses:

They are not, indeed, to be found in the two elder *Folio's*, but they carry the Style, Expression, and Cast of Thought, peculiar to our Author; and that they were not an Interpolation from another Hand needs no better Proof, than that they are in all the oldest *Quarto's*.[58] The first Motive of their being left out, I am perswaded, was to shorten *Hamlet's* Speech, and consult the Ease of the Actor: and the Reason, why they find no Place in the *Folio* Impressions, is, that they were printed from the *Play-house* castrated Copies. But, surely, this can be no Authority for a modern Editor to conspire in mutilating his Author: Such *Omissions*, rather, must betray a Want of *Diligence*, in *Collating*; or a Want of *Justice*, in the *voluntary Stifling*.[59]

---

[56] *1733*, ii. 532 n.; cf. ii. 218 n.; iii. 41 n., 378 n., 451 n.; iv. 225 n., 358 n.; v. 393 n.; vi. 143 n.; vii. 17 n.

[57] The relation of the folio *Hamlet* to the quarto has been a subject of much debate. See G. Blakemore Evans, 'Note on the Text', *Riverside*, p. 1186. J. K. Walton, in *The Quarto Copy for the First Folio of Shakespeare* (Dublin: Dublin University Press, 1971), suggests that the folio text derives from a prompt-book. See also Harold Jenkins (ed.), *Hamlet*, Arden (1982), 13–81. The latest views, that Q2 derives from foul papers and that the folio text derives from a transcript of the prompt-book (which derived from a fair copy by Shakespeare of his foul papers), are found in G. R. Hibbard (ed.), *Hamlet*, Oxford Shakespeare (1987), 67–130, and *Textual Companion*, pp. 396–402.

[58] Cf. Theobald's comment, Nichols, ii. 573: the lines are 'in the oldest quartos, and therefore indisputably genuine'. (The first, 'bad' quarto (1603), which alters and abbreviates the scene, was unknown to Pope and Theobald.)

[59] *1733*, vii. 313 n.; see also vii. 317–18 n. For similar views on the restoration of the full text of *Hamlet*, see Wilson, *MS of 'Hamlet'*, i. 174. Cf. G. R. Hibbard's comments on this passage, General Introduction, *Hamlet*, Oxford Shakespeare (1987), 22–4; Hibbard assumes that the folio text represents Shakespeare's final, revised version of the play. There may still be arguments to be made in favour of restoration of the full text, based on the assumption that readers will want to know all that Shakespeare wrote and that directors will, as usual, make those cuts they believe appropriate. Also, it is possible that the folio cuts (and additions) derive from a period in which Shakespeare's commitment to the play gave way to his commitment to his company and meeting their requirements. In short, Shakespeare's alterations (as a

Theobald supposed that 'The reducing the *Play* to a reasonable Length was the Motive of so many Castrations' in the folio, and his faith in the 1604–5 quarto is very much in advance of his time.[60] Probably he conjectured that the quarto was printed from 'foul papers', since he also speculates that the copy at IV. i. 40 was 'so blind in the Manuscript as not to be guess'd at'.[61] (That Theobald was concerned with quarto copy is evident because the folio omits the entire passage.) Earlier in the play (I. iii. 56–8), he was prepared to appeal to the punctuation of the 'oldest *Quarto*'s' as a confirmation of his understanding of the text.[62]

Probably on the basis of his own experience in the theatre, Theobald believes that the appearance of actors' names in some of the texts is a sign of the prompter's or book-keeper's hand in the copy.[63] More recent theory, which takes into account Shakespeare's intimate relationship with his company, supposes that preservation of actors' names is an indication that 'foul papers' provided copy, and that Shakespeare wrote with particular members of the company in mind.[64] Only the names of actors of minor parts are usually noted, however, and there is a possibility in some cases that names were inserted into 'foul papers' by the book-keeper prior to their transcription for a prompt-book. Such insertions might then appear in texts printed from annotated 'foul papers'. It is also possible that Shakespeare's autograph (even when not completely tidied up) could have been annotated to serve as a prompt-book. Theobald might well have been inclined to make this assumption: he seems to have annotated his own manuscript of *The Perfidious Brother* for use as a prompt-book,[65] and he would have known

man of the theatre of his time) may not have been entirely compatible with his artistic and intellectual interests as an author.

[60] *1733*, vii. 340 n. Cf. Wilson, *MS of 'Hamlet'*, i. 8.

[61] *1733*, vii. 322 n.; cf. *SR*, p. 107.

[62] *1733*, vii. 243 n.

[63] This supposition is shared by E. K. Chambers, *William Shakespeare* (2 vols., Oxford: Clarendon Press, 1930), i. 237: 'But the book-keeper is clearly revealed in several places where the printer has preserved the name of an actor written beside or in substitution for that of the character which he played.'

[64] See Greg, *First Folio*, pp. 114–15.

[65] As Langhans, op. cit., p. 114, points out, some of the notes were probably made during rehearsals and 'The scenic indications were probably entered last; in many cases they were squeezed into the available space on a page.'

from the prompt-book of *The Lady's Triumph* that prompters could use a difficult manuscript.[66] Apart from his own theatrical experience, he might have been inclined to suppose that Shakespeare's autograph sometimes served initially as a prompt-book and then as printer's copy (perhaps after a fresh transcription for a new prompt-book), because such a theory would account for the presence of Shakespeare's false starts and the presence of actors' names in the same printed text. It has been seen that Theobald supposed the text of *Much Ado about Nothing* to derive from 'foul papers'. He also believed that the appearance of the names of the comic actors Kempe and Cowley for Dogberry and Verges in Act IV, Scene ii, is a mark of 'the old Play-house Books'.[67]

Theobald supposes that inconsistency in designation of characters may be attributed to the book-keeper. A stage direction in the good quarto (Q2, 1599) and first folio of *Romeo and Juliet* (V. iii. 22), '*Enter Romeo and Peter*', elicits the comment:

But *Peter* was a Servant of the *Capulets*: besides, he brings the Mattock and Crow to wrench open *Juliet*'s Grave, an Office hardly to be intrusted with a Servant of that Family. We find a little above, at the very Beginning of this Act, *Balthazar* is the Person who brings *Romeo* the News of his Bride's Death: and yet, at the Close of the Play, *Peter* takes upon him to depose that He brought those Tidings. *Utri creditis*, Quirites? —In short, We heard *Balthazar* deliver the Message; and therefore *Peter* is a lying Evidence, suborn'd by the blundering Editors. We must therefore cashier him, and put *Balthazar* on his proper Duty. The Source of this Error seems easy to be accounted for; *Peter*'s Character ending in the 4th Act, 'tis very probable the same Person might play *Balthazar*, and so be quoted on in the prompter's Book as *Peter*.[68]

Theobald's ingenious explanation undoubtedly reflects his own experience of the ways of the theatre. This explanation has been accepted as possible (without reference to Theobald) by W. W. Greg: 'the confusion at V. iii. 22 may have arisen through the book-keeper making a marginal note that the part of Balthazar could be doubled with Peter's. . . .'[69] It should be

---

[66] See ibid. 118, 119: '*The Lady's Triumph* manuscript is a very messy one in several places.' 'The script becomes extremely difficult to follow.'

[67] *1733*, iii. 353 n.

[68] *1733*, vii. 213–14 n.

[69] Greg, *First Folio*, p. 230.

added that Theobald probably thought the prompt-book consisted of Shakespeare's 'foul papers'; later in the scene (V. iii. 108–9) he cashiered lines that anticipate Romeo's conclusion to his final speech,[70] and such anticipations, it has been seen, he associates with 'foul papers'.

Analysis of a printed text for clues about the nature of its manuscript copy is fraught with uncertainty, and discussion of Theobald's thought about such matters is especially difficult because it appears in his notes only incidentally. In the 1720s and 1730s detailed knowledge of technical matters of the theatre was not felt to be consistent with polite learning. Theobald's commentary indicates, however, that he had a much greater faith in the copy for the printed texts than he expresses in his Preface, and, indeed, that he believed some of the plays were probably printed from Shakespeare's autograph. It is evident that he thought much of the abbreviation or omission by the folio of material found in the quartos is owing to 'retrenchment' by the players 'for Brevity's sake',[71] although in the case of *King Lear* he recognizes in his correspondence that such alterations might be 'with the Author's consent'.[72] (The possibility that Shakespeare consented to alterations does not, however, lead Theobald to postulate two versions of *Lear*. He apparently assumes that authorial co-operation in making alterations would be obtained only under duress.) He does not directly discuss the differences between 'good' and 'bad' quartos of the same play, but his account in his Preface of shorthand transcriptions of theatrical performances suggests the lines an account of the 'bad' quartos might have taken.

Probably Theobald's theory of shorthand transcriptions as a source of copy explains in part his rejection of Pope's use of 'bad' quartos as authorities for omitting material in his edition (1725). Of Pope's abbreviation of *Romeo and Juliet* (IV. v. 65–83) he remarks: 'This Speech, tho' it contains good Christian Doctrine, tho' it is perfectly in Character for the Friar, and not the

---

[70] *1733*, vii. 216 n.

[71] *1733*, v. 125 n., 183 n., 202 n., 213 n.; vii. 313 n., 317–18 n., 340 n.

[72] Nichols, ii. 385. For a summary of recent views of Shakespeare as a reviser of *King Lear* and *Othello*, see E. A. J. Honigmann, 'Shakespeare's Revised Plays: *King Lear* and *Othello*', *The Library*, 4 (1982), 142–73, and Gary Taylor and Michael Warren (eds.), *The Division of the Kingdoms: Shakespeare's Two Versions of 'King Lear'* (Oxford: Clarendon Press, 1983).

most despicable for its Poetry, Mr. *Pope* has curtail'd to little or nothing, because it has not the Sanction of the first old Copy' (the 'bad' quarto, Q1 (1597)). Theobald recognized that Pope appealed to the 'authority' of the quartos only when it suited his critical inclination to omit passages. Hence he points out that 'By the same Rule, had he pursued it throughout, we might have lost some of the finest additional Strokes [found in the folio] in the two Parts of K. *Henry IV*'.[73] Theobald is being disingenuous here, for he certainly must have believed that the quartos of the two parts of *Henry IV* have a very different status from that of the first quarto of *Romeo and Juliet*. However, he probably remembered that Pope himself had suggested that the quartos of the two parts of *Henry IV* might have been printed under Shakespeare's supervision,[74] and therefore, in Pope's own terms, any folio additions in these plays especially should be rejected as interpolations.

Theobald realized that Pope's editorial principles consisted of allowing his critical taste to determine what should be included in the plays. Theobald did not, however, respond to Pope's editing by totally rejecting critical taste as a test of authenticity. Instead, he prefers to suggest that Shakespeare's style, as he senses it, is in some passages at variance with his own and Pope's good taste. At the same time, his recognition that he and Pope frequently have differing views on the characteristics of Shakespeare's style indicates how inherently unsatisfactory it is to make editorial decisions solely on the basis of taste. His solution to the problem was to present almost everything found in the good quartos and folio, first, because he believed these texts to have been printed from essentially reliable manuscripts, and, second, because he wished to avoid the arbitrariness of Pope's editing. For example, in *Cymbeline* (a play found only in the folio) Pope degraded the masque (V. iv. 30–122) and marked the passage with his triple daggers as '*plainly foisted in afterwards for meer show, and apparently not of* Shakespear.'[75] Theobald restores the masque and comments that he 'could be as well content' as Pope to omit it,

---

[73] *1733*, vii. 206 n.

[74] See above, p. 138.

[75] *1725*, vi. 219. He also degraded the dialogue between Posthumus and the gaoler (ll. 123–206).

But as 'tis found in the earliest *Folio* Edition, tho' it should have been an Interpolation, and not of SHAKESPEARE's Writing, I did not think, I had any Authority to discard it. I own, to Me, what *Jupiter* says to the *Phantoms* seems to carry the Stamp of our Author: if the other Parts of the *Masque* appear inferior, I heartily wish, this were the only place where we have Reason to complain of Inequalities, either in Style, or the Matter.[76]

This is reasonable editorial conservatism.

Although Theobald had a greater respect for the manuscript copy of Shakespeare's plays than the evidence of his Preface suggests, this respect did not extend to the printers of that copy. Modern editors, having based their texts on the edition that is closest to Shakespeare's manuscript, are extremely unwilling to depart from the readings of their copy-text. This unwillingness, especially in the case of plays derived from the first folio, has been due to a belief that there was fairly careful proof-reading.[77] Reluctance to engage in emendation was also strengthened by publication of the *New English Dictionary* (1928; re-issued in 1933 as the *Oxford English Dictionary*), which often suggests explanations of difficult passages in the earliest texts of the plays. The modern editor is predisposed to explain his copy rather than to alter it. However, the assumption that the folio text was carefully checked against the printer's copy (either a manuscript, or a quarto, or a quarto corrected by reference to a manuscript) has finally been proved to be false.

When it began to be apparent in the early 1950s that the folio was not carefully proof-read, textual theorists were again inclined to emphasize the need for emendation on the basis of bibliographical evidence. In 'Variant Readings in the First Folio of Shakespeare' Charlton Hinman asked, 'If the First Folio is replete with unauthoritative improvements . . . and full also (at least in some plays) of obvious errors that were *not* corrected, does it not follow that editors are justified in somewhat more freedom of emendation than they might otherwise consider their prerogative?' Although Hinman immediately

---

[76] *1733*, vi. 449 n.

[77] See Edwin Eliott Willoughby, *The Printing of the First Folio of Shakespeare*, Supplement to the Bibliographical Society's Transactions, No. 8 (Oxford: Oxford University Press, 1932), pp. 54–70.

acknowledges that editorial freedom can easily be abused, he none the less asserts that 'the evidence provided by the variants in the First Folio may prove considerably to extend the limits within which emendation is a legitimate part of editorial endeavor—and, indeed, one of its primary responsibilities'.[78] In *The Printing and Proof-Reading of the First Folio of Shakespeare* Hinman proved that 'there are only about ten variant readings in the entire Folio which even *suggest* correction of the text by reference to copy; there are but two about which we can be certain'.[79]

The implications of Hinman's early findings were accepted by Alice Walker: 'The assumption that proof-correction was much more scrupulous than it is now known to have been has led to the disastrous state of affairs when greater confidence is placed in the accuracy of compositors than in the common sense and artistic sense of our greatest poet.'[80] It was recognized that, in addition to misreadings of words and phrases in their copy, compositors were prone to errors of omission, interpolation of words, repetition, anticipation, and transposition. Alice Walker estimated that the first folio text of *Antony and Cleopatra* (the sole authority for the play) contains well over 200 errors, although only about 80 such errors are recognized and emended.[81]

A further consequence of this understanding of the nature and accuracy of Shakespeare's early texts has been a reaffirmation of the need for literary expertise in the editor as a means of choosing correctly between conservative reproduction of the copy and emendation. There should also be a reassessment of the work of the best eighteenth-century editors of Shakespeare, and Alice Walker was among the first to advocate a renewed respect for their treatment of the plays:

I do not myself believe that the critical faculty of the best editors of the past was as unprincipled as it is sometimes made out to be. We now

[78] *Shakespeare Quarterly*, 4 (1953), 287. See also Charlton Hinman, 'Shakespearian Textual Studies', in Clifford Leech and J. M. R. Margeson (eds.), *Shakespeare 1971: Proceedings of the World Shakespeare Congress, Vancouver, August 1971* (Toronto: University of Toronto Press, 1972), 37–49, esp. 47–9.

[79] (2 vols., Oxford: Clarendon Press, 1963), i. 331.

[80] 'Principles of Annotation: Some Suggestions for Editors of Shakespeare', *Studies in Bibliography*, 9 (1957), 103.

[81] Ibid. 96.

know that Shakespeare's formative years at the Stratford Grammar
School were spent in the analysis and imitation of Latin poets and
orators, with text-books like the *Epitome* of Susenbrotus to explain the
poet's tools; and we know that in his early work he consciously
applied the lessons he had learnt and that, with maturity, his style
grew bolder and technique second nature. Shakespeare's early editors
had the great advantage of working in much the same tradition and
time may show that where editors between Pope and Johnson shared
common interests with Shakespeare—as in their appreciation of an
antithesis or oxymoron—they contributed more to the solution of
textual problems than is now thought.[82]

Of course, even the most conservative modern editors of
Shakespeare are forced to admit emendations into their texts.
W. W. Greg's statement that 'no emendation can or ought to
be considered *in vacuo*, but that criticism must always proceed
in relation to what we know, or what we surmise, respecting
the history of the text'[83] still provides the basic criterion for
assessing an editor's understanding of this part of his duties. A
number of Theobald's proposed emendations have not received
the consideration they deserve, because the principles underlying his approach to the text have not been recognized. Hence
John Dover Wilson writes: 'But emendation in our day means
something very different from the brilliant shots of a Theobald.'[84]
It is, however, a mistake to assume that Theobald's emendations (whether they have been accepted or rejected) are due
simply to chance. He himself indicates in his Preface to *Shakespeare* an awareness that 'the Art of Criticism' is by some
'esteem'd only an arbitrary capricious Tyranny exercis'd on
Books'. He therefore thought it proper 'to subjoin a Word or
two about those Rules' by which he proceeded and regulated
himself in his edition. It is important to note that he asserts: 'By
This, I flatter myself, it will appear, my Emendations are so far
from being arbitrary or capricious, that They are establish'd
with a very high Degree of moral Certainty.'[85]

Theobald's first rule is to collate: 'I have thought it my

---

[82] 'Principles of Annotation', 100–1.

[83] 'Principles of Emendation in Shakespeare', Annual Shakespeare Lecture of the
British Academy (1928), repr. in J. W. MacKail (ed.), *Aspects of Shakespeare* (Oxford:
Clarendon Press, 1933), 133.

[84] Introduction, Wilson, *MS of 'Hamlet'*, i. 10.

[85] *1733*, vol. i, p. xlii.

Duty, in the first place, by a diligent and laborious Collation to take in the Assistance of all the older Copies.'[86] This included collation of quarto copies of the same edition, if he possessed them, for he realized that corrections were sometimes made in the course of printing.[87] But the purpose of collation was not confined to retrieval of passages omitted elsewhere or to making simple choices among different readings. Not only did he take into account such errors of copyists and compositors as interpolation, eye-skip, transposition, and association,[88] he considered in his collation the relationships of the quartos and folio, and formed theories for some of the plays about the nature of the copy for the quarto and folio texts. These considerations, in addition to his knowledge of secretary script,[89] use of the *ductus litterarum*, and citation of parallel passages, were ready to be brought to bear on his emendations.

An example of the kind of neglected emendation Alice Walker has in mind occurs in *Henry VIII* (III. i. 158). The first folio reads:

> We are to Cure such sorrowes, not to sowe 'em.

In his edition, Theobald comments:

There is no *Antithesis* in these Terms, nor any Consonance of the *Metaphors*: both which my Emendation restores.

> *We are to* ear *such Sorrows, not to* sowe *'em.*

i.e. to weed them up, harrow them out. So our Poet uses this Word in his *Anth.* and *Cleop.* [I. ii. 111]

> *O then we bring forth* Weeds,
> *When our quick Winds lie still; and our Ills, told us,*
> *Is as our* earing.

---

[86] Ibid.

[87] See Theobald's note (*1733*, iii. 499–500) on *2 Henry IV* (IV. i. 93): 'In one of my Old *Quarto*'s of 1600 (for I have Two of the self same Edition; one of which, 'tis evident, was corrected in some Passages during the working off the whole Impression;) after the Line above quoted I found this Verse. . . . I have thought the Verse worth preserving.' As it happens, Theobald mistakenly assumes that the quarto with the additional lines is the corrected version. For an analysis of corrected and uncorrected states, see Greg, *First Folio*, pp. 266 ff.

[88] For examples, see *1733*, i. 6–7 n., 276 n., 299 n., 312 n.; ii. 218 n., 532 n.; iii. 7 n., 41 n., 61 n., 77 n., 81 n., 116 n., 146 n., 330 n., 378 n.; iv. 21 n., 38 n., 73 n., 225 n., 358 n.; v, [4] n.; vii. 17 n., 134 n.

[89] See below, Appendix A.

i.e. as, rooting them up. This Word with us may be deriv'd not only from *arare* to *plow*; but the old *Saxon* Word, *Ear*, which signified a *Harrow*.[90]

Of course, knowledge provided by the *OED* has shown that many of the emendations of the eighteenth-century editors were unnecessary. For example, on *Macbeth* (III. ii. 13–14),

> *We have* scorch'd *the Snake, not kill'd it,*
> *She'll close, and be herself,*

observing that *scorch'd* is to be found in all the editions, Theobald maintains none the less that the reading is corrupt:

What has a Snake, *closing* again, to do with its being *scorch'd*? Scorching would never either *separate*, or *dilate*, its Parts; but rather make them instantly *contract* and *shrivel*. SHAKESPEARE, I am very well perswaded, had this Notion in his head; that if you cut a Serpent or Worm asunder, in several Pieces, there is such an unctuous Quality in their Blood, that the dismember'd Parts, being only placed near enough to touch one another, will cement and become as whole as before the Injury receiv'd. The Application of this Thought is to *Duncan*, the murther'd King, and his surviving Sons. *Macbeth* considers them so much as Members of the Father, that tho' he has cut off the Old Man, he would say, he has not entirely kill'd him, but he'll revive again in the Lives of his Sons. Can we doubt therefore but that the Poet wrote, as I have restor'd to the Text,

> *We have* scotch'd *the Snake, not kill'd it*?

To *scotch*, however the Generality of our Dictionaries happen to omit the Word, signifies, to *notch*, *slash*, *hack*, *cut*, with Twigs, Swords, &c. and so our Poet more than once has used it in his Works.[91]

He ends his discussion with parallels from *Coriolanus* (IV. v. 186) and *Antony and Cleopatra* (IV. vii. 10).

The folio is the sole authority for *Macbeth*, and Theobald recognized that the text derives from a prompt-book.[92] Moreover, he refers elsewhere in the play to 'the Ignorance of the Copyists' in substituting a familiar word for one more abstruse.[93] It

---

[90] *1733*, v. 53–4 n.

[91] Ibid. 425–6 n.

[92] Ibid. 415 n.: Theobald argues that '*Ring the Bell*' (II. iii. 80) is 'a Marginal Direction in the *Prompter*'s Book for him to order the Bell to be rung, the Minute that *Macduff* ceases speaking'. He observes that if this stage direction were a part of the text, Lady Macbeth's speech would begin with 'a broken Line'.

[93] Ibid. 392–3 n.: Theobald shows that the folio reading, 'the *weyward* Sisters' (I. iii.

seems that he believed there was at least one transcription of Shakespeare's manuscript to increase the chances of error, in addition to possible mistakes by the compositor—a set of circumstances which, in combination with his parallel readings, makes his emendation seem very probable. Indeed, Peter Alexander (1951) accepts Theobald's reading, but Dover Wilson's note on the passage in the New Shakespeare *Macbeth* is to the point: '[Theobald's] emendation "scotched" was accepted by all until 1914, when *O.E.D.* showed that "scorch" = "slash with a knife" in 16th and 17th c.' Because of such examples as this, there is now an extreme reluctance on the part of those actually engaged in editing texts to depart from their copy, even though they are aware that chance and the common course of nature will not bring it to pass that the readings of, say, a good quarto are right wherever they are possible. In short, if the eighteenth-century editors emended the texts unnecessarily, a present danger is that their successors may abdicate their editorial responsibilities and, abetted or intimidated by the *OED*, 'produce, not editions of their authors' works at all, but only editions of particular authorities for those works'.[94]

A relatively simple example of Theobald's thought about a quarto and folio text in his attempts to recover what Shakespeare had actually written occurs in Theobald's justification of an emendation in *Much Ado about Nothing* (IV. ii. 36). His theories about the copy for the quarto (Q1, 1600) have been seen above in his first note on the play, where he observes that the ghost-character Innogen is found in the opening stage directions for Act I, Scene i, and Act II, Scene ii, of the editions succeeding Q1. His proposed emendation is consistent with his initial observations. Having objected to Pope's 'Yea, marry, that's the *easiest* Way, let the Watch come forth' as a sophisticated reading, Theobald adds that the 1600 quarto and the first

32) should be printed 'the weïrd sisters' and gives parallels in Chaucer, *Troilus and Criseyde*, iii. 618, Heylin's *Cosmography*, and Holinshed's *Chronicles*.

[94] W. W. Greg, 'The Rationale of Copy-Text', *Studies in Bibliography*, 3 (1951), repr. in *Collected Papers*, ed. J. C. Maxwell (Oxford: Clarendon Press, 1966), 384. Greg is concerned with choices between readings of extrinsic authority, but his remarks also constitute an attack on mechanical reproduction of the copy. Cf. Fredson Bowers, *Textual and Literary Criticism* (1959; repr. Cambridge: Cambridge University Press, 1966), 113–16.

and second folios all read: '*Yea, marry, that's the* eftest *way*, etc.'
In his view,

> A Letter happen'd to slip out at Press in the first Edition; and 'twas
> too hard a Task for the subsequent Editors to put it in, or guess at the
> Word under this accidental Depravation. There is no Doubt, but the
> Author wrote, as I have restor'd the Text;
>
> > *Yea, marry, that's the* deftest *way*, &c.
>
> i.e. the *readiest*, most *commodious* Way. The Word is pure *Saxon*.[95]

Theobald is right in thinking that the folio text was set up from
the good quarto of 1600 (the 'first Edition' referred to in his
note), although there is no evidence that he supposed some
stage directions might have been added to the quarto by reference to a prompt-book. But he does not assume that agreement
in the reading between the folio and the quarto guarantees the
text,[96] since the folio is not an independent witness. In support
of Theobald's belief that a *d* had dropped out, it is worth noting
that in the Capell copy of Q1 at Trinity College, Cambridge,
the spaces on either side of the comma after *mary* are unusually
large, which may indicate adjustment of a loose line.[97] Moreover, although the compositor who set the first quarto of *Much
Ado* was remarkably careless, there was very little proof-reading
of the play, and those corrections that did occur were made
without reference to copy.[98] In addition, in the first folio 'Some
of the reprints (e.g. *Much Ado*) suggest much more naive workmanship than is characteristic of the Folio as a whole'.[99]
Modern editors print *eftest*, perhaps for the same reason given
by H. H. Furness in his note in the New Variorum Edition of

[95] *1733*, i. 464 n. Cf. *1733*, i. 427 n.: 'Thus the whole Stream of the Editions from
the first *Quarto* downwards.'

[96] As he would assume, if R. B. McKerrow's suggestion, that the 18th-century
editors treated the printed texts like classical manuscripts, were correct. See above,
p. 70.

[97] The overwhelming preference of the compositor, now identified as Compositor A,
was for setting commas *without* spaces: approximately 60% of the commas on the page
in question are so printed, 20% have one space, 12% have two (like the comma after
'mary'), while the remaining 8% occur at the ends of lines.

[98] See Charlton Hinman's Introduction to *Much Ado about Nothing*, Shakespeare
Quarto Facsimiles, 15 (Oxford: Clarendon Press, 1971), pp. viii, ix, xvii, and Alan E.
Craven, 'Simmes' Compositor A and Five Shakespeare Quartos', *Studies in Biblio-
graphy*, 26 (1973), 37–60.

[99] Alice Walker, *Textual Problems of the First Folio* (Cambridge: Cambridge
University Press, 1953), 8.

the play (1889): 'To attempt to correct Dogberry is merely to range oneself by his side.' Elsewhere Theobald had said: 'I allow, the Poet meant nonsense; but not nonsense without humour.'[100] His point should be better taken, especially since the *OED*'s citation of *eftest* in this passage as a *hapax legomenon* is suspicious in itself and, in effect, leaves the reader with the doubtful supposition that Shakespeare created a nonce word for Dogberry with no appreciable comic consequences.[101]

In his Preface, as in his correspondence, Theobald faithfully repeats that he does not wish to improve Shakespeare: 'Wherever the Author's Sense is clear and discoverable, (tho', perchance, low and trivial;) I have not by any Innovation tamper'd with his Text; out of an Ostentation of endeavouring to make him speak better than the old Copies have done.'[102] This statement accurately reflects his intentions, but there are instances where, through ignorance or religious or philosophical scruples, he falls short of his editorial principles. But as a rule his emendations are the result of a conscientious endeavour to recover an authorial reading. Of course, in his Preface Theobald is describing what he has done. Once again there is occasion to note that he prefers the term 'literal criticism'—rather than verbal criticism—because of his awareness that textual corruption may arise from compositorial or scribal misreadings of letters.[103] His legal training ensured that he would have no trouble in deciphering secretary script, or in recognizing possible misreadings of secretary script. In this he had a major advantage over Johnson. Like Theobald, Johnson, in his Preface (but not in his *Miscellaneous Observations on Macbeth*, where he follows his literary critical predilections), is cautious in his approach to emendation: 'Conjecture, though it be sometimes unavoidable, I have not wantonly nor licentiously indulged. It has been my settled principle, that the reading of

---

[100] Nichols, ii. 302 (4 Dec. 1729) to Warburton; cf. *1733*, iii. 541 n.: Pistol's 'false *Italian* [*2 Henry IV* (v. v. 96)] is not from the Editors, but purposely from the Author'.

[101] Cf. Blakemore Evans, *Riverside*, p. 355 n.; Evans retains *eftest* and supplies the following note: '*eftest*. It is clear that he means something like "easiest" or "quickest," but not what word he may be mangling.' Peter Alexander (1951) prints *eftest*, but does not include the word in his Glossary. *Complete Works* prints 'eftest', defined as 'easiest' in the Glossary.

[102] *1733*, vol. i, p. xliii.

[103] Ibid. lii.

the ancient books is probably true, and therefore is not to be disturbed for the sake of elegance, perspicuity, or mere improvement of the sense.' Although he is briefer in his account, Johnson does not significantly improve on Theobald's principles, and, indeed, it often seems that Johnson is paraphrasing his predecessor.[104] The following passage is, however, as close as he comes to Theobald's concern for the manuscript behind the veil of print:

For though much credit is not due to the fidelity, nor any to the judgment of the first publishers, yet they who had the copy before their eyes were more likely to read it right, than we who read it only by imagination. But it is evident that they have often made strange mistakes by ignorance or negligence, and that therefore something may be properly attempted by criticism, keeping the middle way between presumption and timidity.[105]

Johnson could only read the compositor's copy 'by imagination'. The same, of course, is true of Theobald, but his imagination (and probably his pen, on occasion) could present him with probable 'traces of the letters' in the analysis of possible misreadings. In *Timon of Athens* (IV. iii. 12), for example, Theobald and Warburton were confronted with '*It is the Pasture lards the* Beggar's *Sides*' in Pope's edition. In what is perhaps his best note Warburton suggested:

This, as the Editors have order'd it, is an idle Repetition at the best; supposing it did, indeed, contain the same Sentiment as the foregoing Lines. But *Shakespeare* meant a quite different Thing: and having, like a sensible Writer, made a smart Observation, he illustrates it by a Similitude thus:

---

[104] See Arthur Sherbo, Appendix C, 'The Preface', *Samuel Johnson, Editor of Shakespeare* (Illinois Studies in Language and Literature, xlii) (Urbana: University of Illinois Press, 1956), 125–8. Sherbo notices some 18 parallel passages, but the list is incomplete. The latter part of Johnson's Preface 'is given over to a statement of what Johnson did or tried to do in the edition. Even here certain similarities to Theobald's Preface are observable' (p. 128).

[105] *1765*, vol. i, sigs. D8^r-D8^v [Yale, vii. 106]. Robert E. Scholes, in 'Dr. Johnson and the Bibliographical Criticism of Shakespeare', *Shakespeare Quarterly*, 11 (1960), 167, supposes Johnson 'was the first editor to give the peculiarities of Elizabethan handwriting any specific attention'. Johnson's interest was very limited, his concern being mainly with confusions arising from such abbreviations as y^t, y^m. In one instance, he notes the difficulty of *lonely* and *lovely*, 'which in the old angular writing can not be distinguished'. See *1765*, i. 41 n., 294 n.; ii. 107 n., 344 n.; vii. 316 n.; viii. 289 n. (cited by Scholes).

> *It is the Pasture lards the* Weather's *Sides,*
> *The Want that makes him lean.*[106]

And the Similitude is extremely beautiful, as conveying this Satirical Reflection; there is no more Difference between Man and Man in the Esteem of superficial or corrupt Judgments, than between a fat Sheep and a lean one.[107]

Theobald praises Warburton's emendation with characteristic generosity, but he also justifies it both by reference to possible misreading of secretary script and by a parallel reading:

I cannot better praise the Sagacity of my Friend's Emendation, than by producing the Reading of the first *folio* Edition, (which, I know, he had not seen,) where we find it thus exhibited;

> *It is the Pasture lards the* Brother's *Sides,* &c.

Every knowing Reader will agree, that this Corruption might much more naturally be deriv'd from Weather's *[i.e.* wether's*], than from* Beggar's*, as far as the Traces of the Letters are concern'd; especially, in the old Secretary Handwriting, the universal Character in our Author's Time.*[108] I will only add, that our Poet, in his *As you like it* [III. ii. 27], makes a Clown say the very same Thing in a more ludicrous manner.

> *That the Property of Rain is to wet, and Fire to burn; that* good
> Pasture *makes* fat Sheep; &c.[109]

Warburton omitted Theobald's justification of the emendation in his edition (1747), as did Johnson in 1765. Presumably they did not see the importance of Theobald's appeal to the 'knowing Reader' and of the parallel reading. Furthermore, after printing Warburton's note without Theobald's justification, Johnson rejects Warburton's reading and adopts the folio version in his text. He observes:

Dr. *Warburton* found the passage already changed thus,

> *It is the* Pasture *lards the* Beggar's *sides,*
> *The want that makes him* lean.

---

[106] The first folio is the sole authority for the play and reads:

> It is the Pastour Lards, the Brothers sides,
> The want that makes him leaue. . . .

The *u* in *leaue* is probably a turned *n*.

[107] *1733*, v. 272 n.

[108] My italics.

[109] *1733*, v. 272–3 n.

And upon this reading, of no authority, raised another equally uncertain.

Alterations are never to be made without necessity. Let us see what sense the genuine reading will afford. Poverty, says the Poet, *bears contempt hereditary*, and *wealth native honour*. To illustrate this position, having already mentioned the case of a poor and rich brother, he remarks, that this preference is given to wealth by those whom it least becomes; *it is the* Pastour *that greases* or flatters *the rich* brother, and will grease him on till *want makes him leave*. The Poet then goes on to ask, *Who dares to say, this man*, this Pastour, *is a flatterer*; the crime is universal; through all the world *the learned pate*, with allusion to the Pastour, *ducks to the golden fool*. If it be objected, as it may justly be, that the mention of Pastour is unsuitable, we must remember the mention of *grace* and *cherubims* in this play, and many such anachronisms in many others.

I would therefore read thus:

> *It is the Pastour lards the brother's sides,*
> *'Tis want that makes him leave.*

The obscurity is still great. Perhaps a line is lost. I have at least given the original reading.[110]

Johnson's reading and interpretation have not been accepted by modern editors. His note reflects his declaration in his Preface that 'my first labour is, always to turn the old text on every side, and try if there be any interstice, through which light can find its way'.[111] This is an excellent first principle, but his interpretation of *Pastour* might have been avoided if he had not impatiently dismissed Theobald's exposition of the nature of Shakespeare's anachronisms.[112] Also, he has not considered the likelihood of *brother*'s being a misreading in secretary script.[113] And, as is usually the case, he fails to draw attention to Theobald's parallel reading.

[110] *1765*, vi. 234–5 n. [Yale, viii. 729–30]. Most modern editors are agreed that *Pastour* is a phonetic spelling of *pasture*. Theobald noted a similar confusion in *Richard II* (III. iii. 100) (Nichols, ii. 399).

[111] *1765*, vol. i, sig. D8ᵛ [Yale, vii. 106].

[112] See *1765*, iv. 494 n. [Yale, viii. 567], and below, p. 192.

[113] New Shakespeare, ed. J. C. Maxwell, accepts *wether's*; Collier's emendation, *rother's*, is graphically implausible (but the existence of Rother Street in Stratford perhaps makes the unfamiliar word attractive). Without mentioning Theobald, C. J. Sisson gives independent support, on the same grounds, to Warburton's emendation. See Sisson, i. 11–12, ii. 173–4. *Textual Companion*, p. 505, maintains that 'Attempts to emend "Brothers" seem misguided' and speculates that 'The lines' combined inappropriateness to their context and appropriateness to another suggest that they

Theobald's use of a 'bad' quarto in conjunction with a good folio text is highly sophisticated. In *Henry V* (I. ii. 173) Theobald uses the 'bad' quarto in such a way as to indicate that he knew Q to be a reported text. In Pope's edition, he was confronted with:

> Playing the Mouse in absence of the Cat,
> To *tear* and havock more than she can eat.

Theobald writes: ' 'Tis not much the Quality of the Mouse to tear the Food it comes at, but to run over and defile it. The old 4to reads *spoile*; and the two first folio's, *tame*: from which last corrupted Word, I think, I have retriev'd the Poet's genuine Reading, *taint*.'[114] There is no question, here, of adopting the 'bad' quarto reading, but Theobald does realize that the garbled version may reflect the sense of the folio's copy. The quarto reading is not what Shakespeare wrote, but it may aid the correction of a folio misreading. The fact that *tame* (perhaps an aphetic form of 'attame' = broach, break into) is now thought to be adequate does not negate the soundness of Theobald's principles in approaching the readings of Q and F. Since a final *e:t* misreading, especially in conjunction with minims, is graphically very plausible, the emendation deserves serious consideration. In the second act of *Henry V* Theobald does adopt a quarto reading. Whereas the folio and his copy-text, Pope, have 'Tho Patience be a tir'd *name*, yet She will plod' (II. i. 23–4), the 'bad' quarto has 'a tired *mare*'. Obviously the folio reading is a compositorial misreading: 'A tir'd *Name plodding*, sure, is a very singular Expression. I make no Doubt, but it is a Corruption of the Press, and that I have restor'd the true Reading from the old *Quarto*.'[115] The quarto, in short, may be used as a guide to the folio compositor's reading (or misreading) of his copy. Thus Theobald confirms a transposition of lines in the folio (IV. iii. 11–14) suggested by Styan Thirlby, because 'the old 4to's plainly lead to such a Regulation'.[116] That Theobald had worked out sophisticated—and

should be relocated. Material was probably added marginally in the copy and misplaced by the compositor.'

114 *1733*, iv. 13 n.
115 Ibid. 21 n.
116 Ibid. 73 n. Theobald's arrangement is accepted.

seemingly very modern—editorial principles in his approach to the two texts can scarcely be doubted.

A further example of Theobald's intelligent use of a good quarto in conjunction with the folio is found in *Hamlet*. He bases the following emendation on the reading or misreading of the quarto (which he thought was printed from good copy),[117] while clearly regarding the folio reading as a sophistication of an obsolete, obscure word. The crux occurs in a speech by Claudius (III. iii. 7) shortly after the play of Gonzago. Pope gave the passage:

> The terms of our estate may not endure
> Hazard so near us, as doth hourly grow
> Out of his *lunacies*.

Pope has followed the second quarto, except that he adopts the folio's *lunacies* for the quarto's reading, *browes*. Theobald writes:

The old *Quarto's* read, —*Out of his* Brows. This was from the Ignorance of the first Editors; as is this unnecessary *Alexandrine*, which we owe to the Players. The Poet, I am persuaded, wrote,

> *as doth hourly grow*
> Out of his Lunes.

i.e. his *Madness*, *Frenzy*. So our Poet, before, in his *Winter's Tale* [II. ii. 28].

> These dang'rous, unsafe Lunes i'th'King!—*beshrew 'em,*
> He must be told of it, &c.

The Reader, if he pleases, may turn to my 10th Remark on that *Play*. Perhaps, too, in the *Merry Wives* of *Windsor*, where all the Editions read [IV. ii. 21–2];

> *Why, Woman, your Husband is in his old* Lines *again.*

We ought to correct;

> *in his old* Lunes *again.*

i.e. in his old Fits of Madness, Frenzy,[118]

Theobald's emendation of *The Merry Wives* has been accepted by some modern editors;[119] as an additional parallel reading he

[117] See above, p. 147.
[118] *1733*, vii. 306 n.
[119] Dover Wilson in the New Shakespeare and Alexander (1951).

might have cited *Troilus and Cressida* (II. iii. 130). In his note on *Lunes* in *The Winter's Tale*, to which he refers his readers, he says: 'I have no where, but in our Author, observ'd this Word adopted in our Tongue, to signify, *Frenzy*, *Lunacy*. But it is a Mode of Expression with the *French.—Il y a de la* lune: (*i.e.* He has got the Moon in his Head; he is frantick.)'[120] Theobald then cites Cotgrave's *Dictionarie of the French and English Tongues* (first published in 1611). Both his derivation of *lunes* and his assertion that its use is confined to Shakespeare are supported by the *OED*, which cites *The Winter's Tale* reading as obsolete in 1611. In his note on *Hamlet* in his edition Theobald does not bother to reproduce the spelling of the quarto, or its lack of capitalization, when he writes *Brows*. But his emendation to *lunes* is graphically plausible. It seems that *Lunacies* is to be ascribed either to 'the sophisticating editor' of the folio or to the preparer of the prompt-book,[121] when confronted with *lunes*, and that *browes* is the quarto compositor's misreading of the unfamiliar word. Theobald's emendation should be accepted, but it has not found its way into most modern editions.[122]

---

[120] *1733*, iii. 90 n.

[121] For complementary views, see Greg, *Editorial Problem*, pp. xxxiii–xxxix, 99; Wilson, *MS of 'Hamlet'*, i. 169–70, 173.

[122] John Munro prints *lunes* in *The London Shakespeare* (London: Eyre & Spottiswoode, 1958); J. H. P. Pafford cites *lunes* (brows) in *Hamlet* as a parallel to *The Winter's Tale* (II. ii. 29) in the Arden edition (1963). Dover Wilson does not discuss *lunes*, although he rejects the folio's *Lunacies* and is clearly ill at ease with *browes*; see Wilson, *MS of 'Hamlet'*, i. 9–11, 74, 132, 169–70; ii. 324, for repeated discussions of the crux; in the New Shakespeare *Hamlet* (2nd edn., repr. 1971), Wilson prints *brows*, notwithstanding his proposed emendation to *brawls* and (a further complication in the acceptance of *brows*) notwithstanding his parallel, 'turbulent and dangerous lunacy' (III. i. 4) (p. 209); in an additional note (p. 304), he defends *brows* by citing a late 17th-century example in the *OED* of *brow* in the figurative sense of 'an unabashed brow, effrontery'. Sisson, ii. 221–2, makes no mention of Theobald's emendation; he rejects Dover Wilson's defence of *brows* and emends to *braves*. Harold Jenkins prints *brows* in the Arden edition (1982). G. R. Hibbard, Oxford Shakespeare (1987), prints *lunacies*, despite the extra foot produced in the line, a reading consistent with his view that the folio text derives from Shakespeare's own revised, fair copy. So do Gary Taylor and Stanley Wells in the *Complete Works*, although they believe (*Textual Companion*, p. 399) that 'A number of features point to a scribal, rather than holograph, transcript [behind F]' and that 'A few verbal sophistications in F, not attributable to the compositors, also point to scribal interference.' If *lunacies* is owing to an interfering scribe, Theobald's emendation is to be preferred, because it is very probable that the quarto's *browes* is a misreading of *lunes*, and *Lunacies* is a likely substitution for *lunes*, but not for *browes*. The parallel readings of *lunes* elsewhere in Shakespeare add to the attractiveness of Theobald's emendation, except, as Wells and Taylor point out (General Introduction, *Textual Companion*, p. 60), 'revising authors

In the eighteenth century *lunes* was accepted by Hanmer, Capell, Steevens, and Malone in their editions. Johnson retains *Lunacies*, but prints Theobald's note (without the parallel readings). He then comments: 'I take *Brows* to be, properly read, *Frows*, which, I think, is a provincial word, for *perverse humours*; which being, I suppose, not understood, was changed to *Lunacies*. But of this I am not confident.'[123] Presumably Johnson thought the change to *Lunacies* was authorial, when he decided to retain the reading.

Johnson does occasionally do justice to Theobald's emendations, as in his comment on Theobald's brilliant emendation of *Macbeth* (I. vii. 6). The first folio reads: 'But heere, vpon this Banke and Schoole of time . . .'. Pope prints: '*Here* only on this bank and school of time . . .'. Theobald recovers the folio line with its 'monstrous Couplement . . . of heterogeneous Ideas' and emends *Schoole* to restore 'a Consonance of Images':

> on this Bank and Shoal *of Time.*

i.e. this *Shallow*, this *narrow Ford* of humane Life, opposed to the *great Abyss* of Eternity. This Word has occurr'd again, before, to us in the Life of King *Henry* VIIIth [III. ii. 436].[124]

Warburton asserted, without giving any reasons, that the reading should be *Shelve*; Johnson prints *Shoal* and adds a note: 'This is *Theobald*'s emendation, undoubtedly right.'[125]

Clearly, Theobald's approach to emendation was far less arbitrary than that of the majority of his contemporaries in the eighteenth century and far more sophisticated than most twentieth-century scholars have realized. Whatever the practice of Rowe, Pope, Hanmer, and Warburton, John Dover Wilson's summary account of eighteenth-century Shakespearian scholarship does not apply to Theobald:

Roughly speaking, any scholar of the Eighteenth Century was

sometimes deliberately replace an arcane word (like "crants", in the second quarto of *Hamlet*, 5.1.226/3197) with a more comprehensible one (like "Rites" in the Folio)'. To conclude, *lunes* is almost certainly a correct emendation of Q2's *browes*, but *lunacies* is to be preferred *if* it is owing to Shakespeare's revision and not to an interfering scribe.

[123] *1765*, viii. 232 n. [Yale, viii, 988].
[124] *1733*, v. 405 n.
[125] *1747*, vi. 353 n.; *1765*, vi. 398 n. [Yale, viii, 767]; *Textual Companion*, p. 544, comments: 'Theobald's reading "shoal", strictly a modernization, has the force of an emendation.'

acquitted if he familiarised himself with one or another of the Folio versions and restored any doubtful passage 'out of his own head.' The marvels they accomplished by this simple process remain an enormous credit to them and no less a wonder to us.[126]

Dover Wilson is characteristically generous in his praise of the eighteenth-century editors, but the approximately 350 major alterations by Theobald generally found in modern texts were not simply inspired, lucky guesses.[127] Perhaps their number may be significantly increased once it is understood that they are a consequence of the application of thought to textual criticism.

Attention has so far been concentrated chiefly on Theobald's efforts to resolve difficulties arising from errors in the transmission of the texts. The second concern of an editor involves those obscurities peculiar to his author's habits of writing which do not arise from accidental textual corruption. The problems of punctuation probably fall midway between these causes of obscurity, if a classification is attempted. Having dealt with the transmission of the text in his Preface, Theobald refers to punctuation before proceeding to a consideration of Shakespeare's other difficulties. Like Johnson, he generally considers the 'pointing' as lying wholly within his power. Unlike Johnson, he punctuates the plays very heavily. For this practice he has been censured,[128] but it is too easily forgotten that by his elaborate punctuation Theobald made Shakespeare much more intelligible to readers in 1734. He 'frequently subjoin'd Notes to shew the *deprav'd*, and to prove the *reform'd*, Pointing'. Doubtless, it was 'a Part of Labour in this Work which I could very willingly have spared myself', but his reasons were practical: 'Without such Notes, these Passages in subsequent Editions would be liable, thro' the Ignorance of Printers and Correctors, to fall into the old Confusion: Whereas, a Note on every one hinders all possible Return to Depravity.'[129]

To appreciate Theobald's point, it should be remembered

[126] General Introduction, *The Tempest*, New Shakespeare (1921; repr. 1969), p. xv.

[127] If calculation is confined to new substantive textual variants found in *Riverside*, Theobald contributed 153 (Rowe 171, Pope 81, Thirlby 10, Hanmer 37, Warburton 19, Johnson 23, Capell 69, and Malone 14). (These figures derive from Marvin Spevack, *A Complete and Systematic Concordance to . . . Shakespeare*, Vol. 9 (Hildesheim: Georg Olms, 1980)). Cf. above, p. 60 n. 42 & Jones, p. 181.

[128] See McKerrow, pp. 120–1 n. 14.

[129] Preface, *1733*, vol. i, pp. xliv–xlv.

that he was the first to pay scrupulous attention to Shakespeare's meaning, and that in the practice of Shakespeare's
previous editors he saw no cause for confidence in the future.
He was aware of the singularity of his concern for the details of
Shakespeare's text. Warburton, indeed, was often above such
trivia as punctuation—as Thomas Edwards points out in
Canon XIII of *The Canons of Criticism*.[130] Although Pope and
his party were quick to express contempt for those who set
commas and points exactly right, there were some who took
punctuation very seriously indeed. What could Theobald do to
satisfy a critic like Styan Thirlby, who scribbled the following
note on *The Merchant of Venice* (IV. i. 382) in the margin of his set
of Theobald's edition?

This monstrous semicolon is not to be endured. The speech at best is
but very indifferently put together but this makes it ten times worse,
and if not absolute nonsense, very little better. And yet I will not
swear that S[hakespeare] did not mean as he seems to have been
understood.

Thirlby, his rage cooled, returns to the matter at the bottom of
the page: 'I am for a comma, though as I said, things will still
hang but odly together.'[131]
   Theobald often pays attention to the dramatic force of the
punctuation in his sources. In *Hamlet* (I. iii. 56–8), when
Polonius gives a second blessing to Laertes and launches into
his 'few precepts', Pope gave the lines thus:

> The wind sits in the shoulder of your sail,
> And you are staid for there. My blessing with you. . . .

Theobald's version runs:

> The wind sits in the shoulder of your sail,
> And you are staid for. There;—
> My Blessing with you. . . .

In his note Theobald writes:

There—where? in the Shoulder of his Sail? For to That must this *local*

---

[130] '*He needs not attend to the low accuracy of orthography or pointing; but may ridicule such
trivial criticisms in others.*' There are 37 examples. Cf. Canon XIV: '*Yet, when he pleases to
condescend to such work, he may value himself upon it*'.
[131] *1733* (Folger PR 2752 1733 c.2), ii. 72. Theobald's semicolon is generally
accepted.

Adverb relate, as 'tis situated. Besides, it is a dragging idle Expletive, and seems of no Use but to support the Measure of the Verse. But when we come to point this Passage right, and to the Poet's Intention in it, we shall find it neither unnecessary, nor improper, in its Place. In the Speech immediately preceding this, *Laertes* taxes himself for staying too long; but seeing his Father approach, he is willing to stay for a second Blessing, and kneels down to that end: *Polonius* accordingly lays his hand on his Head, and gives him the second Blessing. The Manner, in which a Comic Actor behav'd upon this Occasion, was sure to raise a Laugh of Pleasure in the Audience: And the oldest *Quarto*'s, in the Pointing, are a Confirmation that thus the Poet intended it, and thus the Stage express'd it.[132]

Theobald produces a long but useful note. His sense here of the implications of the punctuation of the good quarto for the stage history of the character of Polonius is particularly interesting.

Theobald gives a note in *A Midsummer Night's Dream* (V. i. 113–16) on the punctuation necessary in Quince's delivery of the Prologue to the 'tedious brief scene' of Pyramus and Thisbe. Pope's version reads:

> We do not come as minding to content you,
> Our true Intent is all for your delight,
> We are not here that you should here repent you,
> The Actors are at hand. . . .

Theobald comments:

Thus the late accurate Editor, deviating from all the Old Copies, has, by a certain peculiar Fatality, pointed this Passage. The whole Glee and Humour of the Prologue is in the Actor's making false Rests, and so turning every Member of the Sentences into flagrant Nonsense. And Mr. *Pope* seems very cruel to our Author, (considering, how many Passages, which should have been pointed *right*, he has pointed *wrong*;) that here, when he should point *wrong*, with a strange Perverseness, and unusual Appetite for Sense, he will *point right*.[133]

In Theobald's edition the passage is given:

> We do not come, as minding to content you,
> Our true intent is. —all for your delight,
> We are not here. —that you should here repent you,
> The actors are at hand. . . .

---

[132] *1733*, vii. 243 n.   [133] *1725*, i. 142; *1733*, i. 139 n.

Theobald's hit at Pope is restrained, given Pope's initial response to Theobald's efforts in *Shakespeare Restored* (1726) to reform imperfect punctuation. Of course, there are a great many passages that Theobald discusses in his correspondence, but prints in his edition without comment.

Throughout his edition there is evidence of Theobald's efforts to clarify the text where 'the sense is perplexed, and buried'.[134] By his punctuation, Theobald did much for the understanding and appreciation of Shakespeare; when he provides a note, he was usually right to do so. Johnson was more restrained in his punctuation: after Theobald's labours, the difficulties were less numerous, and Johnson did not have Theobald's experience of the unreformed text. However, having benefited from Theobald's punctuation and elucidation of the text, Johnson ungenerously remarks: 'I have sometimes adopted his restoration of a comma, without inserting the panegyrick in which he celebrated himself for his atchievement.'[135]

---

[134] Nichols, ii. 489.
[135] Preface, *1765*, vol. i, sig. D1ᵛ [Yale, vii. 96].

9. Theobald's Edition: Elucidation of the Text

ALTHOUGH a large part of Theobald's annotation is concerned with his alterations of the received text, he was equally concerned to explain those obscurities resulting from the passage of time. In this part of his work he was probably influenced by Pope's Notes to Homer and, like Pope, hoped his readers would derive pleasure from his extensive commentary. The novelty of providing footnotes to an English author and Pope's attacks in *The Dunciad* caused him, however, to be on the defensive: 'As to my *Notes*, (from which the common and learned Readers of our Author, I hope, will derive some Pleasure;) I have endeavour'd to give them a Variety in some Proportion to their Number.'[1] Altogether Theobald supplied 1,356 notes to the plays. Many of his

. . . Remarks are spent in explaining Passages, where the Wit or Satire depends on an obscure Point of History: Others, where Allusions are to Divinity, Philosophy, or other Branches of Science. Some are added to shew, where there is a Suspicion of our Author having borrow'd from the Antients: Others, to shew where he is rallying his Contemporaries; or where He himself is rallied by them. And some are necessarily thrown in, to explain an obscure and obsolete *Term*, *Phrase*, or *Idea*.[2]

In the last category of his notes Theobald makes especial use of his reading in earlier English literature, and cites parallels not only from Shakespeare but from his English contemporaries and predecessors.

In his Preface Theobald distinguishes three classes of obscurity in Shakespeare: 'There are *Obscurities* in him, which are common to him with all Poets of the same Species; there are Others, the Issue of the Times he liv'd in; and there are Others, again, peculiar to himself.' Theobald discusses each of

---

[1] Preface, *1733*, vol. i, p. xliii.   [2] Ibid., p. xliv.

these classes and attempts to make Shakespeare more comprehensible to eighteenth-century readers by providing familiar
contexts for the problems. Thus the obscurities that Shakespeare has in common 'with all Poets of the same Species' are
linked to Congreve's well-known account of humours in
comedy:

The Nature of Comic Poetry being entirely satyrical, it busies itself
more in exposing what we call Caprice and Humour, than Vices
cognizable to the Laws. The *English*, from the Happiness of a free
Constitution, and a Turn of Mind peculiarly speculative and inquis-
itive, are observ'd to produce more *Humourists* and a greater Variety
of Original *Characters*, than any other People whatsoever. . . .[3]

With this context established for his discussion, Theobald
argues that since humours owe 'their immediate Birth to the
peculiar Genius of each Age, an infinite Number of Things
alluded to, glanced at, and expos'd, must needs become
obscure, as the *Characters* themselves are antiquated, and dis-
used'. It follows that 'An Editor therefore should be well vers'd
in the History and Manners of his Author's Age, if he aims at
doing him a Service in this Respect'.[4] Here Theobald formally
initiates the historical study of Renaissance English literature.

True wit in the eighteenth century was generally associated
with clarity of thought and expression, and Theobald was at
some pains to explain that, in contrast, Elizabethan and Jacobean notions of wit might be causes of obscurity. By alluding to
Locke's analysis of wit in *An Essay concerning Human Understanding*, which had been popularized by Addison in *Spectator* No. 62,
Theobald relates ideas of wit current in Shakespeare's time to
ideas current in the eighteenth century. His discussion anticipates parts of Johnson's account of the metaphysical poets in the
'Life of Cowley':

Besides, *Wit* lying mostly in the Assemblage of *Ideas*, and in the

---

[3] Cf. Congreve's letter (10 July 1695) to John Dennis on humour in comedy printed
in *William Congreve: Letters and Documents*, ed. John C. Hodges (London: Macmillan,
1964), 184–5; the letter was first published by Dennis in *Letters upon Several Occasions*
(1696), 80–96.

[4] Preface, *1733*, vol. i, pp. xlv–xlvi. These passages were also claimed by
Warburton in his set of Theobald's *Shakespeare* now in the library of Trinity College,
Cambridge. They were retained by Theobald in *1740* and may be safely ascribed to
him. See below, Appendix D.

putting Those together with Quickness and Variety, wherein can be found any Resemblance, or Congruity, to make up pleasant Pictures, and agreeable Visions in the Fancy;[5] the Writer, who aims at Wit, must of course range far and wide for Materials. Now, the Age, in which *Shakespeare* liv'd, having, above all others, a wonderful Affection to appear Learned, They declined vulgar Images, such as are immediately fetch'd from Nature, and rang'd thro' the Circle of the Sciences to fetch their Ideas from thence. . . . The ostentatious Affectation of abstruse Learning, peculiar to that Time, the Love that Men naturally have to every Thing that looks like Mystery, fixed them down to this Habit of Obscurity.[6]

Theobald's account of the obscurities in Shakespeare is organized so as to proceed from the general to the particular, from those arising from Shakespeare's being an Elizabethan to those resulting from his individual nature. In his discussion of the third class of Shakespeare's obscurities Theobald is able to transcend a purely rhetorical view of figurative language. Whereas metaphor and simile, when divorced from their eidetic power, tended to be regarded in the eighteenth century simply as means of elevating or diminishing an object by comparison—as in Pope's *Peri Bathous*—Theobald seizes on Shakespeare's figurative style as characteristic of his analogical mode of thought: 'The third Species of *Obscurities*, which deform our Author, as the Effects of his own Genius and Character, are Those that proceed from his peculiar Manner of *Thinking*, and as peculiar Manner of *cloathing* those *Thoughts*.' From his detailed knowledge of the plays, Theobald is able to add: 'With regard to his *Thinking*, it is certain, that he had a general Knowledge of all the Sciences: but his Acquaintance was rather That of a Traveller, than a Native. Nothing in Philosophy was unknown to him; but every Thing in it had the Grace and Force of Novelty.' At the same time, Theobald is glad to be able to recommend Shakespeare by referring to orthodox neo-classical commonplace: 'And as Novelty is one main Source of Admiration, we are not to wonder that He has perpetual Allusions to the most recondite Parts of the Sciences:

[5] Cf. bk. ii, ch. 11, *An Essay concerning Human Understanding*, ed. A. C. Fraser (2 vols., 1894), i. 203. (Of course, Theobald expected his allusion to Locke to be recognized.)

[6] Preface, *1733*, vol. i, p. xlvi.

and This was done not so much out of Affectation, as the Effect of Admiration begot by Novelty.' Theobald concludes:

> Then, as to his *Style* and *Diction*, we may much more justly apply to SHAKESPEARE, what a celebrated Writer has said of MILTON; *Our Language sunk under him, and was unequal to that Greatness of Soul which furnish'd him with such glorious Conceptions.*[7] He therefore frequently uses old Words, to give his Diction an Air of Solemnity; as he coins others, to express the Novelty and Variety of his Ideas.[8]

Theobald's statement that Shakespeare 'coins' words does not imply that Shakespeare invented words previously unknown; his metaphor implies rather that precious metal is melted down and then stamped with a new image (and, perhaps, a new value).[9] However, Theobald is mainly concerned in his account of Shakespeare's thought and language to defend scholarly annotations ('Upon every distinct Species of these *Obscurities* I have thought it my Province to employ a Note, for the Service of my Author, and the Entertainment of my Readers'),[10] although he is also intent on providing reasoned qualifications of such condemnations of Shakespeare's style as that found in Dryden's Preface to his adaptation of *Troilus and Cressida* (1679).[11]

A practical consequence of Theobald's sympathetic approach to Shakespeare's style is his ability to guide his readers into a new understanding of Shakespeare's imagery, whether simple or complex. For example, he restores 'a *Cain*-colour'd beard' in *The Merry Wives of Windsor* (I. iv. 23) and explains the image: '*A cane-colour'd* beard.] Thus the latter Editions. I have restor'd with the old Copies. *Cain* and *Judas*, in the Tapestries and Pictures of old, were represented with *yellow* Beards.'[12] This explanation may be the result of chance observation, but many of Theobald's notes on Shakespeare's images and allusions were the product of considerable research.

[7] Addison, *Spectator*, 297 (9 Feb. 1712).

[8] *1733*, vol. i, p. xlvii.

[9] Cf. Dryden, *Of Dramatic Poesy* (1668), Watson, i. 39; Preface to *Annus Mirabilis* (1662), ibid. 100; 'Defence of the Epilogue' (1672), ibid. 177; 'A Discourse concerning the Original and Progress of Satire' (1693), ibid. ii. 84.

[10] Preface, *1733*, vol. i, pp. xlvii–xlviii.

[11] See above, p. 38.

[12] *1733*, i. 238 n. For other references to pictures and tapestries, see *1733*, ii. 135 n., 230 n.

A good example of the extensiveness of Theobald's efforts to seek out the sources of Shakespeare's imagery is found in his correspondence with Martin Folkes, who had lent him a copy of the first folio and who in 1741 became President of the Royal Society. He was concerned to understand and to explain Shakespeare's numismatic word-play, and this desire led him to Folkes's collection of old English coins.[13] Folkes was glad to respond to the enquiries of a correspondent who was so acute and courteous, and who had first taken the trouble to ascertain all that the best printed sources could afford.[14]

A number of Theobald's notes explain terms of fencing,[15] hunting and falconry,[16] exorcism and witchcraft,[17] and medical and natural history.[18] His interest in Shakespeare's imagery was not confined, however, to antiquarian explanations of its sources. In his correspondence with Warburton he referred to Shakespeare's 'noble *translationes sensuum*',[19] and in his edition he comments at length on *Lear* (IV. i. 23):

> *Might I but live to* see thee in my touch,]

I cannot but take Notice, that these fine *Boldnesses* of Expression are very infrequent in our *English* Poetry, tho familiar with the *Greeks* and *Latins*. We have pass'd another signal One in this very Play [III. ii. 46–8].

> *Such* Sheets of Fire, *such Bursts of horrid Thunder,*
> *Such Groans of roaring Wind and Rain, I never*
> *Remember to have* heard.

For tho the Verb *hear* properly answers to the *Thunder*, the *Wind*, and *Rain*; yet it does not so, but figuratively, to the *Sheets of Fire*. I have observ'd an Instance of this *implex* Sort, exactly parallel, in the *Hero* and *Leander* of *Musæus* the Grammarian.

---

[13] See Nichols, ii. 619–20 (17 Nov. 1731). For notes on coins and word-play in *1733*, see iii. 170 n., 172 n., 452–3 n.; v. 237–8 n.

[14] See *1733*, iii. 170 n., 172 n.

[15] In a note on *As You Like It* (V. iv. 90–1), Theobald observes that Shakespeare's contemporaries 'studied the Theory of the Art, the Grounding of Quarrels, and the Process of giving and receiving Challenges, from *Lewis de Caranza*'s Treatise of Fencing, *Vincentio Saviola*'s Practice of the Rapier and Dagger, and *Giacomo Di Grassi*'s Art of Defence; with many other Instructions upon the several Branches of the Science' (*1733*, ii. 264). See also *1733*, vii. 119 n., 174 n., 340 n., 364 n.

[16] For examples, see *1733*, iii. 71 n.; v. 427–8 n.; vii. 60 n.

[17] See *1733*, iii. 312–13 n.; v. 163–4 n., 180 n., 392–3 n., 438 n.

[18] See *1733*, v. 188 n., 275 n., 395 n.; vi. 100 n.; vii. 315 n.

[19] Nichols, ii. 378.

In addition to this example, Theobald notes a parallel in Aeschylus' *Seven Captains before Thebes*, but more important, perhaps, is his observation that 'The late Learned Dr. *Gataker*, in his Treatise upon the *Style* of the *New Testament*,[20] has amass'd Examples of this Figure in Holy Writ, as well as from Heathen Writers, both *Greek* and *Latin*'.[21] This leads him to suggest in a subsequent comment on Act IV, Scene iii, of *Lear* that '*Shakespeare* might have form'd this fine Picture of *Cordelia*'s Agony from Holy Writ, in the Conduct of *Joseph*; who, being no longer able to restrain the Vehemence of his Affection, commanded all his Retinue from his Presence; and then *wept aloud*, and discover'd himself to his Brethren'.[22]

Theobald's appreciation of Shakespeare's figurative language in relation to his habits of thought is a wholly new development in Shakespearian criticism. Prior to the appearance of Theobald's edition, Thomas Rymer was considered the master of close reading of Shakespeare, as Theobald himself recognizes in a comment on *Othello* (V. ii. 99–101):

> *Methinks, it should be now a huge* Eclipse
> *Of Sun and Moon; and that th'* affrighted *Globe*
> *Should* yawn *at Alteration.*

Theobald quotes Rymer's ridicule of the passage in *A Short View of Tragedy* (1693)[23] and then proceeds to a justification:

> . . . I am afraid, Mr. *Rymer* was not too diligent a Reader of the *Scriptures*. Let the Poet account for the Prophanation, if he has committed any: but it is very obvious to me, his Allusion is grounded on a certain *solemn* Circumstance, when *Darkness* is said to have *cover'd the whole Face of the Land*; when *Rocks* were *rent*, and *Graves open'd*.[24]

Theobald's sensitivity to the implication of Shakespeare's imagery anticipates modern criticism. As W. K. Wimsatt acknowledges, even Johnson was 'rather severely limited as he encountered the immediate surface of Shakespeare's work— either individual scenes of certain sorts or the turns of dialogue, the rhetorical elaborations, the play of words—what today we

---

[20] Theobald refers to Thomas Gataker, *Dissertatio de Stylo Novi Testamenti* (1648).
[21] *1733*, v. 178–9 n.
[22] Ibid. 187 n.
[23] See Zimansky, p. 161.
[24] *1733*, vii. 484–5 n.

should call the verbal texture'.[25] However, neither W. H. Clemen nor Kenneth Muir mentions Theobald in his survey of the history of imagery in Shakespearian criticism.[26]

Many of Theobald's notes are devoted to explicating obsolete or obscure words and phrases by means of parallels in other writers. He was able to explain that 'Eisel' (*Hamlet*, V. i. 276) is vinegar and not, as previously thought, the name of a river;[27] that to be 'one that loves quails' (*Troilus and Cressida*, V. i. 52) is to be 'a Wencher';[28] that '*lac'd Mutton* has been a sort of standard Phrase for *Girls of Pleasure*' (*Two Gentleman of Verona*, I. i. 97);[29] and that to have 'an excellent breast' (*Twelfth Night*, II. iii. 19–20) is to have 'a good Power in singing'.[30] Although such explanations are fairly frequent, a comparison of Theobald's correspondence with the notes printed in his edition shows that his published annotation could have been greatly increased. Three considerations were at work to limit his commentary: first, he was restricted by the space available (as it was, his original agreement with Tonson provided for an edition of six volumes, rather than for the seven that were eventually printed);[31] second, he intended to provide a Glossary to all Shakespeare's works in his proposed volume of the poems;[32] third, he was afraid of being accused of pedantry.

[25] Introduction, *Samuel Johnson on Shakespeare* (New York: Hill and Wang, 1960), p. xx.

[26] W. H. Clemen, 'Imagery in the History of Shakespeare Criticism', *The Development of Shakespeare's Imagery* (London: Methuen, 1951), 10–17; Kenneth Muir, 'Shakespeare's Imagery—Then and Now', *Shakespeare Survey*, 18 (1965), 46–57.

[27] *1733*, vii. 352 n.

[28] Ibid. 100 n.

[29] *1733*, i. 156 n.

[30] *1733*, ii. 480 n.

[31] See below, Appendix B.

[32] See Preface, *1733*, vol. i, p. xliv. Although Theobald's edition of the poems and Glossary was never published, either because of his unwillingness to print Warburton's additional notes, or because of difficulty in filling his subscription list, there is evidence that he had prepared the volume for the press. In a letter (21 Apr. 1737) to the Duke of Bedford (now in the 'Hyde Collection', Somerville, New Jersey) he solicits a subscription 'to that Supplement I am now hastening to publish; w^ch: will both compleat your Grace's Setts, & all the Works of this great Poet'. Item 141 of the *Sale Catalogue* (1744) of his library is described as 'Shakespear's Poems, the 7th Volume, *with a Number of Mr. Theobald's MSS. Notes particularly a large Addition to the Explanation of Shakespear's old Words*'. This volume, edited by George Sewell and based on Gildon's compilation of 1710, was published in 1726. Folger PR 2841 A12a c.2 is a copy of Shakespeare's *Poems* (n.d.) with Theobald's MS notes and Index (see below, Appendix E). Theobald published notes and emendations on the poems in John Jortin

This last consideration restricted all his annotation, although he does, for example, indicate that Pistol's speech in *2 Henry IV* (II. iv. 163–7) parodies *Tamburlaine*,[33] and there are other notes showing where Shakespeare is burlesqued by Beaumont and Fletcher and other contemporaries.[34] He provides fairly detailed information about the historical background of certain plays, which ranges from Shakespeare's use of his sources to an account of London brothels in the sixteenth century.[35]

Theobald's commentary established a new standard for editors of English texts and created new levels of expectation in the reading public, but a regrettable consequence of his fear of being considered a pedant is that often he fails to do himself justice in his accounts of his discoveries. This is particularly evident in the use he makes of his research into the chronology of Shakespeare's plays. Nicholas Rowe acknowledged in his life of Shakespeare that he would have been 'pleas'd, to have learn'd from some certain Authority, which was the first Play he wrote; it would be without doubt a pleasure to any Man, curious in Things of this Kind, to see and know what was the first Essay of a Fancy like *Shakespear*'s.' Rowe continued: 'Perhaps we are not to look for his Beginnings, like those of other Authors, among their least perfect Writings; Art had so little, and Nature so large a Share in what he did, that, for ought I know, the Performances of his Youth, as they were the most vigorous, and had the most fire and strength of Imagination in 'em, were the best.'[36] This kind of 'philosophical' speculation about Shakespeare as a natural genius appealed to eighteenth-century dilettanti, and is of a piece with Pope's proposition that Shakespeare 'gives ground for a very new opinion, That the Philosopher and even the Man of the world, may be *Born*, as well as the Poet.'[37] Edmond Malone is usually considered the first to

(ed.) *Miscellaneous Observations upon Authors, Ancient and Modern* (2 vols., 1731–2), ii. 242–50. Theobald's contributions were identified by Jortin in his own set, now in the Victoria and Albert Museum (Dyce Collection 5377 (7.E.2)).

[33] *1733*, iii. 476–7 n. Theobald notes Shakespeare's parody of a passage in *Soliman and Perseda* (printed in 1599) in *King John* (i. i. 244–5) (*1733*, iii. 176 n.), and of *Cambyses* in *1 Henry IV* (II. iv. 387 ff.) (*1733*, iii. 386 n.).

[34] See *1733*, iv. 136 n., 338 n., 341 n.; vi. 202–3 n.; vii. 256 n., 286 n.

[35] *1733*, iv. 122 n. The note is on *1 Henry VI* (I. iii. 34–5) and draws on Theobald's reading in legal history .

[36] *1709*, vol. i, pp. vi–vii.

[37] See above, pp. 42–3.

have addressed the problem of chronology in his 'Attempt to Ascertain the Order in which the Plays Attributed to Shakespeare were Written' originally published in 1778, although G. Blakemore Evans remarks: 'The problem of chronology, an important approach to an understanding of Shakespeare's development, was first attacked by Capell, though the credit is usually given to Malone.'[38] However, to Theobald belongs the credit of being the pioneer in this area: in his edition he gives suggestions for dating fifteen of the plays.

In a letter to Warburton written a few months after publication of *The Dunciad Variorum*, Theobald apologizes for discussing the probable dates for the first appearances of *The Merry Wives of Windsor* and *Twelfth Night* and wonders if Warburton 'can pardon this digression, and acquit me of pedantry and impertinence'. In his letter Theobald suggests that *Twelfth Night* was first performed in 1604; he believes that there is an allusion to the trial of Sir Walter Ralegh in Sir Toby Belch's advice to Sir Andrew Aguecheek (III. ii. 44–6): 'Taunt him with the *licence of ink*; if thou *thou'st* him some Thrice, it shall not be amiss.' Theobald comments: 'The words quoted seem to me directly levelled at the Attorney General Coke, who, in the trial of Sir Walter, attacked him with all the following indecent expressions: 'All that Hell was by thy instigation, *thou* Viper: for I *thou* thee, *thou* Traytor.' (Here, by the bye, are the Poet's three *thou*'s.)'[39] He supposes that the trial of Ralegh in November 1603 provides a *terminus a quo* (although he also recognizes that the supposed allusion may be the result of subsequent interpolation). He next conjectures that Viola's 'Then, Westward-hoe' (III. i. 134) is an allusion to Webster's and Dekker's *Westward-hoe* (1607), a play that, he observes, contains references to the fall of Ostend in August 1604, and is itself referred to in the Prologue to *Eastward-hoe* (1605) by Chapman, Jonson, and Marston. He thus considers 1605 a *terminus ad quem* and chooses 1604 as a likely date for the appearance of *Twelfth Night*. Theobald's attempt to date the play is no more tenuous than modern attempts to date plays for which there is no external evidence of a performance.[40] In his edition,

[38] *Riverside*, p. 34.
[39] Nichols, ii. 273, 271.
[40] The account of a performance of *Twelfth Night* in the diary (discovered in 1826) of

however, he omits these speculations and refers only to his belief that Shakespeare was glancing satirically at the trial of Ralegh.[41]

The 'still-vext Bermoothes' in *The Tempest* (I. ii. 229) elicits a reference to 'Sir *George Summers*, who in 1609 made that Voyage; and viewing them, probably, first brought the English acquainted with them'.[42] Theobald subsequently notes Jonson's reference to Caliban in the Induction to *Bartholomew Fair*.[43] In *The Merry Wives of Windsor* Theobald comments on 'she is a region in *Guiana*' (I. iii. 69):

If the Tradition be true, (as, I doubt not, but it is;) of this Play being wrote at Queen *Elizabeth*'s Command;[44] this Passage, perhaps, may furnish a probable Conjecture that it could not appear till after the Year 1598. The mention of *Guiana*, then so lately discover'd to the *English*, was a very happy Compliment to Sir *W. Raleigh*, who did not begin his Expedition for South *America* till 1595, and return'd from it in 1596, with an advantageous Account of the great Wealth of *Guiana*. Such an Address of the Poet was likely, I imagine, to have a proper Impression on the People, when the Intelligence of such a golden Country was fresh in their Minds, and gave them Expectations of immense Gain.[45]

The *terminus ad quem* for Theobald was provided by his discovery

---

John Manningham of the Middle Temple indicates that the play was performed as early as 2 Feb. 1602.

[41] *1733*, ii. 503 n. Theobald's reference to the trial of Ralegh was omitted by Warburton in *1747*, but printed without comment by Johnson in *1765*. Theobald may have been right to suppose an allusion to Ralegh's trial; for arguments that the play was revised sometime in the years 1603–6, see John Dover Wilson, the New Shakespeare edition, pp. 92–101, and Greg, *First Folio*, pp. 296–8. Edmond Malone in his 'Essay on the Chronological Order of Shakespeare's Plays', repr. in *1790*, dated the first appearance of *Twelfth Night* in 1614 (I. i. 382–5). *Riverside*, p. 54, suggests 1601–2; *Textual Companion*, p. 123, suggests 1601.

[42] *1733*, i. 14 n. Warburton omits Theobald's reference to Summers's voyage, as does Johnson. Theobald also refers to Summers in his Preface, vol. i, p. x.

[43] Ibid. 44 n. *Bartholomew Fair* was first performed in 1614, when, Theobald notes, Shakespeare 'was retreated from the Scene'. Warburton and Johnson omit Theobald's reference. Edmond Malone, *1790*, I. i. 267, suggested 1612 as a date for *The Tempest*. Evans, *Riverside*, p. 56, and *Textual Companion*, p. 132, propose 1611.

[44] A tradition first recorded by John Dennis in the Dedication of *The Comical Gallant* (1702), sig. A2[r].

[45] *1733*, i. 235 n. Warburton omits Theobald's note, but it is reprinted by Johnson without comment.

of the quarto of 1602.[46] When explaining '*John Drum*'s entertainment' in *All's Well* (III. vi. 38–9), Theobald suggests that
'an old Motley Interlude, (printed in 1601) call'd *Jack Drum*'s
Entertainment; Or, the *Comedy* of *Pasquil* and *Katharine*' is
'perhaps, too late in Time, to come to the Assistance of our
Author'.[47] *The Comedy of Errors* is dated 1591 on the basis of his
recognition of a quibbling allusion (III. ii. 123–4) to the Earl of
Essex's expedition into France to assist Henry of Navarre.[48]
After a discussion of the tradition that Falstaff was originally
called Oldcastle (a discussion including references to *The
Famous Victories of Henry V*, printed in 1598, in which Oldcastle
appears, Jonson's reference to the fat of Falstaff in *Every Man
Out of his Humour*, which 'started first in to publick in 1599',
and the first part of *Sir John Oldcastle, the good Lord Cobham*,
printed in 1600), Theobald concludes that the change in name
in *1 Henry IV* was made 'some Years before' *Sir John Oldcastle*
'appear'd on the Stage'.[49] In a note on *2 Henry IV* (IV. iv.
117–18) Theobald observes a similarity to a passage in Daniel's
The Civil Wars (bk. iv, st. 84), but confesses: 'I don't know the
Date of that Poem being wrote, so cannot say which Poet has
copied from the Other.'[50] He supposes that *Henry V* appeared
before Jonson's *Every Man In his Humour*, first acted in 1598,
because he detects an allusion to Shakespeare's chorus (especially the Prologue to Act II, ll. 35–9) in Jonson's Prologue:

> *He rather prays, you will be pleas'd to see*
> *One such to day, as other Plays should be;*
> *Where neither* Chorus *wafts you o'er the Seas*, &c.[51]

[46] He relates his discovery in a letter of Nov. 1731 (Jones, p. 282). Malone, *1790*,
i. i. 266, suggested 1601. Evans, *Riverside*, p. 52, proposes 1597, with a revision
*c.*1600–1. *Textual Companion*, p. 120, proposes 1597–8.

[47] *1733*, ii. 415–16 n. Warburton omits Theobald's reference to the old play;
Johnson prints his note in full without comment.

[48] *1733*, iii. 32 n. Warburton disregards Theobald's attempt to date the play;
Johnson reprints Theobald's note. Malone, *1790*, I. i. 266, dates the play 1593. Evans,
Riverside, p. 48, suggests 1592–4; *Textual Companion*, pp. 116–17, proposes 1594.

[49] *1733*, iii. 348–9 n. Both Warburton and Johnson omit Theobald's speculations
on the date of *1 Henry IV*. Malone, *1790*, I. i. 266, suggests 1597. Evans, *Riverside*,
p. 52, and *Textual Companion*, p. 120, suggest 1596–7.

[50] *1733*, iii. 515 n. Warburton and Johnson omit Theobald's reference.

[51] *1733*, iv. 19 n. Warburton and Johnson (and most modern editors) omit
Theobald's reference. *Henry V* is assigned to 1599 by Malone, *1790*, I. i. 320, and
Evans, *Riverside*, pp. 52–3, on the basis of an allusion to Essex's Irish campaign of that

Theobald is unsure whether the three parts of *Henry VI* are entirely by Shakespeare:

tho there are several Master-Strokes in these three Plays, which incontestibly betray the Workmanship of *Shakespeare*; yet I am almost doubtful, whether they were entirely of his Writing. And unless they were wrote by him very early, I shou'd rather imagine them to have been brought to him as a Director of the *Stage*; and so to have receiv'd some finishing Beauties at his hand[.] An accurate Observer will easily see, the *Diction* of them is more *obsolete*, and the *Numbers* more *mean* and *prosaical*, than in the Generality of his genuine Compositions.[52]

These views are consistent with those of most modern authorities on these plays, although Theobald is perhaps more willing to leave the matter in doubt. In a subsequent note on *1 Henry VI* (I. ii. 1–2), 'MARS his true moving, ev'n as in the heav'ns, | So in the earth to this day is not known', he suggests a date in the vicinity of 1594, or earlier:

Our Poet, in an hundred Passages of his Works, has shewn us his Acquaintance with *judicial Astrology*; he here gives us a Glimpse of his Knowledge in *Astronomy*. The Revolutions of the Planet *Mars* were not found out till the beginning of the 17th Century. *Kepler*, I think, was the Person, who first gave Light to Discovery upon this Subject, from the Observations of *Ticho-Brahe*, in his Treatise *De Motibus Stellæ* Martis: of which Treatise I have seen no earlier Edition than that from *Frankfurt* publish'd in 1609; at least 15 years, if not more, after the Appearance of this Play.[53]

Theobald provides a *terminus a quo* for *King Lear* in Shakespeare's use of Dr Samuel Harsnett's *Declaration of Egregious Popish Impostures* (1603) in the speeches of Edgar, when he is disguised as Poor Tom. In a lengthy note (for which he apologizes) on Lear's questions, 'Didst thou give all to thy daughters? and art thou come to this?' (III. iv. 49–50), in which he distinguishes between Lear's madness and Edgar's '*assum'd*

year (first noted by Gerard Langbaine, *An Account of the English Dramatick Poets* (1691), 457). *Textual Companion*, p. 121, proposes 1598–9.

[52] *1733*, iv. 110 n. Warburton omits Theobald's note; Johnson reprints it without comment.
[53] Ibid. 116 n. Warburton and Johnson omit Theobald's note. Malone, *1790*, I. i. 266, proposes 1589; Evans, *Riverside*, p. 48, suggests 1589–90, revised 1594–5; *Textual Companion*, p. 112, suggests 1592.

Passion', Theobald ventures to assure his readers that Edgar's 'whole Frenzy is Satire levell'd at a modern Fact, which made no little Noise at that Period of Time: and consequently, must have been a rapturous Entertainment to the Spectators, when it was first presented'. After a summary of Harsnett's account of the Jesuits' fraudulent exorcisms, Theobald suggests: 'This Transaction was so rife in every Body's Mouth, upon the Accession of King *James* the 1st to the Crown; that our Poet thought proper to make his Court, by helping forward the Ridicule of it.' This suggests a *terminus ad quem* of about 1604.[54]

Timon of Athens presented Theobald with greater difficulty: he was not 'able to trace the Time, when this Play of our Author's made its first Appearance', but he presumes it to have been written 'before the Death of Q. *Elizabeth*', because of an apparent allusion to the play 'in a Piece, call'd, *Jack Drum's Entertainment* . . . play'd by the Children of *Powles*, and printed in 1601.—*Come, come, now I'll be as sociable as* Timon *of* Athens'.[55]

Theobald follows a suggestion made by Edward Ravenscroft in 1687 that *Titus Andronicus* was not originally by Shakespeare;[56] he finds support for this view in Jonson's Induction to *Bartholomew Fair*, 'which made its first Appearance in the year 1614' and 'couples *Jeronymo*[57] and *Andronicus* together in Reputation, and speaks of them as Plays then of 25 or 30 Years standing'. This reference implies a first production between 1584 and 1589, and '*Andronicus* must have been on the Stage, before *Shakespeare* left *Warwickshire* to come and reside in *London*'. However, Theobald acknowledges 'that he afterwards introduc'd it a-new on the Scene, with the Addition of his own

[54] *1733*, v. 163–4 n. Theobald gives the printer and date of Harsnett's *Declaration*: 'Printed by *James Roberts*, in 1603.' Warburton (*1747*, vi. 99) refers to Harsnett without mentioning Theobald and without realizing the chronological implications of the work. Edmond Malone, *1790*, I. i. 353, mentions Harsnett (without reference to Theobald) and proposes 1605 (ibid. 267). Evans, *Riverside*, pp. 54–5, suggests a date of 1605. *Textual Companion*, p. 128, dates *The History of King Lear* 1605–6 and a revision, distinguished as *The Tragedy of King Lear*, 1610.

[55] *1733*, v. 303 n. Warburton and Johnson omit Theobald's note. Malone, I. i. 267, proposes 1609; Evans, *Riverside*, p. 55, suggests 1607–8; *Textual Companion*, pp. 127–8, proposes Middleton as a collaborator, 1604–6.

[56] Ravenscroft's suggestion appears in the 'Address' before his version of *Titus Andronicus* (1687) and is discussed by Langbaine, *Account* (1691), pp. 464–5.

[57] Thomas Kyd's *Spanish Tragedy*.

masterly Touches, is incontestable: and thence, I presume, grew his Title to it'.[58]

Theobald recognizes that the apparitions in *Macbeth* (IV. i) are a compliment to King James and appends a note to 'some I see, | Thăt twofold balls and treble scepters carry' (ll. 120–1):

it will not be amiss to observe, that this fine Play, tis probable, was not writ till after Q. *Elizabeth*'s Death. These Apparitions, tho very properly shewn with Regard to *Macbeth*, yet are more artfully so, when we consider the Address of the Poet in complimenting K. *James* I. here upon his uniting *Scotland* to *England*: and when we consider too, the Family of the *Stuarts* are said to be the direct Descendants from *Banquo*.[59]

In the course of defending Othello's account of his wooing of Desdemona and his tale of 'men whose heads | Do grow beneath their shoulders' (I. iii. 144–5), which had been ridiculed by Rymer[60] and degraded by Pope,[61] Theobald suggests a period for the play's composition. He quotes from Ralegh's *Discoverie . . . of Guiana* (1596): 'They are call'd *Ewaipanomaws*, they are reported to have their *Eyes* in their *Shoulders*, and their *Mouths* in the middle of their *Breasts*. It was not my Chance to hear of them, till I was come away; and if I had but spoken one word of it while I was there, I might have brought one of them with me, to put the *Matter out of Doubt*.' Theobald also refers to Lawrence Kemys's confirmation of Ralegh's tale in *A Relation of the Second Voyage to Guiana* (1596): Kemys 'mentions the same People; and, speaking of a Person who gave him considerable Informations, he adds, "*He certified me of the* headless

---

[58] *1733*, v. 307–8 n. Warburton omits Theobald's note; Johnson reprints it in full from *1733* in his general note on the play (*1765*, vi. 364–5) and comments: 'That *Shakespeare* wrote any part, though *Theobald* declares it *incontestable*, I see no reason for believing.' J. C. Maxwell, Arden (1950), favours George Peele's authorship of Act I and a date of 1589–90. Eugene M. Waith, Introduction, Oxford Shakespeare (1984), p. 20, believes that *Titus* 'is entirely by Shakespeare' and that it was first performed in 1590–2. Evans, *Riverside*, p. 49, proposes 1593–4; *Textual Companion*, pp. 113–15, suggests 1592.

[59] *1733*, v. 443–4 n. Warburton (*1747*, vi. 396 n.) notes the compliment to James I, but without referring to Theobald; Johnson reprints Warburton's note. Malone, *1790*, I. i. 267, Evans, *Riverside*, p. 55, and *Textual Companion*, pp. 128–9, suggest a date of 1606.

[60] In *A Short View of Tragedy* (1693), Zimansky, pp. 132–3.

[61] *1725*, vi. 491.

Men, *and that their* Mouths *in their* Breasts *are exceeding* wide." '
Theobald points out that

Sir *Walter*, at the time that his Travels were publish'd, is styled
Captain of her Majesty's Guard, Lord Warden of the *Stannaries*, and
Lieutenant General of the County of *Cornwal*. If we consider the
Reputation, as the ingenious *Martin Folkes* Esq; observ'd to me, any
thing from such a Person, and at that time in such *Posts*, must come
into the World with, we shall be of Opinion that a Passage in *Shakespeare* need not be *degraded* for the Mention of a Story, which, however
strange, was countenanc'd with such an Authority. *Shakespeare*, on the
other hand, has shewn a fine Address to Sir *Walter*, in sacrificing so
much Credulity to such a *Relation*.

He further suggests, on the basis of Shakespeare's use of these
accounts, that 'they do in some Measure fix the Chronology of
his writing *Othello*, as well as the *Tempest*: for as neither of them
could be wrote before the Year 1597; so the Mention of these
Circumstances should persuade us, they appear'd before these
Travels became stale to the publick, and their Authority was too
narrowly scrutiniz'd.'[62]

Theobald's methods in his attempts to date Shakespeare's
plays were sound and anticipate those of Capell and Malone. He
was not aware of the three most important sources of information known to later scholars: the Stationers' Register, Philip
Henslowe's diary, and Francis Meres's *Palladis Tamia* (1598),
but of the plays he discusses, he appears egregiously mistaken
only in his dating of *Henry VIII*, which he believes was written
in the time of Queen Elizabeth and revised after the accession
of James I. His argument is based on his critical judgment and
has some point: the praises of Anne Boleyn in Act II, Scene iii,
do appear, as he says, to be deliberate compliments to Queen
Elizabeth's mother.[63] His further supposition, that the continuation of Cranmer's speech after V. iv. 38 is a later addition
complimenting James I, deserves consideration. As he remarks,
'The Transition here from the Complimentary Address to
King *James* the First is so abrupt, that it seems obvious to me,

---

[62] *1733*, vii. 392–3 n. Warburton and Johnson omit Theobald's note. Malone,
1790, I. i. 267, dates *Othello* in 1611. Evans, *Riverside*, p. 54, suggests a date of 1604;
Textual Companion, p. 126, proposes 1603–4. For Theobald's suggestion of a later date
for *The Tempest*, see above, p. 180 & n. 43.

[63] See *1733*, v. 39 n.

that Compliment was inserted after the Accession of that Prince.' After quoting King Henry VIII's expostulation over the Princess Elizabeth (V. iv. 55, 63–5),

> Thou speakest Wonders.
>
> .   .   .   .   .   .
>
> O Lord Archbishop,
> Thou'st made me now a Man. Never, before
> This happy Child, did I get any Thing,

he pertinently remarks of Cranmer's intervening account of her chaste life and death: 'Whether the King would so properly have made this Inference, upon hearing that a Child of so great Hopes should dye without Issue, is submitted to Judgment.'[64] As in this instance, however, Theobald's interest in chronology is generally to provide a context for Shakespeare's art. He does not discuss Shakespeare's development as a dramatist at length. The focus is on Shakespeare's relation to his own time. Theobald presents him not as an inexplicable natural prodigy, but as a playwright producing works that reflect the environment in which they were written.

Theobald's sense of the historical context of Shakespeare's career also gives balance to his account of that vexed question in the eighteenth century, Shakespeare's classical learning. Although Ben Jonson allowed Shakespeare '*small* Latine, *and lesse* Greeke',[65] later in the seventeenth century Milton's depiction of 'sweetest *Shakespeare*, fancy's child' warbling 'his native Wood-notes wild'[66] gave support to the view that he was without any classical education. (The tradition recorded by John Aubrey that Shakespeare 'understood Latine pretty well: for he had been in his younger yeares a schoolmaster in the countrey'[67] was not generally known.) Nicholas Rowe declared flatly that 'It is without Controversie, that he had no knowledge

---

[64] Ibid. 99–100 n. Theobald's theory of revision and supporting arguments were accepted without acknowledgement by Malone in *1790*, I. i. 331–2, who proposed a date of 1601; modern editors see the play as a collaboration with Fletcher; Evans, *Riverside*, p. 56, proposes 1612–13; *Textual Companion*, pp. 133–4, proposes 1613 for *All Is True*.

[65] 'To the memory of my beloued, The Author', *Mr. William Shakespeares Comedies, Histories, & Tragedies* (1623), sig. A4ʳ.

[66] 'L'Allegro', ll. 133–4.

[67] *Aubrey's Brief Lives*, ed. Oliver Lawson Dick (London: Secker and Warburg, 1949), 276.

of the Writings of the Antient Poets'. For Rowe, this lack of knowledge is evident

from his Works themselves, where we find no traces of any thing that looks like an Imitation of 'em; the Delicacy of his Taste, and the natural Bent of his own Great *Genius*, equal, if not superior to some of the best of theirs, would certainly have led him to Read and Study 'em with so much Pleasure, that some of their fine Images would naturally have insinuated themselves into, and been mix'd with his own Writings; so that his not copying at least something from them, may be an Argument of his never having read 'em.[68]

Subsequently, Rowe does admit that 'There is one Play of his, indeed, *The Comedy of Errors*, in a great measure taken from the *Menœchmi* of *Plautus*' but he does not acknowledge his indebtedness to be a contradiction of his previous statement and merely comments: 'How that happen'd, I cannot easily Divine, since, as I hinted before, I do not take him to have been Master of *Latin* enough to read it in the Original, and I know of no Translation of *Plautus* so Old as his Time.'[69]

Rowe's failure to note other parallels with the classics is difficult to credit, and Charles Gildon, while decrying Shakespeare's 'want of a thorough Knowledge of the Art of the Stage', was quick to maintain that 'there are many Arguments to prove, that he knew at least, some of the *Latin* Poets, particularly *Ovid*'. In addition to the matter of *The Comedy of Errors*, he cites the characters in the Roman plays as proof of Shakespeare's acquaintance with their historians. Gildon concludes that Shakespeare 'was capable of reading at least, the *Latin* Poets'.[70] In contrast, John Dennis asserted: 'I believe he was able to do what Pedants call construe, but that he was able to read *Plautus* without Pain and Difficulty I can never believe.' Dennis was even more distressed than Gildon by Shakespeare's neglect of 'the Rules of Art', especially his lack of decorum in the representation of Greek and Roman characters: Shakespeare 'runs counter to the Instructions which *Horace* has given for the forming the Character of *Achilles*',[71] and 'Where', asks Dennis,

---

[68] *1709*, vol. i, p. iii.

[69] Ibid., p. xv.

[70] 'An Essay on the Art, Rise and Progress of the Stage', *The Works of Mr. William Shakespear, Volume the Seventh* (1710), pp. x, vi.

[71] *Ars Poetica*, ll. 120–2.

'is the *Impiger*, the *Iracundus*, or the *Acer*, in the Character of *Shakespear*'s *Achilles*? who is nothing but a drolling, lazy, conceited overlooking Coxcomb.' Dennis subsequently gives what is probably the basis of the eighteenth century's preference for an unlearned Shakespeare. Dennis's commitment to the rules was such that he could not conceive that Shakespeare might consciously reject them and, therefore, 'he who allows that *Shakespear* had Learning and a familiar Acquaintance with the Ancients, ought to be look'd upon as a Detractor from his extraordinary Merit, and from the Glory of *Great Britain*'. Clearly, it is 'more honourable for this Island to have produc'd a Man, who without having any Acquaintance with the Ancients, or any but a slender and a superficial one, appears to be their Equal or their Superiour by the Force of Genius and Nature', than 'to have bred one who knowing the Ancients, falls infinitely short of them in Art, and consequently in Nature it self'.[72]

Dennis's arguments placed Pope in a difficult position: to acknowledge Shakespeare's familiarity with any of the Latin poets was also to suggest that his neglect of the rules in Horace was deliberate. Pope preferred to avoid addressing this question directly, and Theobald had good reason to comment of Pope's Preface in a letter to Warburton that 'The question of Shakespeare's Learning, I believe you'll find so very doubtfully decided by him, that the argument will put you in Mind of— *Jean a dancé mieux que Pierre, et Pierre a dancé mieux que Jean*'.[73] Theobald's commitment to neo-classical dramatic theory, as we have seen, was not so strong as to make him believe that had Shakespeare known the rules, he would have felt compelled to follow them.[74] Even in his Preface to his neo-Aristotelian adaptation of *Richard II* (1720) he was prepared to argue that Shakespeare knew both Greek and Latin, '*unless any One can find a Way how He should come at the Knowledge of the* Greek *and* Roman *Stories, any other Way than by understanding the Language of their Writers*'.[75] His subsequent discovery of North's translation of

---

[72] Letter 3, *Essay on the Genius and Writings of Shakespear*, *The Critical Works of John Dennis*, ed. E. N. Hooker (2 vols., Baltimore: Johns Hopkins Press, 1939–43), ii. 13–14.

[73] Jones, p. 265 (25 Apr. 1730).

[74] See above, pp. 40–1.

[75] Sig. Aa2ᵛ.

Plutarch (1579)[76] lessened the strength of his proofs, but not his conviction. In the Preface to his edition, Theobald takes note of Rowe's discovery that Shakespeare 'was bred for some Time at a Free-School; the very Free-School, I presume, founded at *Stratford*: where, we are told, he acquired what *Latin* he was Master of'. Still following Rowe, Theobald records the tradition that Shakespeare's father was obliged 'thro' Narrowness of Circumstance, to withdraw him too soon from thence', and he was 'unhappily prevented from making any Proficiency in the Dead Languages'. According to Theobald, however, this is 'A Point, that will deserve some little Discussion'.[77]

Although in his Preface to his adaptation of *Richard II* (1720) Theobald asserted that he '*could, with the greatest Ease imaginable, produce above* 500 *Passages*' from *Coriolanus*, *Julius Caesar* and *Antony and Cleopatra* to '*evidence* [Shakespeare's] *Intimacy with the* Latin *Classicks*',[78] in the Preface to his edition he merely remarks:

> Tho' I should be very unwilling to allow *Shakespeare* so poor a Scholar, as Many have labour'd to represent him, yet I shall be very cautious of declaring too positively on the other side of the Question . . . of his Knowledge in the dead Languages. And therefore the Passages, that I occasionally quote from the *Classics*, shall not be urged as Proofs that he knowingly imitated those Originals; but brought to shew how happily he has express'd himself upon the same Topicks.

Theobald is prepared in his Preface to suppose that Shakespeare might have had 'but a slender Library of Classical Learning', and he was further prepared to temper his beliefs by 'considering what a Number of Translations, Romances, and Legends, started about his Time, and a little before; (most of which, 'tis very evident, he read)',[79] but many of his parallels in his notes with Cicero, Horace, Juvenal, Lucretius, Ovid, Plautus, Seneca, and Virgil imply direct translation. The view that prevailed in the eighteenth century was, however, that of a Shakespeare without classical learning. This view was most forcefully argued by Richard Farmer in *An Essay on the Learning*

---

[76] See Nichols, ii. 500 (19 Feb. 1730), *1733*, v. 303 n.; vi. 231–2 n.
[77] *1733*, vol. i, p. v.
[78] Sig. Aa4ᵛ.
[79] *1733*, vol. i, pp. xxviii–xxix.

of Shakespeare (1767), and it was not until the twentieth century that Theobald's assessment of Shakespeare's learning came to be generally accepted. As T. W. Baldwin remarks:

His parallels are generally so sound that even Dr. Farmer ignored them, and, with few exceptions, are quoted with approval to this day. The same sense of relationships which enabled him to restore so many of Shakespeare's passages also shows itself here. Had others been so critical, we might have been spared Dr. Farmer and his train.[80]

Theobald's assumptions about Shakespeare's learning have important consequences for his editing. For example, in the quarto and folio texts of *Love's Labour's Lost* (V. i. 27–9) an exchange between Holofernes and Sir Nathaniel appears as follows:

Cura. Laus Deo, bene intelligo.
Peda. Bome boon for boon prescian, a little scratcht, 'twil
    serue.

Whereas Pope left the passage essentially unchanged, Theobald emended and supplied a note:

Nath. Laus deo, bone, intelligo.
Hol. Bone?—*bone,* for *bene*; *Priscian* a little scratch'd; 'twill serve.

The Curate, addressing with Complaisance his brother Pedant, says, *bone*, to him, as we frequently in *Terence* find *bone Vir*; but the Pedant thinking, he had mistaken the Adverb, thus descants on it.

Bone?—bone for *bene*. Priscian *a little scratch'd: 'twill serve.*

Alluding to the common Phrase, *Diminuis* Prisciani *caput,* apply'd to such as speak false *Latine*.[81]

Before such an emendation can be made, there has to be an assumption that Shakespeare could make an elementary distinction between good and bad Latin. Theobald was more than willing to make such assumptions, and his text benefits accordingly.

At the same time, readers of Theobald's edition might also

---

[80] *William Shakespere's Small Latine & Lesse Greeke* (2 vols., Urbana: University of Illinois Press, 1944), i. 60–1. For discussion of parallels adduced by Theobald, see ibid. 485, 487, 489, 508, 527–31, 536–7, 539–40, 600. See also S. Schoenbaum, *Shakespeare's Lives* (Oxford: Clarendon Press, 1970), 728–32.

[81] *1733*, ii. 148 n. Cf. J. W. Binns, 'Shakespeare's Latin Citations: The Editorial Problem', *Shakespeare Survey*, 35 (1982), 126.

be led to accept the idea of a Shakespeare who had a grounding in the learned languages. Earlier in *Love's Labour's Lost* (IV. ii. 125) Holofernes, to whom Theobald and subsequent editors assign the speech, engages in brief critical discourse on the *Canzonet* (Theobald's emendation into anglicized Italian of the quarto's meaningless *cangenct* and the folio's *cangenet*). In the folio, the passage reads:

Here are onely numbers ratified, but for the elegancy, facility, & golden cadence of poesie *caret*: *Ouiddius Naso* was the man. And why in deed *Naso*, but for smelling out the odoriferous flowers of fancy? the ierkes of inuention imitarie is nothing: So doth the Hound his master, the Ape his keeper. . . .

Theobald's emendation and note on the passage depend on a necessary assumption that Shakespeare knew both Latin and something of the critical traditions associated with its literature. (On the immediately preceding page of the edition he had pointed out an allusion to Horace.) His note also displays the occasional arrogance that mars his edition:

Sagacity with a Vengeance! I should be asham'd to own myself a piece of a Scholar, to pretend to the Task of an Editor, and to pass such Stuff as this upon the World for genuine. Who ever heard of *Invention imitary*? Invention and Imitation have ever been accounted two distinct Things. The Speech is by a Pedant, who frequently throws in a Word of *Latin* amongst his *English*; and he is here flourishing upon the Merit of Invention, beyond That of Imitation, or copying after another. My Correction makes the Whole so plain and intelligible, that, I think, it carries Conviction along with it.[82]

In Theobald's edition the passage reads:

Here are only numbers ratify'd; but for the elegancy, facility, and golden cadence of poesie, *caret: Ovidius Naso* was the man. And why, indeed, *Naso*; but for smelling out the odoriferous flowers of fancy? the jerks of invention? *imitari*, is nothing: so doth the hound his master, the ape his keeper. . . .[83]

Associated with the question of Shakespeare's classical learning were the anachronisms to be found in his plays, especially

---

[82] *1733*, ii. 131 n.

[83] Ibid. 131–2. Pope had modernized the spelling of the passage and printed: 'the jerks of invention imitary is nothing' (*1725*, ii. 130).

those with classical settings. Rowe, Dennis, and Pope found in them proof that Shakespeare lacked learning. Theobald disagreed, finding that they occurred 'not thro' Ignorance, as is generally supposed, but thro' the too powerful Blaze of his Imagination; which, when once raised, made all acquired Knowledge vanish and disappear before it'.[84] When Theobald views the plays in their original context as popular entertainment, he accounts for Shakespeare's anachronisms with telling arguments that reveal his historical and critical understanding:

In all *Anachronisms*, as in other Licences of Poetry, this Rule ought certainly to be observ'd; that the Poet is to have Regard to *Verisimilitude*. But there is no *Verisimilitude*, when the *Anachronism* glares in the face of the common People. For this Falshood is, like all other Falshoods in Poetry, to be only tolerated, where the Falshood is hid under Verisimilitude. No sober Critick ever blamed *Virgil*, for instance, for making *Dido* and *Aeneas* contemporary. (Such a *Prolepsis* may be justified by the examples of the greatest Poets of Antiquity.) But had he made *Aeneas* mention *Hamilcar*, what Man in his Senses would have thought of an Excuse for him? For the Name of *Hamilcar*, tho a Foreigner, was too recent in the Acquaintance of the People; as he had for five Years together infested the Coast of *Italy*; and after that, begun the second *Punic* War upon them. The Case of our Author differs in his mentioning *Machiavel* in some of his Plays, the action of which was earlier than that Statesman's Birth. For *Machiavel* was a Foreigner, whose Age, we may suppose, the common Audience not so well acquainted with; as being long before their time, and, indeed, very near the Time of the Action of those Plays. Besides, He having so establish'd a Reputation, in the time of our Author, amongst the Politicians; might well be suppos'd by those, who were not Chronologers, to be of much longer Standing than he was. This, therefore, was within the Rules of Licence; and if there was not Chronological Truth, there was at least Chronological Likelihood: without which a Poet goes out of his Jurisdiction, and comes under the Penalty of the Criticks Laws.[85]

This is a sensible and sophisticated account of Shakespeare's anachronisms, designed to appeal to readers accustomed to neo-classical rules of art.

What is perhaps surprising in Theobald's Preface is the lack of any extended account of Shakespeare's drama in relation to

---

[84] Preface, *1733*, vol. i, p. xxx. See also ibid., vol. i, pp. l–li.
[85] *1733*, iv. 112 n.

neo-Aristotelian theory or classical dramatic practice. It is clear from his discussion here and in his notes that he was disinclined to believe that Shakespeare wrote in ignorance of the classics. Instead of Pope's ambiguity on the general subject of Shakespeare's learning or Pope's assertion that Shakespeare wrote 'without that knowledge of the best models, the Ancients, to inspire him with an emulation of them',[86] Theobald maintains: 'Whether we view him on the Side of Art or Nature, he ought equally to engage our Attention: Whether we respect the Force and Greatness of his Genius, the Extent of his Knowledge and Reading, the Power and Address with which he throws out and applies either Nature, or Learning, there is ample Scope both for our Wonder and Pleasure.' As opposed to Pope's distress over Shakespeare's figurative language, Theobald argues on behalf of the variety of Shakespeare's imagery and its appropriateness to his range of characters:

If his Diction, and the cloathing of his Thoughts attract us, how much more must we be charm'd with the Richness, and Variety, of his Images and Ideas! If his Images and Ideas steal into our Souls, and strike upon our Fancy, how much are they improv'd in Price, when we come to reflect with what Propriety and Justness they are apply'd to Character! If we look into his Characters, and how they are furnish'd and proportion'd to the Employment he cuts out for them, how are we taken up with the Mastery of his Portraits! What Draughts of Nature! What Variety of Originals, and how differing each from the other![87]

In deliberate contrast to Pope's view that Shakespeare as an actor shared the views of his fellow players, and 'They have ever had a Standard to themselves, upon other principles than those of *Aristotle* . . . Players are just such judges of what is *right*, as Taylors are of what is *graceful*',[88] Theobald again praises Shakespeare's characters: 'Each of Them are the Standards of Fashion for themselves: like Gentlemen that are above the Direction of their Tailors, and can adorn themselves without the Aid of Imitation.'[89]

Theobald's praise of Shakespeare provides the rationale of

[86] See above, p. 44.
[87] Preface, *1733*, vol. i, pp. ii–iii.
[88] See above, p. 44.
[89] Preface, *1733*, vol. i, p. iii.

Johnson's dismissal of the rules of art in favour of his representation of Shakespeare as the poet of general nature in his Preface to *Shakespeare* (1765). Continuing his account of Shakespeare's characters, Theobald tells his readers: '*Shakespeare*'s Clowns and Fops come all of a different House: they are no farther allied to one another than as Man to Man, Members of the same Species: but as different in Features and Lineaments of Character, as we are from one another in Face, or Complexion.'[90] In the body of Theobald's Preface the governing principles of his critical praise are sustained. Shakespeare's mastery of character in itself renders him the supreme dramatic poet:

His Fire, Spirit, and Exuberance of Imagination gave an Impetuosity to his Pen: His Ideas flow'd from him in a Stream rapid, but not turbulent; copious, but not ever overbearing its Shores. The Ease and Sweetness of his Temper might not a little contribute to his Facility in Writing; as his Employment, as a *Player*, gave him an Advantage and Habit of fancying himself the very Character he meant to delineate. He used the Helps of his Function in forming himself to create and express that *Sublime*, which other Actors can only copy, and throw out, in Action and graceful Attitude.[91]

For Theobald, negative criticism pales in the face of Shakespeare's achievement; consequently it is restricted to very few lines:

The Genius, that gives us the greatest Pleasure, sometimes stands in Need of our Indulgence. Whenever this happens with regard to *Shakespeare*, I would willingly impute it to a Vice of *his Times*. We see Complaisance enough, in our own Days, paid to a *bad Taste*. His *Clinches*, *false Wit*, and descending beneath himself, seem to be a Deference paid to *reigning Barbarism*. He was a *Sampson* in Strength, but he suffer'd some such *Dalilah* to give him up to the *Philistines*.[92]

This passage constitutes Theobald's negative criticism, and although it anticipates Johnson's comic elaboration of Shakespeare's stylistic faults that concludes with 'the fatal *Cleopatra* for which he lost the world, and was content to lose it',[93] it

---

[90] *1733.*
[91] *1733*, vol. i, p. xvi.
[92] Ibid.
[93] *1765*, vol. i, sig. B3[r] [Yale vii. 74].

differs significantly in its brevity. After an account of Shakespeare as a lover of music, Theobald dilates on Shakespeare's
'grand touches of Nature . . . that do not appear superficially
such; but in which he seems the most deeply instructed; and to
which, no doubt, he has so much ow'd that happy Preservation
of his *Characters*, for which he is justly celebrated'.[94] Shakespeare's achievement entirely overbalances the criticisms of the
neo-Aristotelians, and Rymer and Gildon, their representatives
in his Preface, are dismissed in the tail of a paragraph. Rymer
'writes with great Vivacity, and appears to have been a Scholar',
but Theobald cannot perceive that his knowledge of the art
of poetry 'was any deeper than his Acquaintance with *Bossu*
and *Dacier*, from whom he has transcribed many of his best
Reflexions'. Gildon is treated with equal lack of deference as
'One attached to *Rymer* by a similar Way of Thinking and
Studies'. Both are dismissed in terms that are Johnsonian in
their reference: 'They were Both of that Species of Criticks,
who are desirous of displaying their Powers rather in finding
Faults, than in consulting the Improvement of the World.'
Their concerns are merely 'the *hypercritical* Part of the Science
of *Criticism*'.[95]

From a modern perspective, a major fault of the edition is the
frequency with which Theobald ridicules Pope's editorial endeavours. To adopt this view is, however, to ignore Theobald's
real need to make Pope's aspersions in *The Dunciad* (1729)
rebound upon himself. The provocation was indeed great, and,
as Theobald remarked, 'there are Provocations, which a Man
can never quite forget'. Although Theobald is often harsh in
his counter-attacks on Pope ('His Libels have been thrown out
with so much Inveteracy, that, not to dispute whether they
should come from a *Christian*, they leave it a Question whether
they *could* come from a *Man*'), there is also a surprising amount
of good humour. He was, no doubt, willing to 'devote a part of
my Life to the honest Endeavour of quitting Scores', but in the
same paragraph he was prepared to acknowledge that 'The
Indignation, perhaps, for being represented a *Blockhead*, may
be as strong in Us as it is in the Ladies for a Reflexion on their

---

[94] Preface, *1733*, vol. i, pp. xx–xxi.   [95] Ibid., vol. i., p. xlviii.

Beauties'. This virtual admission of his own vanity is not only disarming to the reader, it enabled Theobald to maintain a remarkably balanced perspective on his dispute with Pope. Some of the absurd humour of *The Dunciad* seems to have struck Theobald himself as humorous, and he could be amused by the flights of a wanton imagination even as he felt obliged by the requirements of form to engage in ripostes: 'It is certain, I am indebted to Him for some *flagrant Civilities*.'[96] Possibly each man felt a degree of sympathy for the positions of his opponent even as he laboured to extricate himself from the predicaments created by the other, and in his correspondence, when puzzling over a passage in *The Comedy of Errors*, Theobald was prepared to see himself approximating to Pope's portrait in *The Dunciad*: 'Believe me, I had toiled myself into the very abyss of dullness upon this passage, and met with no ground.'[97] There may not have been a love–hate relationship between Pope and Theobald, but there are amongst their formal expressions of contempt occasional suggestions of the kind of attraction sometimes felt by opponents. Indeed, Theobald seems ironically to acknowledge this even in his Preface: 'It has been my Fate, it seems, as I thought it my Duty, to discover some *Anachronisms* in our Author; which might have slept in Oscurity but for *this Restorer*, as Mr. *Pope* is pleas'd affectionately to style me. . . .'[98]

If Theobald was not inclined to parade his learning in his commentary, he was likely to emphasize the logic in his thinking. In general, he was concerned to obviate Pope's charges of blockheadedness. He was, however, also imitating the style of one of the heroes of his youth, Richard Bentley.[99] The results of this imitation are unfortunate both for his style and, on two notorious occasions, for his text, where he comes perilously close to Bentley's performance in his edition of *Paradise Lost* (1732). Ariel's song in *The Tempest* (V. i. 88) is emended from 'Where the bee sucks, there *suck* I' to 'Where the bee sucks, there *lurk* I' on the grounds that Ariel, 'a Spirit of a refin'd ætherial Essence', could not be 'intended to want Food'. In the same song, Ariel flies 'After *Sunset*, merrily', rather than

[96] Preface, *1733*, vol. i, pp. xxxvi–xxxvii.
[97] Nichols, ii. 309 (6 Dec. 1729). Cf. Pope's representation of Theobald in *The Dunciad* discussed above, p. 94.
[98] Preface, *1733*, vol. i, p. xlix.
[99] For an analysis of Bentley's influence on Theobald, see Jones, ch. 2.

Summer, because bats hibernate, rather than migrate.[100] All
that can be said in favour of these emendations is that they do
at least indicate close attention to the meaning of the lines.[101]

For the most part, the errors in Theobald's text and commentary are of the kind that could only be avoided after successive generations of scholars had charted Elizabethan and
Jacobean English usage. He himself was aware of this liability
to error and consequently tended to be cautious. For example,
there is his comment on *3 Henry VI* (V. i. 42–4):

> Alas, that Warwick had no more fore-cast,
> But while he thought to steal the single ten,
> The King was slily finger'd from the Deck. . . .

Theobald's note reads: 'Tho there may seem no Consonance of
Metaphors betwixt a *single Ten* and a *Deck*, the latter Word
being grown obsolete, and not acknowledg'd by our Diction-
aries in the Sense here required; yet *Deck*, in all our *Northern*
Counties, is to this day used to signify a *Pack* or *Stock* of
Cards.'[102]

Theobald was aware of the larger implications for the English
language of his work as an editor of Shakespeare. In his
Preface, after a lengthy defence of verbal criticism, he declares
his belief that

If the *Latin* and *Greek* Languages have receiv'd the greatest
Advantages imaginable from the Labours of the Editors and Criticks
of the two last Ages; by whose Aid and Assistance the Grammarians
have been enabled to write infinitely better in that Art than even the
preceding Grammarians, who wrote when those Tongues flourish'd
as living Languages: I should account it a peculiar Happiness, that,
by the faint Assay I have made in this Work, a Path might be chalk'd

---

[100] *1733*, i. 66–7 nn.

[101] Cf. Johnson's comment on *A Midsummer Night's Dream* (III. i. 170) (*1765*, i.
132 n.. [Yale, vii. 151]):

> 'The honey-bags steal from the humble-bees,
> And for night-tapers crop their waxen thighs,
> And light them at the fiery glow-worm's eyes. . . .

I know not how *Shakespeare*, who commonly derived his knowledge of nature from his
own observation, happened to place the glow-worm's light in his eyes, which is only in
his tail.'

[102] *1733*, iv. 379 n.

out, for abler Hands, by which to derive the same Advantages to our own Tongue: a Tongue, which, tho' it wants none of the fundamental Qualities of an universal Language, yet as a *noble Writer* says, lisps and stammers as in its Cradle; and has produced little more towards its polishing than Complaints of its Barbarity.[103]

This passage stands out in its context in the Preface. In the midst of an account of the tribulations of his life of scholarship, Theobald remains firmly committed to his belief in the dignity and importance of his labours as a service not only to Shakespeare and his readers, but to the English language. If Pope's *Windsor Forest* (1713) marks the self-conscious beginnings of eighteenth-century English imperialistic pretensions having Roman origins, Theobald's Preface intimates a possible dominance of English, comparable to that of Latin, as 'an universal Langauge'. This awareness of the larger implications of his work, which distinguishes him as an editor from Pope and Warburton, inspired his detailed attention to his text and begins with his declaration in *Shakespeare Restored* (1726) that '*SHAKESPEARE* stands, or at least ought to stand, in the Nature of a Classic Writer'.[104] Not until Johnson's *Dictionary* (1755) was the idea of scholarship devoted to English language and literature explored and realized with comparable commitment and understanding. Theobald's edition taught Englishmen to read Shakespeare with care and respect, both at the level of the individual line and with appreciation of his larger purposes—purposes that in their romantic, imaginative power might transcend the concerns of neo-Aristotelian criticism. Again, it was not until Johnson's Preface to *Shakespeare* (1765) that these views of Shakespeare's achievement were more fully articulated.

---

[103] Preface, *1733*, vol. i, p. lxii. Theobald's reference is to Shaftesbury's 'Soliloquy: or, Advice to an Author' (1710), repr. in *Characteristicks*, 5th edn. (3 vols., 1732), i. 217.

[104] Introduction, *SR*, p. v. See above, p. 67.

10. Epilogue: Theobald's Last Years and Reputation

THE change in attitudes brought about by Theobald's *Shakespeare* can be gauged by David Mallet's poem, *Of Verbal Criticism*, which was dedicated to Pope, with his permission, and published in 1733. Mallet thought his readers would accept a representation of Theobald as an editor of Shakespeare as one 'Condemn'd to dig and dung a barren soil, | Where hardly tares will grow with care and toil' (ll. 59–60). Mallet caused Theobald no distress, who in his Preface quoted Falstaff on Poins: '*Hang him, Baboon! his Wit is as thick as* Tewkesbury *Mustard; there is no more Conceit in him, than is in a* MALLET.'[1] What had been intended as a buttress for Pope was now a source of embarrassment.

The period of his life that Theobald devoted to producing his edition of *Shakespeare* was both the most rewarding and, perhaps, the most stressful. To be lampooned in *The Dunciad* in itself had been trying, although he managed to survive that ordeal with dignity. More taxing was the need to earn his living from day to day while maintaining the progress of his work. He was fortunate to have the patronage of Sir Robert Walpole and Frederick, Prince of Wales. In February 1730 'by his Royal Highness's Command' he made a presentation copy of *Orestes: A Dramatic Opera*,[2] and subsequently he dedicated the published version to Walpole. In his dedication (1731) he thanks Walpole for his generous response to 'a late Sollicitation' and for not being willing 'to suffer any Degree of Merit to pine in Obscurity . . . by curing that false and ungenerous Notion' upon which the nobility 'proceed when they call a Man dull, because he is poor; and poor, because he is dull'. His being identified with poverty and dullness was, of course, owing mainly to Pope, and this argument, he feels, is 'A Piece of Sophistry which they have copied from some bad Wits among us, who

---

[1] Preface, *1733*, vol. i, pp. lii–liii.   [2] Jones, p. 264.

. . . consider Success as the only Argument and Test of Merit'.[3]

Henry Fielding, who at this time was also jockeying for Walpole's patronage, wrote an Epilogue for Theobald's opera in which he implored the ladies,

> Once in Age, at least, your Smiles dispense
> To *English* Sounds, and Tragedy that's Sense.
> These are Variety to you, who come
> From the *Italian Opera*, and *Tom Thumb*.[4]

As news spread that work on the edition was proceeding, support for Theobald increased. At the same time, the reaction against Pope and *The Dunciad* also strengthened. The rising tide of support for Theobald is reflected by Fielding in an epistle addressed to George Lyttelton in which he attacked Pope:

> Why, when thou lashest Tibbald's lifeless Lays,
> Dost thou not give the Solid Critick Praise?
> His Name with Shakespeare's shall to Ages Soar
> When thou shalt jingle in our Ears no more
> Shakespeare by him restor'd again we see
> Recover'd of the Wounds he bore from thee.
> And sure much brighter must his Merit shine
> Who gives us Sha[kes]peare's Works, than his who thine.[5]

There were others interested in the progress of his work. As early as February 1730 Theobald referred to 'A certain parcel of Free-masons, that are very zealous to have me of the order'.[6] Probably at the instigation of Martin Folkes, who was Deputy Grand Master in 1725, he afterwards joined the Quator Coronati Lodge No. 2076, and the connection was to his advantage. Shortly before publication of the edition, the Grand Master of the London Freemasons, the Earl of Strathmore, 'recommended to the Bretheren Br. Theobald's' *Apollo and Daphne* and 'desired they would all come clothed' to a performance.[7]

---

[3] Sigs. A2^r–A2^v.

[4] See Charles Woods, 'Fielding's Epilogue for Theobald', *Philological Quarterly*, 28 (1949), 419–24, and Bertrand A. Goldgar, *Walpole and the Wits: The Relation of Politics to Literature, 1722–1742* (Lincoln: University of Nebraska Press, 1976), 99–102.

[5] Isobel Grundy (ed.), 'New Verse by Henry Fielding,' *PMLA* 87 (1972), 244, ll. 124–31.

[6] Nichols, ii. 517.

[7] 'Minute Book No. 2', *Quator Coronatorum Antigrapha: Masonic Reprints of the Quator*

In addition to theatrical ventures as a means of earning income, Theobald enjoyed the patronage of 'my good Friend' the fifth Earl of Orrery. While work on the edition was in progress, Orrery employed Theobald to regulate and transcribe the family papers.[8] Theobald also addressed a poem to Orrery lamenting the death of the fourth Earl, probably his most generous patron, and urging the son to 'Be, what your Father was; & sweetly blend | A double Grace, the Patron and the Friend!'[9] The Earl, following the practice of his father, 'made the Whole set of them Golden Verses'.[10] Theobald had thought he might have separate dedications to each volume of his Shakespeare, 'but my Lord Orrery has been beforehand wth. me, & bespoke a part of its Patronage; & I think I can do no less than compliment him wth the Whole, turn my Address into an Epistle Dedicatory'.[11] Although he feared more 'Drydenisms', Theobald's dedication indicates a very warm and intimate association with the Orrerys, even as he claims 'Your Lordship's Patronage as it were by Descent from your Noble Father'.[12]

Such public and private support was necessary if Theobald were going to fill his subscription list and become solvent. A letter from him to a William Archer (11 May 1734) indicates that the list was entirely filled.[13] Included were the Prince of Wales, the Princess of Wales, eight dukes, seven duchesses, one marquis, one marchioness, and twenty earls. There were those, such as the Earl of Tyrconnel, who hesitated to have their names included for fear of offending Pope.[14] On the other hand, those whom Pope offended were likely to react in a manner advantageous to Theobald. As Theobald remarked to

Coronati Lodge, No 2076, London, vol. x, ed. W. J. Songhurst (Margate: W. J. Parrett, 1913), 69; 237 (13 Dec. 1733). The Brethren apparently attended the performance dressed in full Masonic regalia.

[8] Jones, p. 298 (21 Mar. 1732). See also ibid. 326, 333, 337. Some of the volumes of letters transcribed by Theobald are now in the Houghton Library, Harvard University.

[9] *An Epistle Humbly Addressed to the Right Honourable John, Earl of Orrery* (1732), p. [6].

[10] Jones, p. 306 (4 July 1732).

[11] Ibid. 312 (10 Mar. 1732).

[12] *1733*, vol. i, sig. A3^v.

[13] Now in the Beinecke Library, Yale University. To Theobald's subscription money of 1,100 guineas (see above, ch. 7 n. 74) should be added gifts of 100 guineas from the fifth Earl of Orrery for the Dedication and 20 guineas from the Prince of Wales (Jones, p. 327).

[14] Jones, pp. 305–6 (4 July 1732).

Warburton: 'Pope, as you'll find, has lent me an accidental lift by his Poem on Taste: for the Duke of Chandos, whom I never knew or approach'd, has subscrib'd for 4 Setts of my Shakespeare on Royal Paper.'[15] In addition to his monetary rewards, publication of the edition gave Theobald the satisfaction of a public repudiation of Pope's aspersions on his character and abilities in *The Dunciad*. Even *The Grub-Street Journal*, which previously had been very hostile, finally proved to be at a loss for criticism. In No. 229 (16 May 1734), while finding fault with Theobald's Greek conjectures in his Preface,[16] Mr. Bavius allowed Theobald 'the title, he so incontestably possesses, of the best English critic'.

The period immediately following publication of his *Shakespeare* was undoubtedly the most satisfactory of Theobald's life. The Freemasons sponsored a performance of *2 Henry IV* for the 'Entertainment of the Grand Master' and for the benefit of the Editor of Shakespeare in May 1734.[17] Indeed, his association with the Masons seems to have played a significant part in his life for the next few years. In April 1736, when the Earl of Loudoun was invested as Grand Master, Theobald was elected one of the twelve Grand Stewards of the Grand Lodge—perhaps the apex of his social career. This election involved him in the high society and lavish entertainments of the Masons. To give an instance, on 28 April 1737 the twelve Grand Stewards gathered at the house in Pall Mall of The Right Honourable Edward Earl and Viscount Darnley, along with the Earl of Loudoun GM, the Duke of Richmond, the Earl of Craufurd, the Earl of Weymes, and Lord Grey. They then

Together with vast Appearance of former Grand Officers & other Bretheren as well of the Nobility as others properly cloathed Who proceeded in a regular manner in Coaches & Chariots to Fishmongershall in Thames Street   The Grand Master being in a Chariot richly carved & gilt drawn by six beautiful Grey Horses having three Setts of Musick properly disposed playing before them that preceeding the Grand Master consisting of a pair of Kettle Drums four Trumpets & four French Horns   The others of a pair of Kettle Drums two Trumpets & two French Horns each.

[15] Ibid. 298 (21 Mar. 1732); Pope's 'Poem on Taste' is the *Epistle to Burlington, Of the Use of Riches* (Dec. 1731).

[16] *1733*, vol. i, pp. liii–lxii.

[17] Jones, p. 326. See also *LS*, pt. 3, i. 394; the bretheren were 'desir'd to meet at the Castle Tavern, Drury Lane, cloath'd; thence to go in Procession, as usual, to the Play'.

Following the election of Darnley as Grand Master for the year, 'the twelve present Stewards were called in & had thanks returned them in the name of the whole Lodge for their great Care & Conduct in providing so elegant & plentiful an Entertainment   And their Healths were drank with Ceremony.'[18]

It would be pleasing to record that Theobald's last years were spent in affluence and that he continued to be appreciated by his contemporaries. Such was not the case. As early as 1737 William Hogarth, who was a subscriber to the edition, published 'The Distrest Poet', which in the first issue (3 March 1737) presented the poet writing a copy of verses with a title alluding to Theobald's early poem, 'The Cave of Poverty' and with Pope's verse portraits in *The Dunciad* as a motto. Hogarth was evidently persuaded to alter his print, and the second issue (15 December 1740) erased the verses by Pope and substituted 'Riches a Poem' for 'Poverty a Poem'. However, the identification of Theobald with poverty and dullness had been renewed by publication of Hogarth's print. Indeed, by 1740 Theobald was again in serious financial difficulties. Contemplating the lost income of his neglected law practice, he admitted to Lord Rockingham's daughter, Lady Monson, that 'If I have not made all the Advantages, which might have accrued from so favourable a Situation in Life, it is, that Nature had not done her Part, and all Soils are not equally susceptible of Improvement'.[19] In 1741 the taxable value of his dwelling in Wyan's Court, Great Russell Street, was reduced from twenty-eight pounds to fourteen, and by 1744 the rate had been reduced from two shillings in the pound to ten pence.[20]

He had, of course, continued to attempt to maintain his life of scholarship by means of the theatre. His pantomimic afterpieces generally continued to be successful, but provided only an irregular source of income. His adaptation of Webster's *The Duchess of Malfi* as *The Fatal Secret* (1735), first performed on 4 April 1733, managed only two performances, its fate being to appear 'in a Season when the Weather was warm, and the

---

[18] *Quator Coronatorum Antigrapha*, ed. Songhurst, x. 286–7.

[19] Dedication, *The Happy Captive: An English Opera* (1741), sig. A2[r].

[20] Camden Public Library, Holborn Library (32–8 Theobalds Road, London WC1X 8PA), Rate Books for the Parish of St Giles in the Fields in the County of Middlesex, pts. i and ii (1730–45), 2, 15.

Town in a political Ferment'.[21] He furnished the 'Vocal Parts' of an *Entertainment call'd Merlin; or, The Devil of Stone-Henge,* which was performed on 12 December 1734, but which ran for only seven performances. In 1739 the *London Daily Post and General Advertiser* reported (26 September), 'We hear, that Mr Theobald has given the last Hand to his Tragedy, called, The Death of Hannibal, attempted in Imitation of Shakespear's Manner, and that it is designed to appear on the Stage this Season.'[22] However, the play was never staged. In 1740 *Orpheus and Eurydice (with the Metamorphoses of Harlequin), an Opera* was performed at the Theatre Royal with music by John Frederick Lampe. There were 324 performances in the course of the century. *The Happy Captive, an English Opera,* performed 16 April 1741 with music by Galliard, was an amusing satire on Italian opera, which failed.[23] In May 1741 there was another revival of *Double Falshood* for the benefit of 'the last Editor of Shakespear'.[24] The proceeds from these ventures were not sufficient to meet his needs. His last theatrical piece was *Harlequin Captive,* which had one performance at Daniel and Smith's Great Theatrical Booth in Mayfair on 1 May 1744.[25]

There were other disappointments: he published the second edition of his *Shakespeare* in 1740, but the proceeds were again insufficient. His translation of Aeschylus, although completed, remained unpublished. Sir Robert Walpole, it is true, acceded to his petition (21 August 1739) for a place for his son, Lewis, in the Office of the Pells,[26] but he failed to find a sinecure for Theobald himself. In May 1741, when the benefit performance of *Double Falshood* was being staged, Theobald wrote to the Duke of Newcastle 'that I am once more encouraged to address your Grace on an Emergency. The Situation of my Affairs upon a Loss & Disappointment, obliging me to embrace a Benefit at this late & disadvantageous Season, it lays me under

[21] Preface, *The Fatal Secret* (1735), quoted *LS*, pt. 3, i. 285.

[22] *LS*, pt. 3, ii. 789.

[23] See Roger Fiske, *English Theatre Music in the Eighteenth Century* (London: Oxford University Press, 1973), 207.

[24] *LS*, pt. 3, ii. 917.

[25] *Index to the London Stage 1660–1800,* compiled by Ben Ross Schneider, Jr. (Carbondale: Southern Illinois University Press, 1979); *LS*, pt. 3, ii. 1107.

[26] Cambridge University Library, Cholmondeley (Houghton) Collection, C.H. 2917.

a Necessity of throwing Myself on the Favour of the Publick, & the kind Assistance of my Friends and Well-wishers.'[27]

The fifth Earl of Orrery sought to cultivate the company of other literary men, including Pope and Warburton. In 1735 he wrote to Pope, assuring him that 'I shall always endeavour to deserve your Freindship: You shall have my Hand and Heart'.[28] In 1741 the Earl confided to Thomas Birch that 'I really think it an honour to be remembered by Mr Warburton. He has my sincere respects, & has long had my admiration and esteem.'[29] As part of a further bid for Pope's friendship, Orrery corresponded with the Earl of Arran in 1743, soliciting support for the conferring of an honorary DD by Oxford on Warburton, which had before been 'unaccountably' refused by Convocation.[30] (After glimpsing Warburton's *Shakespear*, Orrery observed to Birch: 'My house is too little to hold any more Shakespears', but he did 'have room for the divine legation of Moses'.)[31]

A final social recognition of Theobald's contribution to the understanding and appreciation of Shakespeare was his being asked to write the Prologue to the benefit play, performed on 10 April 1739 at Covent Garden, for erecting a monument to Shakespeare in Westminster Abbey.[32] His last scholarly project was an edition of the works of Beaumont and Fletcher. His contract was with Jacob Tonson jun. and Somerset Draper, and he announced his agreement in the *London Daily Post* for 13 May 1742. Thomas Seward, a Canon of Lichfield, responded to his advertisement, as did the Revd John Sympson. Almost immediately there were problems with Seward, who had Warburton's vanity, although not his malice. Upon Theobald's omitting 'several Emendations which seem still to me more deserving of Notice than many which are inserted', Seward took advantage of his friendship with the proprietors, Tonson

[27] Jones, p. 346.

[28] *Correspondence*, iii. 481 (10 Aug. 1735).

[29] British Library, Add. MS 4303, fo. 86ᵛ (31 Oct. 1741).

[30] Harvard University, Houghton Library, MS Eng. 218.2, iv. 345 (15 Jan. 1743).

[31] British Library, Add. MS 4303, fo. 124ᵛ (26 May 1747). (A transcript of this letter is at Harvard University, Houghton Library, MS Eng. 218.2, v. 44). Orrery refers to Warburton's *The Divine Legation of Moses Demonstrated* (2 vols., 1738–41).

[32] See *LS*, pt. 3, ii. 768. The Prologue was printed in *The London Daily Post and General Advertiser* (12 Apr. 1739).

and Draper, to exact a written promise from Theobald that he would have 'a full Liberty to publish what Postscript I pleas'd at the end of each Volume'.[33] The critical standards of the edition as a whole immediately fell. It was published posthumously in 1750.

He died as a result of jaundice on 18 September 1744. His death was recorded by his old friend, John Stede, the prompter, as 'very remarkable, not only in that he went off quietly without agonies, but also that he was so composed as not to alter the disposition of his body, being in an easy indolent posture, one foot out of bed, and his head gently supported by one hand'. According to Stede, 'He was of a generous spirit, too generous for his circumstances; and none knew how to do a handsome thing, or confer a benefit, when in his power, with a better grace than himself. He was my antient friend of near 30 years acquaintance. Interred at Pancras the 20th, 6 o'clock P.M. I only attended him.'[34] Perhaps stung by Pope's description of him in *The Dunciad*, he had kept his books 'unpawn'd', but a little over a month later, beginning on 23 October, his library was sold by public auction in the course of four evenings in 631 lots. Lot 460 consisted of 'One hundred ninety-five old English Plays in Quarto, some of them so scarce as not to be had at any Price, *to many of which are Manuscript Notes and Remarks of Mr. Theobald's*, all done up neatly in Boards, in single Plays'. The remaining volumes were advertised for sale on 11 May 1747.[35]

The collapse of Theobald's social life was due to poverty and the combined influence of Pope and Warburton. It was scarcely possible to be the avowed friend of Theobald and to expect their friendship. Indeed, after Pope's death Warburton alone made a formidable opponent to Theobald's reputation. However, Thomas Edwards's *Supplement to Mr. Warburton's Edition of Shakespear* (1747) devastated Warburton's credentials as an editor and critic, and Lord Orrery wrote to Birch, 'Such a blow cannot be recovered. The last cannon, carries with it very severe observations: and ends with as sharp a Thing as possible. I

---

[33] Thomas Seward, 'An Account of the present Edition', *Works of Beaumont and Fletcher* (10 vols., 1750), i. 1.

[34] Nichols, ii. 745 n. There is no record of his burial in the parish registers.

[35] See below, Appendix E.

dare say, Mr Warburton will answer his adversary, but in what manner, is hard to guess.'[36] In fact, Warburton made no reply, and Thomas Seward ventured to reaffirm 'the Distinction Mr. *Theobald* gain'd in the learned World, who had no other Claim to Honour but as a *Critic* on *Shakespear*', and to assert that 'his *Fame* remains fresh and unblasted tho' the *Lightning* of Mr. *Pope* and the *Thunder* of Mr. *Warburton* have been both lanch'd at his Head'.[37] It was Johnson, in the latter part of his career, who effectively ruined Theobald's reputation among later scholars in the eighteenth century and most twentieth-century academics.

The fundamental importance and novelty of Theobald's methods of elucidating his texts are indirectly attested to by Johnson in the period immediately preceding publication of the *Dictionary* (1755). It is also clear that Thomas Warton perceived the connection between Theobald's pioneering researches and Johnson's *Dictionary*. What becomes apparent is that Johnson's later reluctance to do Theobald justice, especially in the citation of parallels, is due in part to his unwillingness to acknowledge any similarity between Theobald's duty as an editor and his own drudgery as a lexicographer. Theobald instituted the practice of citing parallels as a means of explicating obscure English words, and Johnson in the *Dictionary* followed his practice on an unprecedented scale.

In 1754 Thomas Warton published the first edition of *Observations on the Faerie Queene of Spenser*, a work which makes very considerable use of parallel readings as a means of elucidation. On 16 July 1754 Johnson wrote to congratulate Warton:

I now pay you a very honest acknowledgement for the advancement of the literature of our native Country. You have shown to all who shall hereafter attempt the study of our ancient authours the way to success, by directing them to the perusal of the books which those authours had read. Of this method Hughes[38] and Men much greater than Hughes seem never to have thought. The Reason why the authours which are yet read of the sixteenth Century are so little understood is that they are read alone, and no help is borrowed from those who lived with them or before them. Some part of this ignorance

[36] British Library, Add. MS 4303, fo. 145^v (received 13 Dec. 1748).

[37] Preface, *Works of Beaumont and Fletcher* (10 vols., 1750), vol. i, p. lviii.

[38] John Hughes, the editor of Tonson's edition of Spenser (1715).

I hope to remove by my book [the *Dictionary*] which now draws towards its end.[39]

Although in the *Dictionary* Johnson was more concerned with the standards of excellence exemplified by his citations than with a historical approach to the language, he was, of course, thoroughly aware of the importance of the historical approach to language and literature. In the Preface to the *Dictionary*, when he indicates that he has extracted 'the diction of common life from Shakespeare', he was principally concerned with Shakespeare as an exemplary source. But his historical concerns take precedence over exemplary usage in the year following publication of the *Dictionary*. In his *Proposals for Printing the Dramatick Works of William Shakespeare* (1756) he observes:

When a writer outlives his contemporaries, and remains almost the only unforgotten name of a distant time, he is necessarily obscure. Every age has its modes of speech, and its cast of thought; which, though easily explained when there are many books to be compared with each other, becomes sometimes unintelligible and always difficult, when there are no parallel passages that may conduce to their illustration. Shakespeare is the first considerable authour of sublime or familiar dialogue in our language. Of the books which he read, and from which he formed his stile, some perhaps have perished, and the rest are neglected. His imitations are therefore unnoted, his allusions are undiscovered, and many beauties, both of pleasantry and greatness, are lost with the objects to which they were united, as the figures vanish when the canvass has decayed.[40]

Some account of Theobald's researches would have been appropriate in Johnson's brief history of the editing of Shakespeare in the *Proposals*. Instead, Johnson dismisses him as one who 'considered learning only as an instrument of gain', who 'made no further enquiry after his authour's meaning, when once he had notes sufficient to embellish his page with the expected decorations', and launches into an account of his own qualifications as an editor arising from his years working on the *Dictionary*:

With regard to obsolete or peculiar diction, the editor may perhaps

---

[39] No. 53, *The Letters of Samuel Johnson*, ed. R. W. Chapman (3 vols., Oxford: Clarendon Press, 1952), i. 56.

[40] Yale, vii. 52–3.

claim some degree of confidence, having had more motives to consider the whole extent of our language than any other man from its first formation. He hopes, that, by comparing the works of Shakespeare with those of writers who lived at the same time, immediately preceded, or immediately followed him, he shall be able to ascertain his ambiguities, disentangle his intricacies, and recover the meaning of words now lost in the darkness of antiquity.[41]

Thomas Warton, a man totally devoid of pretensions, felt that Johnson had treated Theobald unfairly in his *Proposals*. Furthermore, Warton was not prepared to accept credit for the discovery of Theobald's methods of elucidating Elizabethan texts—notwithstanding Johnson's letter to him in 1754 on the occasion of the first edition of *Observations on the Faerie Queene*. In the second, enlarged edition of the *Observations* (2 vols., 1762), Warton added a postscript which did justice to Theobald's pioneering work. Warton also pointedly rebuked Johnson for his treatment of Theobald by quoting from Johnson's *Proposals* before launching into his own defence of the man. In order to elucidate Spenser, Warton says that he has searched his contemporaries and 'examined the books on which the peculiarities of his style, taste, and composition, are confessedly founded'. He fears that he may be censured for his prolixity of examples, but a commentator must bring to bear on his author 'those books, which though now forgotten, were yet in common use and high repute about the time in which his authors respectively wrote, and which they consequently must have read'. If these books are neglected, 'many allusions and many imitations will either remain obscure, or lose half their beauty and propriety: "as the figures vanish when the canvas is decayed." '[42] Having quoted Johnson, Warton launches into his defence of Theobald:

Pope laughs at Theobald for giving us, in his edition of Shake-speare,[43] a sample of

'———— All such READING *as was never read.*'

But these strange and ridiculous books which Theobald quoted, were unluckily the very books which Shakespeare himself had studied; the knowledge of which enabled that useful editor to explain so many

[41] Ibid. 56.

[42] *Observations on the Faerie Queene*, 2nd edn. (1762), ii. 264; cf. Johnson, *Proposals*, quoted above, p. 208.

[43] Actually, it was in *Shakespeare Restored* (1726).

difficult allusions and obsolete customs in his poet, which otherwise could never have been understood.[44]

Warton gives as an example Pope's mistaking the 'dreadful sagittary' in *Troilus and Cressida* for Teucer and defends Theobald's reference to *The Recuyell of the Histories of Troy* as Shakespeare's source.[45] He then makes his main point:

If Shakespeare is worth reading, he is worth explaining; and the researches used for so valuable and elegant a purpose, merit the thanks of genius and candour, not the satire of prejudice and ignorance. That labour, which so essentially contributes to the service of true taste, deserves a more honourable repository than The TEMPLE of DULNESS.[46]

Warton hoped to exorcise the ghost of Shaftesbury from scholarship.[47] Of course, general agreement that 'Shakespeare is worth reading' was an essential prerequisite for Warton's argument, and Theobald played a central role in bringing about this consensus. To Warton it was evident that Pope's satire was 'false satire'. Also implicit in Warton's account is the view that Johnson's failure to do justice to his predecessor is reprehensible.[48]

Indeed, when Johnson himself was still an aspiring scholarly hack, his views of Theobald were very different. In the *Miscellaneous Observations on Macbeth* (1745) he had said of Theobald: 'some of his amendments are so excellent, that, even when he has failed, he ought to be treated with indulgence and respect.'[49] Johnson's thought here is echoed and expanded in his Preface to *Shakespeare*, but, unfortunately, without reference to Theobald:

an emendatory critick would ill discharge his duty, without qualities very different from *dulness* [*my italics*]. In perusing a corrupted piece, he must have before him all possibilities of meaning, with all possibilities of expression. Such must be his comprehension of thought, and such his copiousness of language. Out of many readings possible, he

[44] Warton, op. cit., ii. 264–65.

[45] See above, pp. 98–9.

[46] Warton, op. cit., ii. 265.

[47] See above, pp. 52–3.

[48] For a more complaisant reading of Johnson's treatment of his predecessor, see Donald T. Siebert, Jr., 'The Scholar as Satirist: Johnson's Edition of Shakespeare', *Studies in English Literature*, 15 (1975).

[49] Note III, Yale, vii. 8.

must be able to select that which best suits with the state, opinions, and modes of language prevailing in every age, and with his authour's particular cast of thought, and turn of expression. Such must be his knowledge, and such his taste. Conjectural criticism demands more than humanity possesses, and he that exercises it with most praise has very frequent need of indulgence.[50]

When comparing Pope and Theobald as editors in the Preface, he says: '*Theobald*, thus weak and ignorant, thus mean and faithless, thus petulant and ostentatious, *by the good luck of having* Pope *for his enemy*, has escaped, *and escaped alone*, with reputation, from this undertaking' (my italics). The sentence meiotically acknowledges the justice of contemporary views that as an editor of Shakespeare Theobald was superior to both Pope and Warburton—but it is the conclusion of Johnson's paragraph that gives insight into his condemnation of Theobald: 'So willingly does the world support those who solicite favour, against those who command reverence; and so easily is he praised, whom no man can envy.'[51] The ambivalence in Johnson's attitude to scholars and scholarship is evident. By 1765, he himself wished to 'command reverence'—not as a commentator beating 'his little gold to a spacious surface', nor as a 'retired and uncourtly Scholar', nor yet as 'a harmless drudge' providing parallel readings to illustrate words, but as a commanding personality in the larger arenas of life. The painful memories of his own poverty when a scholarly hack and of his proud repudiation of condescension vitiate his judgement of one who aspired no higher than to be a scholar.

In the conclusion of his Preface to *Shakespeare*, Theobald declared: 'as no Labour of Mine can be equivalent to the dear and ardent Love I bear for *Shakespeare*, so, if the Publick shall be pleas'd to allow that He owes any Thing to my Willingness and Endeavours of restoring Him; I shall reckon the Part of my Life so engag'd, to have been very happily employ'd.' He was willing 'to be try'd by my Country in the Affair'.[52] His country found in his favour: despite the ridicule of Pope, the malignity

---

[50] *1765*, vol. i, sig. C8ᵛ [Yale, vii. 94–5].

[51] *1765*, vol. i, sigs. D1ᵛ–D2ʳ [Yale, vii. 96]. See also Arthur Sherbo, 'Johnson's Indebtedness to Others', *Samuel Johnson, Editor of Shakespeare*, Illinois Studies in Language and Literature, 42 (Urbana: University of Illinois Press, 1956), ch. 3.

[52] *1733*, vol. i, p. lxviii.

of Warburton, and the contumely of Johnson, continuing demand for his *Shakespeare* produced nine editions by 1773.

APPENDIX A. *Special Hands in the Eighteenth Century*

Hilary Jenkinson notes that the plain secretary hand 'lasted in some places well into the eighteenth century'.[1] George Bickham sen., in the Preface to *British Youth's Instructor* (1754), says that by the late seventeenth century and early eighteenth century the round hand prevailed over the secretary hand and was 'practised by all degrees of men, in all employments, *the law only excepted*' (my italics).[2] The better schools took into account the possible needs of their pupils, either as potential lawyers or as future landowners. Theobald's acquaintance, William Stukeley (1687–1765), received his early education at the Free School at Holbeach in Lincolnshire, where 'in penmanship, I became a great proficient, & could write court, secretary, or any other hand, in great perfection'.[3] He learned to write in 1694. Stukeley may have been exceptionally proficient, but his writing-master, a Mr Coleman, was not unusual in what he taught, judging by advertisements in the newspapers, e.g. *Mist's Journal* (25 September 1725): 'Philip Pickering, Writing Master . . . at the Golden Pen in Pater-Noster-Row . . . teacheth all the useful Hands of Great Britain . . . and also qualifies young Gentlemen for . . . Attorneys Clerks.' *Mist's Journal* (1 January 1726): 'Writing in all Hands of Great Britain . . . carefully taught by William Brooks . . . at the Hand and Pen in Wardour Street.'

After the Acts regulating the training and practice of lawyers and attorneys (2 Geo. II, c. 23; 4 Geo. II, c. 26; 6 Geo. II, c. 14), study and use of the old hands fell into abeyance, with the result that by 1776 Andrew Wright felt it necessary to publish *Court Hand Restored; or, the Student's Assistant in Reading Old Deeds, Charters, &c.* Wright's comments in his Introduction are interesting, especially when it is remembered that Theobald's training as an attorney was before the Acts discarding the use of Latin and special hands:

---

[1] *The Later Court Hands in England from the Fifteenth to the Seventeenth Century* (Cambridge: The University Press, 1927), 67.

[2] Quoted by Ambrose Heal, *A Biographical Dictionary of the Old English Writing Masters and Bibliography of English Copy Books, 1500–1800* (Cambridge: The University Press, 1931), p. xxxiii.

[3] Bodleian Library, MS Eng. Misc. e. 121, fo. 7^r.

Although it is universally agreed that the Public have reaped some advantages by the Acts of the 4th Geo. II. c. 26. and 6th Geo. II. c. 14. requiring all Law-Pleadings, Deeds, &c. to be thereafter written in English; yet the Tax growing from these advantages is becoming so excessive, that few persons are now to be found capable of reading or explaining old Deeds and Charters, with any satisfaction to themselves or others.

This great inconvenience must have arisen from the Acts above mentioned; for, it being vainly imagined after the passing of those Acts, Court-Hand and Latin were unnecessary accomplishments for a Lawyer, young gentlemen were frequently articled to Attornies and Solicitors without the knowledge of either: and even called to the Bar without learning to read the Court-Hand, or the Abbreviations of it. The inconveniences brought on by this neglect were in some measure solved *pro tempore* by Old Practitioners then living, who were in Business when the Law Pleadings were in Latin, and were familiar with the contractions; but time having gradually deprived the Law of those valuable Gentlemen of the profession, I believe it may with truth and modesty be affirmed, from the numerous applications that are made to me on that subject, that the Reading of the old Law-Hands is at this day very nearly (if not altogether) become obsolete, though useful. I make this declaration with some concern; for although it is not necessary, as the Law now stands, to *write* the Court or any other of the old Law-Hands; yet, as Records written in those hands are daily produced in Evidence in the Courts of Law, the being able to *read* them with propriety and certainty cannot be an unnecessary accomplishment, not only for young Students, Stewards of Manors, and others, but also for the most dignified characters in the profession; as, in the cases of Quo Warranto's and Election Business, Records and old Charters are almost constantly referred to: and he who best understands the Abbreviations, bids fairest for a true explanation of the matter in question.[4]

As Dr J. H. Baker remarks (see above, ch. 2 n.15), the secretary hand is easier to read than court hand, and mastery of court hand implies mastery of secretary script. It seems certain that Theobald's training as an attorney would have made him quite capable of writing out a doubtful passage in secretary script when pondering 'the Traces of the Letters' and testing an emendation by means of the *ductus litterarum*.

[4] pp. 1–2.

APPENDIX B. *The Agreement between Theobald and Tonson for Publishing Shakespeare (Bodleian Library, MS Rawl. D. 729)*

ARTICLES of Argument [*sic*] had made concluded and Agreed on this Twenty sixth day of October in the Fifth year of ye Reign of our Sovereign Lord George ye second by ye grace of God of great Britain ffrance and Ireland King Defender of ye Faith &c Anoq: Dom: 1731 BETWEEN Jacob Tonson Citizen & Stationer of London (in behalf of himself & others ye Proprietors of ye Copy Right of Shakespears Plays) of ye one part of and Lewis Theobald of Great Russ[ell] street in the Parish of St Giles's in the fields and County of Middx Gentleman of ye other part.

IMPRIMIS Whereas ye Said Lewis Theobald hath with great Labour Diligence and Expence of Time prepared to Exhibit a Correct Edition of ye s^d Shakespear's Plays and hath compiled Notes to prove his several Corrections of the Text as well as to explain the difficult Passages ther^{e}of.

AND WHEREAS the said Lewis Theobald hath agreed w^t.^{h}. ye said Jacob Tonson in behalf of himself and ye other Propr[i]etors as above mentioned for selling and Assigning his said Notes & corrections and other Additions on the Terms herein after for that purpose Specified and Expressed WHEREUPO[N] the s^d. Jacob Tonson hath Covenanted and Agreed (with what reasonable Dispatch may be) to print of [*sic*] one Edition of the ~~first and Second~~ said Shakespears Plays (vizt. of all his Plays contained in the first and second Folio Editions of the said Poets Works) in six Volumes in Octavo together with all the Notes and Corrections of the s^d Lewis Theobald at the charge and Expence of him ye s^d Jacob Tonson in behalf of himself and ye s^d. other proprietors Now it is agreed ~~that~~ between the said Parties that in Consideration of the s^d ~~Parties~~ Notes and corrections and other Additions hereby intended to be sold and Assigned as afores^d. to ye s^d Jacob Tonson and the s^d. other Proprietors

Ite[m] the s^d. Jacob Tonson in behalf of himself and ye s^d. other Proprietors shall alow and give 400 perfect and compleat Copy's of y^e

s^d edition (so to be printed) in sheets and on the paper now produced as a Specimen & marked as such with the names of ye s^d. J: Tonson & Lewis Which 400 Copy's are to be free and Clear to the S^d L: Theobald of and from all expences either for paper or printing the s^d. Edition or any part thereof & it is also agreed for the Considerations afores^d. that ye s^d J: Tonson in behalf of himself and the s^d. other proprietors shall farther ^{give} & alow to ye s^d. L: Theobald one Hundred more compleat and perfect copy's of ye said Edition to be printed of [*sic*] on a fine Royal paper without any Expence whatsoever to the s^d Lewis Theobald for or on Account of ye Printing thereof or of opening ye Chases or Margins of ye Respective Sheets in order to ye same or of any other part of Workmanship requisite in ye printing of ye s^d Edition only ye s^d Lewis Theobald is to pay for and answer ye Expence of ye Royal Paper requisite & to be employed for and in ye s^d 100 Copies last abovementioned which Royal Paper he ye s^d Lewis Theobald doth hereby promise & agree to pay for at ye end of Six Months next after ye same shall be brought and delivered to ye printer from ye merchant or stationer.

Item It is also agreed by and between the Parties to these Presents That ye s^d. Lewis Theobald shall and will within two Calender Months from the day of ye date of these presents deliver ye s^d. work compleat for ye press unto ye s^d. J Tonson & that he ye s^d J Tonson shall not be ~~alowed~~ obliged to begin to print the s^d ~~Book~~ ^{Work} or any part thereof untill such time as ye s^d. L: Theobald shall have so deliver'd ye s^d. whole work compleat for ye pres unto ye s^d. J Tonson as afores^d. And that then ye s^d. work shall be printed at two or more printing Houses with ye utmost dispatch.

Item It is convenanted and agreed by ye s^d. J Tonson in behalf of himself & ye s^d. other Propr^{i}etors that so soon as ye s^d. L: Theobald shall have prepared and published his proposals for taking in Subscriptions for his Copies of ye s^d Edition he ye s^d. J. Tonson[1] & the s^d. other Proprietors shall at their respective Shops and Dwelling Houses take in Subscriptions for the s^d Lewis Theobalds s^d Copies for his use Benefit & Behoof & shall deliver out his printed Receipts & Proposals for the same for & during the Time while the s^d. Edition is printing & until it is perfected for Publication.

Item. It is agreed by the Parties to these presents that the L[i]st of the s^d Lewis Theobalds Subscribers Catalogue of the s^d. Shakespears Editions of his Plays such Indexes & Glossaries of obscure Words & also all such Prefaces & Dedications as the s^d. Lewis Theobald shall think fit to Prefix or add to any of ye respective six Volumes[2] are to be

---

[1] At this point the handwriting appears to change.

[2] When the edition was finally published in Jan. 1734, there were 7 volumes.

construed a part of the s^d Edition & to be printed & incerted as a part thereof without any manner of Expence whatsoever to the s^d Lewis Theobald save the additional charge in the Paper for his one hundred Copies beforementioned to be printed & wrought off on fine Royal Paper.

Item It is agreed by the Parties to these Presents that the s^d Jacob Tonson on behalf of himself & the s^d other Proprietors shall not print or cause or procure to be printed any Copies of the s^d Edition of Shakespears Plays on either of the same Papers (or equal to it) fixt & stipulated for the Subscription books of the s^d Lewis Theobald other than the Five Hundred Copies to be printed for the use & Benefit of the s^d Lewis Theobald nor shall the s^d Jacob Tonson in behalf of himself or the s^d other Proprietors publish or Sell or cause to be published or Sold any one printed Copy of the s^d Edition till the Expiration of six Weeks after the s^d Lewis Theobald has had his five hundred Copies abovementioned perfected & ready to be deliverd out to his Subscribers.

Item It is agreed on the part & behalf of the s^d Lewis Theobald & he the s^d Lewis Theobald for the consideration abovementioned doth hereby fully & absolute[ly] Grant Bargain Sell Assign Transfer & set over unto the s^d Jacob Tonson his Ex'tors Adm' & Assign[gns] all his s^d Notes [&] Corrections so to be printed in the s^d Edition & [*illegible*] all & every such Index & Indexes Glossaris & Glossaries of obscure Words Preface & Pref[aces] Dedication & Dedications as shall or may be prefixed or added to the s^d six Volumes [in] any or either of them And all his Copy Right Interest & Claims of in or to the same & every of [*illegible*] & every part thereof To have & to hold the same & every of them & every part thereof unto the s^d Jacob Tonson his Executors Adm'. & Assigns as his & their own proper[ty] Goods & Chattells for ever for the Benefit of himself & the s^d. other Proprietors.

AND LASTLY the s^d. Lewis Theobald doth hereby covenant & agree to & with the s^d Jacob Tonson his Ex'tors Adm'. & Assigns that he the s^d Lewis Theobald his Ex'tors Adm'. or Assigns shall not nor will at any time hereafter print or publish or Cause or procure to be printed or published all or any or either of the s^d. Notes Corrections Indexes Glossaries Prefaces & Dedications or any part thereof or of any or either of them either alone or together with any other Work either as the same shall be printed & published with the s^d six Volumes of the s^d Plays or with any alteration or alterations Addition or Additions whatsoever——

And the s^d Parties to these presents for the due performance of all Clauses Articles Covenants & Agreements herein abovementioned have bound themselves & their respective Heirs Ex'tors & adm.^rs to each other in the Penal Sum of one Hundred Pounds of lawful Money of Great Britain In Witness whereof they have hereunto interchangeably set their Hands & Seals the Day & Year first above

Sealed & deliverd in the Presence of

Tho˙Glenister[3]

Jacob Tonson

Som. Draper[4]

Lew Theobald

[3] The Rate Book for the Parish of St Giles-in-the-Fields (p. 34) for this period, now in the Camden Public Library, Holborn Library (32–8 Theobalds Road, London WC1X 8PA), indicates that Thomas Glenister was a neighbour of Theobald who resided in Lyon Street, Blomesbury.

[4] Somerset Draper was a friend and eventually a partner of the Tonsons, as well as a financial adviser to David Garrick. See George Winchester Stone, Jr. and George M. Kahrl, *David Garrick: A Critical Biography* (Carbondale and Edwardsville: Southern Illinois University Press, 1979), 57, 112–14.

APPENDIX C. *Sale of the Copyright of* Double Falshood

A convenient guide to the literature surrounding *Double Falshood; or, The Distrest Lovers. A Play, As it is Acted at the Theatre-Royal in Drury-Lane. Written Originally by W. SHAKESPEARE; And now Revised and Adapted to the Stage By Mr. THEOBALD, the Author of Shakespeare Restor'd* (1728) may be found in *Four Plays Ascribed to Shakespeare . . . An Annotated Bibliography*, compiled by G. Harold Metz (New York: Garland, 1982). Although the only book-length study of the relationship between *Double Falshood* and *Cardenio* by Shakespeare and Fletcher asserts that *Double Falshood* is a forgery by Theobald,[1] there is a growing consensus that Theobald did indeed possess manuscripts of a play that he initially believed to be by Shakespeare and that he revised these for the stage.[2] The arguments in favour of this view are summarized by John Freehafer:

> largely on the basis of new evidence, it appears that Theobald did indeed possess three manuscripts of *Cardenio*; that *Cardenio* was written by Shakespeare and Fletcher; that it was based on the 1612 Shelton translation of *Don Quixote*; that *Cardenio* was cut and perhaps altered during the Restoration period, then altered by Theobald; that Theobald's lack of forthrightness in dealing with the authorship of the play resulted from his obligation to support his patron's erroneous belief that the original play was wholly by Shakespeare and his desire to protect his reputation as a Shakespeare scholar; and that Theobald probably destroyed no manuscripts of *Cardenio*.[3]

I entirely agree with these views. In particular, it seems highly likely to me that when Theobald sold the copyright of *Double Falshood* to John Watts, he also relinquished the original manuscripts, since the cost of these constituted a part of the expense that entitled him to the copyright of the play in the first place. As Freehafer observes: 'When

---

[1] Harriet C. Frazier, *A Babble of Ancestral Voices: Shakespeare, Cervantes, and Theobald* (The Hague: Mouton, 1974).

[2] Evans, *Riverside*, p. 31 n. 14, observes: 'In the case of *Cardenio*, we possess a drastic revision of the play published by Lewis Theobald in 1728 under the title *The Double Falsehood, or The Distress'd Lovers*, but the three manuscripts of *Cardenio* that he claimed to have owned have disappeared.' See also *Complete Works*, p. 1341, and *Textual Companion*, pp. 132–3.

[3] '*Cardenio*, by Shakespeare and Fletcher', *PMLA*, 84 (1969), 513.

Watts bought Theobald's rights . . . he must have received the three manuscripts that Theobald was known to have.' It also seems very likely that 'Watts may have bought Theobald's patent and manuscripts to protect the monopoly in Shakespeare's plays presided over by Tonson, who was Watts's chief client and Pope's friend'.[4]

One of Theobald's manuscripts may have survived into the later eighteenth century since, as Brean S. Hammond has pointed out,[5] an advertisement in *The Gazetteer* (31 March 1770) for a revival of the play claims: 'The original Manuscript of this play is now treasured up in the Museum of Covent-Garden Playhouse.' This manuscript presumably was burned in the great fire at the theatre on 19 September 1808.

I am grateful to Laetitia Yeandle of the Folger Shakespeare Library for drawing my attention to the uncatalogued, original assignment (31 July 1728) by Theobald of his rights in the play to John Watts:

> Know all Men by these Presents, That Lewis Theobald, Gent: of the Parish of S[t]: Giles's in the Fields in the County of Middlesex, For and in Consideration of the Sum of One Hundred Guineas of Lawfull Mony of Great Britain to him in Hand paid by John Watts of London, Stationer, He the said Lewis Theobald, Gent: hath Bargain'd, Sold and Assigned, and set Over, and by these Presents doth Bargain, Sell, Assign and Sett Over, all that the full and sole Right and Title, of, in and to the Copy of a Play, Intitled, Double Falshood, or the Distrest Lovers, Written Originally by W: Shakespeare, and now Revised and Adapted to the Stage by the said Lewis Theobald, Gent: the Author of Shakespeare Restor'd, To have and to hold the said Copy of the said Play unto the said John Watts, his Heirs and Assigns for Ever, notwithstanding any Act or Law to the Contrary. In Witness whereof the said Lewis Theobald, Gent: hath hereunto sett his hand and seal this Thirty First Day of July 1728—

> Lew: Theobald

Witnesses, Tho.[s] Smith Cowell.
Mary Ward

[4] Ibid. 512, 513.

[5] 'Theobald's *Double Falshood*: An "Agreeable Cheat"?', *Notes and Queries*, 229 (1984), 2–3.

APPENDIX D. *Warburton's Claims concerning Theobald's Preface and Notes*

Although Nichol Smith was mistaken in believing that incapacity prompted Theobald to ask Warburton for assistance in writing the Preface,[1] none the less, if Theobald is to be faulted, it is in this matter. Theobald was wrong to include three passages of Warburton's composition in his Preface to *1733*—without *public* acknowledgement —as a means of flattering Warburton into docile acceptance of his handling of the text and notes. It was in this context that he had acceded to Warburton's importunities: 'Let those preacquainted Friends frankly know, I embraced them [Warburton's passages in the Preface] in a just preference to what I could myself produce on the Subject.' Although his flattery of Warburton is consistently maintained in this response to Warburton's first view of the printed edition, Theobald is careful to establish that Warburton himself wished the passages to be included: 'They came a free Gift to me. . . . Nor would I have chose tacitly to usurp the Reputation of them: but as I formerly hinted, & you join'd with me in sentiment, it would have looked too poor to have confess'd Assistances towards so slight a Fabrick as my Preface.'[2] Warburton's attempt to gain additional public credit to that which Theobald had already allowed him ended in stalemate. After the two men finally quarrelled over notes and emendations by Warburton that Theobald had rejected,[3] Warburton claimed in a letter to Thomas Birch (24 November 1737) that 'almost all' of Theobald's 'Preface (except what relates to Shakespeare's Life, and the foolish Greek conjectures at the end) was made up of notes I sent him on particular passages, and which he has there stitched together without head or tail'.[4]

In addition to the claims he made in his letter to Birch, Warburton also marked his set of Theobald's *Shakespeare*, indicating passages he wished to be thought his. Nichol Smith has charged Theobald with 'theft' on the basis of those passages by Warburton used in the

---

[1] See above, pp. 127–8.

[2] Jones, p. 324 (5 Mar. 1734).

[3] See Ibid. 324–5 (5 Mar. 1734), Nichols. ii. 634 (17 May 1734), Jones, pp. 343–4 (18 May 1736).

[4] Nichols, ii. 81. Birch had himself benefited from scholarly correspondence with Theobald as recently as 10 Aug. 1737 (Nichols, ii. 654–5).

Preface to *1733* known definitely to be his.[5] Concerning Warburton's claims in his set of *Shakespeare*, Nichol Smith argues:

> Warburton could have had no evil motive in marking those passages in his *private* copy; and there is surely a strong presumption in favour of a man who deliberately goes over seven volumes, carefully indicating the material which he considered his own. It happens that one of the passages contains an unfriendly allusion to Pope. If Warburton meant to be 'dishonest'—and there could be no purpose in being dishonest before he was Theobald's enemy—why did he not disclaim this allusion some years later? The simple explanation is that he marked the passages for his own amusement while he was still on friendly terms with Theobald. They are thirteen in number, and they vary in length from a few lines to two pages. Four of them are undoubtedly his, and there is nothing to disprove that the other nine are his also.[6]

The unfriendly allusion to Pope (whenever it was claimed by Warburton) is irrelevant to Nichol Smith's argument.[7] It is also imperceptive to argue that Warburton carefully went through his set of Theobald's *Shakespeare* marking passages simply for his own amusement: care was taken to ensure that Warburton's claims were known and associated with the volumes. Hence Edward Capell came to write the following note in the first volume: 'This copy of Mr. Theobald's edition was once Mr. Warburton's; who has claim'd in it the Notes he gave to the former which that former depriv'd him of and made his own, and some Passages in the Preface, the Passages being put

---

[5] For the passages in Theobald's Preface claimed by Warburton, see Smith, pp. xlvii–xlviii and n. The volumes (large paper) are in the Capell Collection [L 1–7 Shakespeare], Trinity College, Cambridge. Robert M. Ryley, 'Warburton's Copy of Theobald's *Shakespeare*', *Transactions of the Cambridge Bibliographical Society*, 7 (1980), gives an incomplete account of the volumes. He considers 'some' of Warburton's claims to notes in the edition and excludes 'entries in the Preface' because he was not 'able to add to the evidence cited by Smith' (p. 450). I should perhaps add, apropos of Ryley's observation that those who have discussed these volumes lacked 'any first-hand knowledge of the volumes', that I have myself examined them.

[6] Smith, p. xlviii.

[7] As Warburton explained in a letter to Richard Hurd (12 Jan. 1757), 'Those villains, if any such there be, who upbraid me with my acquaintance and correspondence with the Gentlemen of *The Dunciad*, know I at the same time proclaimed it to the world, in *Tibbald's* Edition of Shakespeare, in Mr. Pope's life-time. Till his *Letters* were published, I had as indifferent an opinion of his morals as they pretended to have. *Mr. Pope knew this, and had the justice to own to me that I fairly followed appearances when I thought well of them, and ill of him* [*my italics*]. He owned indeed that, on reading that Edition, he was sorry to find a man of genius got amongst them; for he told me he was greatly struck with my notes. This conversation happened to pass in company, on one of them saying, they wondered I would give any thing to such a fellow as *Tibbald*. Mr. Pope said immediately, there was no wonder at all: I took him for an honest man, as he had done, and on that footing had visited him' (Nichols, ii. 741 n.).

between hooks, and the Notes sign'd with his name.'[8] However, of the thirteen passages Warburton marked in the Preface, ten were included in Theobald's Preface to the second edition of his *Shakespeare* (1740). If these ten passages were in fact Warburton's, Nichol Smith's accusation might be justified, and, indeed, he makes them central to his allegation. Apart from the fact that one of these passages is of major importance in determining Theobald's influence through stated editorial policy, Nichol Smith's charge is serious in itself and important in determining Theobald's (or Warburton's) place in the history of Shakespearian scholarship. Nichol Smith's views continue to be influential and have led Brian Vickers to attribute to Warburton key passages in Theobald's Preface;[9] in addition, Arthur Sherbo, also following Smith, supposes that Warburton's 'help' was at Theobald's 'insistence'.[10] It is, therefore, necessary that Warburton's general claims and Nichol Smith's assessment of them be addressed.

Theobald had initially intended the writing of his Preface to 'come last in play', but after Warburton's offer of help, he changed his priorities. In a letter of 4 December 1731, which Warburton retained, he thanked him for his kind assurances regarding the Preface. In the interim he had already 'rough-hewn the Exordium & Conclusion' and included a transcript of the latter. Before proceeding with his transcript, he paid what were now his customary respects to Warburton's critical skills: 'I beg earnestly, Dear S^r., you will not be tender of altering, everywhere; (except in my Acknowledgm^{ts} to my Friends). . . .' It was, needless to say, in his acknowledgements that Theobald would have Warburton's closest attention. After an abbreviated account of his negotiations with Tonson (designed to ease the Tonsons' relations with Pope) and thanks to Dr Styan Thirlby of Jesus College, Cambridge, and Hawley Bishop[11] for their assistance, he pays tribute to Warburton:

> To these I must add the indefatigable Zeal & Industry of my most ingenuous [*sic*] & ever-respected Friend, the Rev^d. M^r. Warburton of Newarke-upon-Trent. This Gentleman from the Motives of his frank & communicative Disposition, voluntarily became a Labourer in the Vineyard: not only read over the whole Author for Me with the exactest care; but enter'd into a long & laborious Epistolary Correspondence, to which I owe no small part of my best Criticisms upon my Author. The Number of

[8] Vol. i, sig. A5^v.

[9] See *Shakespeare: The Critical Heritage, Volume 2, 1693–1733* (London: Routledge & Kegan Paul, 1974), 485–6.

[10] *The Birth of Shakespeare Studies* (East Lansing, Mich.: Colleagues Press, 1986), 3.

[11] Hawley Bishop was a graduate of St John's College, Oxford. See Sherbo, *op. cit.*, p. 5.

Passages amended, & admirably explain'd, wch. I have taken care to distinguish with his Name, will shew a Fineness of Spirit, & Extent of Reading, beyond all the Commendations I can give them.

He concludes: 'How great a Share soever of my praise, I must lose from myself, in confessing these Assistances; & however my own poor Conjectures may be weaken'd by the Comparison wth theirs; I am very well content to sacrifice my Vanity to the Pride of being so assisted, & the Pleasure of being just to their Merits.'[12]

It might be supposed that Warburton was reduced to embarrassed silence after reading Theobald's encomium, but such was not the case. Theobald's disingenuous apology at the end of his transcript— 'Forgive me, my dearest Friend, that I have inserted what relates to y^{r}self, & believe that I had certainly declin'd it, only that I am determin'd to submit the Whole to you'—was apparently lost on his correspondent, who was concerned that his being depicted as 'a Labourer in the Vineyard' might prompt some readers to suppose that he had been neglecting his clerical duties for Shakespeare.[13] In letting Warburton see these high compliments at this stage, Theobald hoped to ensure his own editorial freedom and to avoid conflict with Warburton.

Upon first seeing the draft of this part of Theobald's Preface, Warburton responded with three more letters in rapid succession. Concerning the content of the Preface, two things become apparent. First, despite Theobald's apparent deference to Warburton's criticisms in his reply, when he came to print the Preface he made only one change on Warburton's account, and that was in order to avoid embarrassing him by omitting the allusion to the 'Labourer in the Vineyard'. Second, Theobald intended that the Preface should be his own work:

> I make no Question of my being wrong in the disjointed Parts of my Preface, but my Intention was, (after I had given you the Conclusion, & the Manner in wch. I meant to start) to give you a List of all the other general Heads design'd to be handled, then to transmit to you, at proper Leisure, my rough Working off of each respective Head, that you might have the Trouble only of refining & embellishing wth: additional Inrichments: of the general Arrangement, wch. you should think best for the whole; & of making the proper Transitions from Subject to Subject, wch. I account no inconsiderable Beauty. If you think right to indulge me in this Scheme, my next shall be employ'd in Prosecution of it.[14]

[12] Jones, pp. 283, 286; see also p. 289.

[13] Ibid. 288, 286. The biblical allusion was omitted from the printed Preface (*1733*, vol. i, pp. lxvi–lxvii).

[14] Jones, pp. 289–90 (18 Dec. 1731).

In his last sentence, Theobald again makes it clear that he has no wish to take unfair advantage of Warburton, while the whole burden of his letter contradicts Warburton's claim in his letter to Thomas Birch virtually to have written the Preface himself. If the remainder of Theobald's Preface was forwarded to Warburton in a form comparable to that part which he had already received, it is unlikely that there was anything for Warburton to do, beyond gratifying his own insistent eagerness to contribute. At the same time, nothing here indicates that Theobald felt incapable of writing his own Preface. Rather, it is likely that he was beginning to regret his initial, tactical response to Warburton's offer of assistance.

Theobald writes in his next letter, dating from the latter part of December 1731, that he intends 'very soon to trouble you with a prosecution of the *Preface*'.[15] A transcript has not survived, but then Warburton would not have been inclined to preserve a document disproving his later claims.[16]

Nichol Smith's reasons for proclaiming Theobald a thief are insufficient, except that he says *four* passages in the Preface to *1733* are undoubtedly Warburton's, whereas Theobald omitted only three Warburtonian passages in the Preface to his second edition (1740), after the two men had quarrelled. If, indeed, Theobald did in *1740* print without acknowledgement a passage that was undoubtedly Warburton's, there might be grounds for believing with Smith that 'there is nothing to disprove that the other nine are his also'. But, in fact, Nichol Smith only accounts for *three* such passages in his Introduction, and these are *all* omitted in the later Preface. What is presumably the hypothetical fourth passage is described in Nichol Smith's Introduction as 'a passage in the Preface . . . conveyed from one of Warburton's letters published by Nichols and Malone'.[17] This, however, is the same passage mentioned previously as 'the comparison of Addison and Shakespeare . . . taken from a letter

---

[15] Nichols, ii. 626.

[16] Theobald's correspondence (including letters preserved by Warburton) is virtually complete for the period before the edition was published, except for transcripts of the Preface, which would have settled the question of who contributed what to the Preface. On the other side, the only Shakespearian letters of Warburton to have survived are those which were overlooked by Theobald when he returned his assistant's letters, and which, as it happens, contain nothing damaging to Warburton. All were written after the edition was published in Jan. 1734. To these may be added transcripts made by Warburton of 53 notes and emendations to Shakespeare—which Theobald did not want to have associated with his edition—and 'cavillings' at 13 notes in the printed work. Warburton's other letters, which he received back from Theobald, would have given a complete picture of what Theobald rejected, as well as making Warburton's general position in relation to Theobald clear.

[17] pp. xlvii–xlviii, passim.

written by Warburton to Concanen in 1726–27'—which was omitted in *1740*.[18]

Of the remaining ten passages Warburton marked in the Preface, but for which there is no proof of his authorship, some were retained complete by Theobald in his second edition and others only in part. However, these alterations cannot be taken as indicative of Warburton's authorship, because Theobald also omitted or abbreviated passages not claimed by Warburton. Therefore, on the same evidence, it may be supposed with equal probability that, having excised the three passages deriving from Warburton, in the rest of the Preface Theobald was merely abbreviating his own work. On the other hand, notwithstanding Nichol Smith's claim, there is evidence that a passage referring to Bentley's edition of *Paradise Lost* (1732),[19] which was claimed by Warburton, but retained by Theobald in *1740*, was by Theobald. In his letter written immediately after publication of the edition, Theobald responds to Warburton's fears that Bentley (who was a subscriber) might be offended: 'As to D[r] Bentley (whatever the penetration of some readers may devine on this head) in Shaking off the Similitude betwixt our tasks, I hope that neither he, nor his Friends will see cause to suspect any Sneer. The Stating the Difference was absolutely necessary on my own side, & I think I have avoided saying anything derogatory on his.'[20] The passage referred to is obviously Theobald's. Moreover, it is known that Theobald not only made a point of visiting Bentley some time about 4 July 1732, when he was remodelling his *Prolegomena* into a Preface, but also had anticipated his remarks in his Preface in letters to Warburton written before Warburton had seen Bentley's *Paradise Lost*.[21] There can be little doubt that Warburton, once it became clear that Bentley was not going to resent the passage (or was dead), decided he would like to have it thought his own. To this passage may be added the one containing references to Rymer,[22] which is no more than a recasting of views

---

[18] *Pace* Nichol Smith, Warburton's comparison of Addison and Shakespeare was far from being stolen by Theobald. Warburton must have transcribed the passage from his own papers for inclusion in the Preface, since the letter itself was later found by Dr Gavin Knight, the first Librarian of the British Museum, when, in 1750, he took over a house in Crane Court, Fleet Street, that Concanen had previously occupied. It was subsequently made public by Mark Akenside (who loathed Warburton) as part of a deliberate attempt to embarrass him. See Mark Akenside, *Ode to Thomas Edwards, Esq; On the Late Edition of Mr. Pope's Works. M.VCC.LI.* (1761), st. v, p. [5] n.; Johnson, *Lives*, ed. G. B. Hill (3 vols., Oxford: Clarendon Press, 1905), iii. 413 nn.; Edmond Malone, *Supplement to the Edition of Shakespeare's Plays Published in 1778* (2 vols., 1780), i. 222–6; Nichols, ii. 195–8. See also above, p. 104.

[19] Preface, *1733*, vol. i, pp. xxxix–xl.

[20] Jones, p. 324 (5 Mar. 1734). See above, pp. 131–2.

[21] Jones, pp. 306, 278, 299, 305.

[22] Preface, *1733*, vol. i, p. xlviii. Retained in *1740*.

previously expressed by Theobald in letters to Warburton. Indeed, in one of his letters (28 March 1730) Theobald gives Warburton a 'sample' of the older critic, from which it seems that at the time Warburton was unacquainted with *A Short View of Tragedy*.[23] Warburton either deluded himself or, more likely, when his account of his first meeting Theobald is remembered, wished to delude others into thinking the passages were his.

John Churton Collins, without having examined Warburton's marked set of Theobald's *Shakespeare* at Trinity College, Cambridge, was very much inclined to reject Warburton's claims: 'If in this copy, which we have not had the opportunity of inspecting, Warburton has laid claim to more than Theobald has assigned him, we believe him to be guilty of dishonesty even more detestable than that of which the proofs are, as we have shown, indisputable.'[24] For stating this view, Churton Collins was severely taken to task by Nichol Smith:

> An inspection of the Cambridge volume is not necessary to show that a passage in the Preface has been conveyed from one of Warburton's letters published by Nichols and by Malone.[25] Any defence of Theobald by an absolute refusal to believe Warburton's word can be of no value unless some proof be adduced that Warburton was here untruthful, and it is peculiarly inept when Theobald's own page proclaims the theft.[26]

Nichol Smith does not discuss Churton Collins's 'proofs' of Warburton's 'dishonesty' directly. Collins was concerned with Warburton's commentary in *1747*, where Warburton attempted to confirm the misrepresentation of Theobald he had begun in his Preface.[27] Warburton's eagerness betrayed him, because his commentary frequently proves him a thief and a liar: what Warburton prints here may be compared with Theobald's extant letters to him. The following examples could easily be multiplied. In the folio text of *Twelfth Night* (I. iii. 98–9) Sir Toby says of Sir Andrew's hair: 'it will not coole my nature'. Warburton had addressed himself to this passage with his usual ingenuity, and Theobald replies (8 April 1729):

> I dare say, I hardly need subjoin my correction to your sagacity.
>
> *Sir And.*—Oh, had I but follow'd the Arts!
> *Sir Tob.* Then hadst thou had an excellent head of hair.
> *Sir And.* Why, would that have mended my Hair?
> *Sir Tob.* Past question; for thou seest it will not *curl by* Nature.

[23] See Nichols, ii. 583–4; see also 493–4.

[24] 'The Porson of Shakespearian Criticism', *Essays and Studies* (1895), 270 n.

[25] Ryley, op. cit., p. 449, observes that Nichol Smith's own knowledge of the volumes 'was confined to a list, provided for him by Aldis Wright, of passages in Theobald's Preface bracketed by Warburton'.

[26] Smith, pp. xlvii–xlviii.

[27] See above, pp. 4–5.

It means no more, I think, than, if Sir Andrew had had art enough in him to tie up his hair, it had not hung so lank as it did by Nature; and what immediately follows, seems to me an unexceptionable confirmation of this.

Sir And. But it becomes me well enough, does't not?
Sir Tob. Excellent; it hangs like Flax on a Distaff.[28]

Warburton attempted to mislead the readers of his edition (1747) into thinking the emendation his own: '*thou seest, it will not* COOL MY *nature.*] We should read, *it will not* CURL BY *nature*. The joke is evident.'[29] The deception succeeded with Johnson, but in his revision of Johnson's edition published in 1778 George Steevens set the record straight: 'This emendation is Theobald's though adopted without acknowledgment by Dr. Warburton.'[30]

In the folio text of *All's Well That Ends Well* (I. iii. 171) there is the reading:

> now I see
> The mistrie of your *louelinesse*, and finde
> Your salt teares head. . . .

Theobald comments to Warburton (20 December 1729): 'I make no scruple but you will read with me, LONELINESS; of which the Countess had above received intelligence from her Steward. . . .'[31] Warburton was glad to adopt the emendation as his own: '*The mystery of your* loveliness,] We should read *loneliness*, or delight in solitude, as is the humour of lovers.'[32]

On *2 Henry VI* (II. iii. 62)—'Here's a cup of CHARNECO'— Theobald commented (22 January 1730): 'I do not know what liquor this might be. Our Dictionaries take no notice of it. I find it mentioned, amongst several other wines, in an old tract, called "The Discovery of a London Monster, called the Black Dog of Newgate. Imprinted at London by G. Eld, for Robert Wilson, 1612."'[33] After disputing Sir Thomas Hanmer's interpretation of the word, Warburton presented Theobald's information as his own: charneco was 'a common name for a sort of sweet wine, as appears from a passage in a pamphlet, intitled, *The discovery of a London Monster, called the black dog of Newgate, printed* 1612'.[34]

[28] Nichols, ii. 211; cf. *1733*, ii. 465–6n.
[29] *1747*, iii. 125n.
[30] iv. 165n.
[31] Nichols, ii. 343.
[32] *1747*, iii. 23n.
[33] Nichols, ii. 437. There is no note on the passage, *1733*, iv. 233.
[34] *1747*, v. 37n.

In addition to pillaging Theobald's emendations and commentary, Warburton presented Theobald as being generally incapable of appreciating Shakespeare. On Hotspur's speech in *1 Henry IV* (I. iii. 201–8) beginning, 'By heaven, methinks it were an easy leap | To pluck bright honour from the pale-fac'd moon', Warburton remarks:

> *Gildon*, a critic of the size of *Dennis*, &c. calls this speech, without any ceremony, *a ridiculous rant and absolute madness*. Mr. *Theobald* talks in the same strain. The *French* critics had taught these people just enough to understand where *Shakespear* had transgressed the rules of the *Greek* tragic writers; and, on those occasions, they are full of the poor frigid cant, of *fable, sentiment, diction, unities*, &c. But it is another thing to get to *Shakespear*'s sense: to do this required a little of their own.[35]

That this note misrepresents Theobald is evident from his Shakespearian criticism in *The Censor*. In *1733*, Theobald had commented on the speech, but with a purpose different from that ascribed to him by Warburton:

> This bold *Rhodomontado* of *Hot-spur*, however, by the mouthing of an Actor, it may be always crown'd with Applause; I find, and not without some Justice, was carp'd at and ridicul'd in our Author's Time. In *Beaumont* and *Fletcher*'s *Knight* of the *burning Pestle*, (the *Rehearsal* of those Days,) a Grocer's Wife brings her Prentice *Ralph* to the *Play-house* to act a Part; and encouraging him to exert, says, *Hold up thy Head*, Ralph; *Shew the Gentlemen what Thou can'st do: Speak a* huffing *Part: I warrant you, the Gentlemen will* accept *of it*. And then *Ralph* repeats this whole Speech of *Hot-spur*.[36]

Occasionally Warburton went out of his way to attribute a reading to Theobald: '*But on the cause.*—Mr. *Theobald* Vulg. *And on the cause*—].'[37] Elsewhere Warburton remarks of a passage: 'Mr. *Theobald* says, he *cannot, for his heart, comprehend the sense of this phrase*. It was not his heart but his head that stood in his way.'[38] As it happens, Warburton does explain the meaning (*Love's Labour Lost*, V. ii. 465) correctly, but this is the exception, not the rule. Warburton's commentary suggests that Theobald's superiority as an editor, coupled with his frequent correction of Warburton in his letters, produced in Warburton an angry frustration. Perhaps their correspondence forced him to recognize that, despite his ambition, he had a second-rate mind. If, as is probable, Theobald was aware of Warburton's frustration as work on the edition drew to a close, his handling of the Preface ceases to be surprising. At the same time, Churton Collins's

[35] *1747*, iv. 116 n.
[36] *1733*, iii. 361 n. See the Induction, ll. 76–80, *Knight of the Burning Pestle*, ed. Michael Hattaway (London: Methuen, 1969).
[37] *1747*, vii. 406 n.
[38] *1747*, ii. 272 n.

unwillingness to believe Warburton no longer appears 'peculiarly inept'. Most important is that Theobald may be safely credited with the statements of editorial principle found in his Preface.[39]

[39] See above, ch. 8.

APPENDIX E. *Theobald's Shakespearian Collection*

In a letter to *The Censor*, a fictitious correspondent, 'Nicholas Talisman', observes 'that *Daniel Browne* had made a fine Penny by old *Books*'.[1] The *Catalogue of the Library of Lewis Theobald, Deceas'd* [1744] suggests that a significant part of Theobald's income went on 'old *Books*'. There are many tantalizing entries among the 631 lots listed in the *Catalogue*, such as lot 102, 'A Volume of old plays', and lot 417, 'A Volume of Plays'. These volumes may account for all the extant copies of plays associated with Theobald. Most tantalizing of all is lot 460: 'One hundred ninety-five old English Plays in Quarto, some of them so scarce as not be had at any Price, *to many of which are Manuscript Notes and Remarks of Mr. Theobald's*, all done up neatly in Boards, in single Plays.' The copy of the *Catalogue* in the Bodleian has prices paid for the different lots, except for lot 460, which suggests that the collection was not sold at this auction.

George M. Kahrl and Dorothy Anderson suggest that David Garrick may have been 'the purchaser of lot 460'.[2] This suggestion does not, however, seem likely. In a Postscript to *The Works of Beaumont and Fletcher* (1750), Thomas Seward says that 'Since Mr. *Theobald*'s Death, I received his valuable Collection of old *Quarto*'s'.[3] If the collection actually belonged to Seward, it presumably passed to his daughter, Anna Seward, 'the Swan of Lichfield', since on 4 October 1781 Seward revised his will and bequeathed to her 'all my real estates, and all the residue of my goods, etc.'.[4] Anna Seward's will (1809) determined that her 'whole stock of Household Furniture Plate Books Pictures Drawings and other effects' be sold by public auction.[5] However, according to Margaret Ashmun, Anna Seward's

[1] *Censor*, 5 (20 Apr. 1715), i. 36. Daniel Browne is identified by Henry R. Plomer, *A Dictionary of the Printers and Booksellers Who were at Work in England, Scotland and Ireland from 1688 to 1725* (1922; rpr. Oxford: The Bibliographical Society, 1968), 53, as a 'bookseller in London, Black Swan and Bible, next door to the Queen's Head, without Temple Bar, 1672–1729'.

[2] *The Garrick Collection of Old English Plays: A Catalogue with an Historical Introduction* (London: British Library, 1982), 17. The authors associate 17 plays in the Garrick Collection with Theobald.

[3] (10 vols., 1750), i. 372.

[4] Aleyn Lyell Reade, *Johnsonian Gleanings* (11 pts., London: privately printed for the author, 1909–52), pt. 7, pp. 172–3.

[5] Lichfield Joint Records Office, MS Anna Seward's Will (1809), p. 13.

books, plate, and furnishings went to Sarah Seward (Mrs Burrowes) at Stradone House, the seat of the Burrowes family in county Cavan.[6] If Theobald's collection remained with these descendants of the Seward family, it was destroyed in 1921, when Stradone House was burned by the IRA. Margaret Ashmun also notes that 'Some volumes may have gone, on Miss Seward's death, to the Rev. Mr. Henry White, who was a collector of books and manuscripts'.[7] White's books and papers were acquired by the Huntington Library, and there is no trace of Theobald's collection among them.[8]

It is possible that lot 460 passed into the hands of Jacob Tonson. When Johnson came to edit Shakespeare, he had in his possession Theobald's copy of the second folio, which may have been lent or given to him by Tonson (this is on the authority of George Steevens—see below). This volume is now No. 20 of the collection in the Folger Library. Perhaps Tonson also lent Theobald's collection to Thomas Seward, when he became the principal editor of Beaumont and Fletcher after Theobald's death.

When Theobald was at work on his *Shakespeare* he was greatly assisted by his friends. As he acknowledges in his Preface, Martin Folkes 'furnish'd me with the first *folio* Edition of *Shakespeare*, at a Time when I could not meet with it among the Booksellers; as my obliging Friend *Thomas Coxeter*, Esq; did with several of the old 4to single Plays, which I then had not in my own Collection.'[9] These statements suggest that Theobald was an active purchaser of Shakespeariana in the course of his editing.

The most detailed description of the Shakespearian collections employed by Theobald in the course of his editing remains that provided by himself: 'A TABLE OF The several EDITIONS OF SHAKESPEARE'S PLAYS, Collected by the EDITOR.'[10] Altogether he borrowed or collected twenty-nine early quartos.[11] The following items are identified by the numbers assigned by Greg, *Bibliography*. Included in his collection were eight first 'good' quartos: *Romeo and Juliet* (1599) (Greg 143(b)), *2 Henry IV* (1600) (Greg 167(aI) and (aII)), *Much Ado about Nothing* (1600) (Greg 168(a)), *A Midsummer-Night's Dream* (1600) (Greg 170(a)), *The Merchant of Venice* (1600)

[6] *The Singing Swan: An Account of Anna Seward* (New Haven: Yale University Press, 1931), 268.

[7] Ibid. 268–9.

[8] Letter (22 Apr. 1974) to me from Alan Jutzi, Assistant Curator of Literary Manuscripts, Huntington Library, who catalogued the Henry White collection.

[9] *1733*, vol. i, p. lxvii.

[10] *1733*, vol. vii, sig. Ii4^r.

[11] He lists 28 quartos, but he had *2HIV* in both corrected and uncorrected states (Nichols, ii. 418–19; *1733*, iii. 499 n.) making 29 pre-1623 quartos in all. It is presumably a typographical error that leads McKerrow, p. 110, to state that 'he had obtained, or borrowed, 38 quartos'.

(Greg 172(a)), *Hamlet* (1605) (Greg 197(b)), *Othello* (1622) (Greg 379(a)). The were three reprints deriving from 'good' quartos: *Titus Andronicus* (1611) (Greg 117(c)), *Richard II* (1598) (Greg 141(b)), and *1 Henry IV* (1599) (Greg 145(c)). He also had *Lear* (1619, dated 1608) (Greg 265(b)). His six 'bad' quartos (excluding his reprints of earlier volumes in his possession) were represented by *[T]he true Tragedy of Richard Duke of York* (1600) (i.e. Q2 *3 Henry VI*) (Greg 138(b), see also Greg 119(b)***), *The Whole Contention between the two famous Houses, Lancaster and York* [1619] (i.e. Q3 *2 & 3 Henry VI*) (see Greg, *Bibliography*, iii. 1107), *Richard III* (1597) (Greg 142(a)), *Romeo and Juliet* (1597) (Greg 143(a)), *Henry V* (1619, dated 1608) (Greg 165(c)), and *Merry Wives* (1602) (Greg 187(a)).[12]

Copies of extant Shakespearian quartos associated with Theobald are first identified (where possible) by the numbers in H. C. Bartlett and A. W. Pollard, *A Census of Shakespeare's Plays in Quarto, 1594–1709*, revised and extended (New Haven: Yale University Press, 1939), hereafter cited as *Census* No., and by the numbers assigned by Greg. Of the forty-eight sixteenth- and seventeenth-century Shakespearian titles known to have been in Theobald's possession, perhaps twelve may be identified.

1. MR. WILLIAM SHAKESPEARES COMEDIES, HISTORIES, & TRAGEDIES. Published according to the True Originall Copies. *LONDON* Printed by Isaac Iaggard, and Ed. Blount. 1623.

The first folio loaned by Folkes is apparently the Spencer folio now in the John Rylands Library, Manchester, which has a MS note on a flyleaf: 'Bought at M^r. Folkes's sale Sat: Feb:21. 1756. N.B. This was the Book Mr Theobald made use of in ['for' *superimposed*] his edition.' In the top right corner, above this note, are initials 'J[?]:M.'. According to Sidney Lee, *Shakespeares Comedies, Histories & Tragedies: A Census of Extant Copies* (1902), No. 48, this folio was sold for three guineas at the Folkes sale (2 Feb. 1756) to George Steevens, who made it over to the second Earl Spencer, *c.*1790. The book is surprisingly clean, unlike Theobald's copy of the second folio (1632), now Folger No. 20, which was also in the possession of Johnson. Theobald apparently acquired his own copy of the first folio, since the second sale catalogue of his library lists a first folio with MS notes by him: Item 393, 'Shakespeare's Works, *with a great Number of Manuscript Additions, Corrections,* &c. *all wrote by Mr. Theobald, Editor of*

---

[12] He also collected *The First Part of the Troublesome Reign of John, King of England* (1591) (Greg 101–2(a)) and *The Second Part of the Troublesome Reign of John, King of England* (1591) (Greg 101–2(a)), which he refers to, *1733*, iii. 200 n., 237 n., as 'the Old Sketch of' and 'first rough Model' of *King John*, but without discussing authorship.

Shakespear 3l 3s. 1623.'[13] (Folkes's copy was borrowed some time between 20 and 27 May 1729, as appears from Theobald's initial references to a first folio in his correspondence.)

2. M^R. WILLIAM SHAKESPEARES COMEDIES, HIS-TORIES, and TRAGEDIES. Published according to the true Originall Copies. *The second Impression. LONDON*, Printed by *Tho. Cotes*, for *Robert Allott*, and are to be sold at the signe of the Blacke Beare in Pauls Church-yard. 1632.

Folger No. 20. The British Library has a copy of the first folio (C. 39. i. 12), which has associations with Theobald's second folio. There is a MS note by George Steevens: 'Ex dono Jacobi Tonson, Bibliop: 1765 It belonged to Mr Theobald. From him it devolved to Dr Johnson, who did not much improve its condition.' Dr J. D. Fleeman tells me in a letter (13 May 1974) that the leaf with Steevens's note in the British Library first folio comes from Folger No. 20. Annotations in the British Library folio suggest that someone made notes by referring to Theobald's *Shakespeare* (1733). See also Donald Greene, *Samuel Johnson's Library: An Annotated Guide*, English Literary Studies Monograph Series No. 1 (University of Victoria, BC, 1975), 102–3.

3. THE Tragedie of King Richard the Second . . . Printed for *Mathew Law*, and are to be sold at his shop in Paules Church-yard, at the signe of the Foxe. 1615.

National Library of Scotland, Bute 507. Title-page: 'George Steevens'. The writing of the collation appears (it is collated more or less with edit. 1598 for Andrew Wise) to be the same as that attributed to Theobald by Bartlett and Pollard in Bute 511, *Richard III* [1612] (*Census* No. 1047) (Greg 142(e))—if the Bute 511 attribution is correct, then Bute 507 was also Theobald's (Greg 141(e)).

4. THE TRAGEDIE of King Richard the third . . . Printed by Thomas Creede, and are to be sold by Mathew Lawe, dwelling in Pauls Church-yard, at the Signe [*what follows supplied in MS*] 'of the Foxe 1612'. 1612.

National Library of Scotland, Bute 511. Inlaid, with notes (according to Bartlett and Pollard) by Theobald, Steevens, and Forster; book-plate of 3rd Marquis of Bute. (See note on Bute 507.) There is the following MS note on the inlay of sig. A1^v: 'This is the identical Play of Richard the Third from which Mr. Steevens copied his, in the publication of Shakespere's Quarto's printed in 1766. with all the

---

[13] *A Catalogue of the Libraries of one of the Judges Lately Deceas'd, of Mr William Pate . . . and Mr. Lewis Theobald, Editor of Shakespear, (Amongst which last Parcel are several with Large MSS. Notes, Corrections and Additions, by Mr. Theobald . . . . .) Which will begin to be Sold . . . On Monday the Eleventh of May, and continue selling all the Summer.* [1747], p. 18. A copy is in Durham University Library.

various readings &c. as done by Mr. Theobald, This copy being one of those belonging to (and collated by) that Gentleman. I bought this curious old Quarto at Mr. Steevens sale, with an imperfect copy of that printed in 1602.' There are signs of collation throughout— *possibly*, as suggested by the note above, in Theobald's hand. The Theobald association is accepted by Bartlett and Pollard. (*Census* No. 1047) (Greg 142(e))

    5. A Midsommer nights dreame . . . Imprinted at London, for *Thomas Fisher*, and are to be soulde at his shoppe, at the Signe of the White Hart, in *Fleetestreete*. 1600.

This copy is now in the library of Trinity College, Cambridge, and has the following note on the title-page: 'Collated with the other Old Quarto, with the same Title, printed by James Roberts in 1600. L.T.' The collations are in the margins. Presented by Edward Capell, June 1779. (*Census* No. 748) (Greg 170(a))

    6. The most excellent Historie of the *Merchant of Venice* . . . Printed by *I.R.* for Thomas Heyes, and are to be sold in Paules Church-yard, at the signe of the Greene Dragon. 1600.

National Library of Scotland, Bute 494. Note on title-page: 'Carefully collated w:th the other Editions of the same Date, printed by J Roberts. L: Theobald.' Signs of Theobald's collation throughout; signature of Geo. Steevens on title; book-plate of 3rd Marquis of Bute. (*Census* No. 610) (Greg 172(a))

    7. The most excellent HISTORIE OF THE Merchant of Venice . . . Printed for *William Leake*, and are to be solde at his shop at the signe of the Crown in *Fleetstreet*, between the two Temple Gates. 1652.

National Library of Scotland, Bute 496. Title-page: 'L.T.'; sig. A2^v: 'By Sir Antony'. Book-plate of 3rd Marquis of Bute. (Also belonged to Farmer.) (*Census* No. 675) (Greg 172(eII))

    8. THE MERRY VVIVES OF WINDSOR. With the humours of Sir *Iohn Falstaffe* . . . Printed by *T. H.* for *R. Meighen*, and are to be sold at his Shop, next to the Middle-Temple Gate, and in S. *Dunstans* Church-yard in *Fleet-street*, 1630.

National Library of Scotland, Bute 499, which has the following MS note, sig. A2^v (p. 2), apparently in Theobald's hand: 'Luce, is a fish in fresh Water, as Lakes, marshes &c & there is also a Marine fish of the same Name. vid: Gesner.' (The only note in the volume; cf. Theobald's discussion of 'Luce' in Nichols, ii. 240–1: 'Gesner tells us, there is a marine and a fresh-water species'; not associated with Theobald by Bartlett and Pollard.) (Greg 187(d))

    9. THE TRAGEDY OF HAMLET, PRINCE OF DENMARK. Newly imprinted and inlarged, according to the true and perfect

Copy lasted Printed . . . Printed by *R. Young* for *John Smethwicke*, and are to be sold at his Shop in Saint *Dunstans* Church-yard in Fleet-street, under the Diall. 1637.

Now in the Dyce Collection in the Victoria and Albert Museum: Dyce Coll. 8965 (25. D. 63): *Hamlet*. 1637. Flyleaf: 'This Copy was once the property of that valuable injured Editor, Lewis Theobald. See the collations and Remarks in his handwriting, *passim*. J. Boaden.' (*Census* No. 55) (Greg 197(g))

10. M. William Shake-speare, *HIs* True Chronicle History of the life and death of *King Lear*, and his *three Daughters* . . . Printed by *Jane Bell*, and are to be sold at the East-end of *Christ-Church*. 1655.

This copy is in the University Library, University of Illinois at Urbana-Champaign, x822.33 T3 1655. Title-page: 'Collated throughout exactly with the old Quto printed in 1608. L.T.' (Greg 265(e))

11. THE Tragœdy of Othello, The MOORE of VENICE . . . Printed for *William Leak* at the *Crown* in *Fleet-street*, between the two Temple Gates, 1655.

Houghton Library, Harvard University. Call No. 13408. 124. 10*. Title-page: 'L.T.' MS note on flyleaf: 'Although this copy wants one leaf [sig. M4], it is very interesting, having belonged to Theobald, & having his autograph initials on the title-page. J.O. Halliwell.' MS note, sig. A1ᵛ: 'Bought it [*illegible word*] out of Theobald's Colections 5d 1767'. There are no signs of collation by Theobald. (*Census* No. 865) (Greg 379(e))

12. A Collection of POEMS . . . By MR. WILLIAM SHAKE-SPEARE . . . Printed for *Bernard Lintott*, at the *Cross-Keys* between the Two Temple Gates in Fleetstreet. n.d. [1709, 1711].

With Theobald's MS notes and Index. Folger Library, PR 2841 A12a c. 2 Sh. Col.

Index

Discussion of an emendation or a restoration is indicated by **E** or **R** after the title of the play and the page reference. *See under* Shakespeare, *Works*.